The Power of Index Funds

Canada's Best-Kept Investment Secret

Ted Cadsby, MBA, CFA

Published in 1999 by Stoddart Publishing Co. Limited
34 Lesmill Road, Toronto, Canada M3B 2T6

Distributed by:
General Distribution Services Ltd.
325 Humber College Boulevard, Toronto, Ontario M9W 7C3
Tel. (416) 213-1919 Fax (416) 213-1917
Email cservice@genpub.com

03 02 01 00 2 3 4 5

Canadian Cataloguing in Publication Data

Cadsby, Ted
The power of index funds: Canada's best-kept investment secret

ISBN 0-7737-6083-0

1. Index mutual funds — Canada. I. Title.

HG4530.C327 1999 332.63'27 C99-931456-4

The author, in his capacity as a senior executive of the CIBC group of companies, is responsible for the development, management, and sales of CIBC mutual funds; however, the opinions and recommendations expressed in this book are exclusively his, and do not necessarily represent those of CIBC.

Cover design: Angel Guerra
Design and typesetting: Kinetics Design & Illustration

Printed and bound in Canada

We acknowledge for their financial support of our publishing program the Canada Council, the Ontario Arts Council, and the Government of Canada through the Book Publishing Industry Development Program (BPIDP).

Contents

Introduction

Hasn't It All Been Said Before?

Get a plan.
Pay yourself first.
Invest in stocks for the long run.
Diversify your investments.
Don't time the markets.
Make your RRSP contribution every year.
Maximize your foreign content.

The basics are repeated over and over in every newspaper, book, magazine, and radio or television investment program. Not that the basics don't warrant repetition. They are all principles to live by.

And yet the basics don't address some of the most important questions investors have about how exactly to choose investments. This means the conversations I have with investors tend to go over the same territory, again and again. Here are two typical discussions:

Chat #1: With an investor who relies on an adviser for investment advice

Investor: I don't know if I'm in the right mutual funds.

Ted: How did you pick them?

Investor: They were recommended to me by my adviser.

Ted: Are you comfortable with the advice you're getting? Do you think he or she has put you in good funds?

Investor: I'm not sure. He switches me every so often, from fund to fund. I don't know if I'm ever in the best funds. *How do I know if I'm getting good advice on my funds and doing as well as I could be?*

Chat #2: With an investor who makes their own investment decisions

Investor: I've read some of the books that come out every year, the ones that recommend which funds are best. But they all seem to recommend different funds.

Ted: How do you end up choosing?

Investor: I have some funds with my bank and I bought a few others that I read about in the newspaper, through my discount brokerage account.

Ted: Are the funds doing well? Are you satisfied with your returns?

Investor: Not really. The funds I bought last year that got very high ratings ended up having terrible performance. One fund had a 26 percent return in the year before I bought it, and it was minus 16 percent the year after. Can you believe it? I calculated my returns for the past year and found that I would have done better in an average balanced fund. *How do I know which funds are going to do well?*

I'm not the least bit surprised that investors are confused. So many mutual funds. So many mutual fund experts. So much information and hype. In the 1980s, when the baby-boom generation began to pay off its mortgages and think about retirement, the financial-planning industry was born and grew rapidly, regularly re-inventing itself to satisfy consumers' insatiable demands for advice. Some of that advice has come in the form of "how to" books on investing (including this one).

Now there are legions of books that claim to give you the definitive list of the best mutual funds available in Canada. These books are updated annually and many are supplemented with monthly or quarterly newsletters and web sites to provide frequent updates. The implication is that readers should know which funds are best at any moment in time. It may seem odd for an industry that espouses long-term time horizons to offer instantaneous, real-time updates on which funds are hot. Some of the national newspapers even publish the daily "winners" and "losers," in case you didn't get a chance to log onto the Net the night before.

It wasn't many years ago that I myself was victim to the noise and hype over which funds to invest in. For a few years it really frustrated me that every time I invested in a good fund, it turned out that I didn't end up generating the kinds of returns I expected. Every year I would sit down to examine my portfolio, and separate the funds that were performing well from the funds that were not. It always seemed that most of the funds fell short of my expectations. Where they earned 20 percent the year before I bought them, they earned only 5 percent the year after I invested. Where they easily beat the market index, such as the TSE 300, before I bought them, they badly underperformed the index after I bought them. I became very frustrated with the annual ritual of changing my fund holdings. I wondered why someone with my investment experience found it so hard to get the returns I wanted.

Although most everyone agrees on the basic principles of investing, *there is almost no agreement on how exactly and specifically someone is supposed to maximize their long-term returns.* Why is there no easy way to determine which funds are going to generate the best returns? Why is it that the great performers often end up underperforming? Is it really that complicated or mysterious? Is there no simple answer, perhaps one that is having difficulty penetrating the clutter and noise of an industry that is scrambling to meet the growing demand for financial advice?

There *is* a simple answer. It's called *passive* management, also known as *indexing* because it is an investment method that ends up replicating the performance of market indexes. The strategy is simple but powerful: Instead of actively researching and picking stocks that they hope will outperform an index such as the TSE 300 or the S&P 500, index managers buy and hold the same stocks, in the same proportions, that are in the index. And the amazing thing is that more often than not, **index funds outperform actively managed mutual**

funds. Once I discovered indexing for myself, I never looked back. And I never will.

Surprisingly few investors understand the power of indexing. This is despite the fact that the second largest mutual fund company in the world is Valley Forge, Pennsylvania–based Vanguard, which grew its business by championing indexing. The largest mutual fund company in the world is Boston-based Fidelity, and the January 18, 1999, edition of *Business Week* estimated that almost three-quarters of its fund sales were from sales of index funds. The second largest institutional money manager in the world is San Francisco–based Barclays Global Investors, whose specialty happens to be indexing.

Indexing is certainly getting noticed by the financial press. Here is a very small sample of the many headlines you might have seen.

> "Year in and year out, the market outperforms most fund managers" (*Canadian Business*)
>
> "Vanguard. That low-cost religion hauls in $1 billion a week. Should you join?" (*Forbes*)
>
> "How to own the broad market" (*Fortune*)
>
> "Index funds are cheap, easy — and they're changing the way Americans invest" (*Business Week*)

Indexing may be making headlines, but it still has a low profile in the Canadian market, compared with actively managed funds. Passively managed funds are not as profitable for the mutual fund industry. Commissioned brokers and planners make less money selling index funds. Mutual fund experts get less publicity recommending index funds. Mutual fund companies make less money promoting index funds.

But the fact is that indexing is the best way to maximize your long-term returns. Who doesn't want that? You don't have to be rich, or poor for that matter, to have "maximum returns" as an investment goal. And there is enough product variety in indexing to allow you to build a portfolio of stocks, bonds, and cash that allows you to maintain the best balance for your individual needs.

Indexing may not necessarily be the best way to ensure you never lose money (although I will show that it is often less risky than many active funds). Some investors may be looking to maximize income or preserve their capital above all else. But most investors with long time horizons are seeking to maximize the growth of their investments, in order to live comfortably and prosperously throughout their retirement years, and that's why indexing should be interesting to them. If you want to maximize your long-term returns, you can't afford to ignore indexing.

I have written this book for a broad audience, hoping that it will be useful for sophisticated investors but accessible to all. I have tried to explain the concepts as simply as I could, without sacrificing the details that are necessary to support the ideas and put them into action.

Each chapter builds on the previous one, so my recommendations in the last six chapters will put into action all of the arguments established in the first four. The research and analysis that support my claims come from many sources, not all of which I have noted because many are hard-to-find academic papers. The sources that are easier to get hold of, however, are listed in Appendix 4 for your reference and interest. My approach has been to synthesize the best research and thinking I could find, to arrive at the most logical conclusions.

I realize that everyone has a different way of investing. Some people deal exclusively with their bank, while others have brokers or planners they rely on for guidance. Still others do everything on their own. The advice in this book is applicable to all three types of investors. Even if you have an adviser that you trust, indexing is something you should explore with her, if she is not already using a form of indexing in your portfolio.

The power of indexing is relevant for every single investor. Without exception.

Before going any further, let me make one thing perfectly clear: This is not a product pitch. As I am a senior executive of the CIBC group of companies with responsibility for managing the CIBC family of mutual funds, you may wonder about my intentions. But I want to assure you that my objective in writing this book is not to sell more CIBC index funds. My purpose is to educate; I want to let investors in on a secret that I discovered for myself a few years ago. That said, it shouldn't be surprising that some of the funds I recommend in this book *are* CIBC products, since CIBC happens to offer some of the best index products and services in Canada. And although I believe that, for many people, the best way to index is by investing in index funds, I will also be discussing alternative methods of indexing. My principal mission will be accomplished if you index a good portion of your investments, no matter which type of products you use or which company you choose to deal with.

To make this book as easy to read as possible, I have structured much of the content in dialogue form. Each chapter begins with an overview of the discussion that will follow, and ends with a brief summary entitled "The Bottom Line." I've also included appendices at the back of the book to help you explore, if you wish, some of the details of my recommendations and other related topics.

The discussions will occur between me and a fictional couple in their late thirties. Of the two, the wife, Brenda, is a little more knowledgeable about investments. She has done some reading in the past and is responsible for most of the household finances. She relies on her bank as well as a financial planner for most of her investment decisions. About half of her money is invested in bank mutual funds, while the other half is invested in mutual funds recommended by a planner. Bob, her husband, is interested in the investment process and concerned about their retirement plan. He is a little worried about some of their investments because they appear to have underperformed when he compares them with the returns of other funds in the newspaper. Although he has been content to let Brenda control the family investments up to now, he is getting anxious that they are not in the right mutual funds and that their returns are not being maximized.

The background scenario is straightforward. A friend of Brenda and Bob's has asked me if I would mind talking to them one evening after work, because they are confused about the advice they have received and not sure where to turn or whom to trust. Always eager to help, I arrive at their home just after dinner and we embark on a long and interesting conversation that takes us into the late evening. Throughout the conversation, we explore the power of indexing and a few related topics, such as how to get advice and how to build a portfolio based on indexing. The trick with indexing is not "if," but "where."

Here is a brief overview of what I cover in this book: In the first few chapters, I explain indexing, briefly show how it evolved in the investment industry, and demonstrate how and why it is such a powerful investment technique. Then, for the more skeptical reader, I address (and, if I've done my job right, refute) every possible argument against indexing. In the final chapters you will learn exactly how to choose index products, build a personalized portfolio (and I'll be very specific), and find good help if you need more comprehensive advice.

And because I believe that there is still a place in many investment portfolios for non-indexed — that is, actively managed — funds, I also look at how to properly determine which ones are the best to combine with indexed investments. By the end of the book, you'll have what you need to understand and appreciate the specific portfolio recommendations that I make.

Before we begin, there are just a few terms that need to be defined so we start off on equal footing:

Equities: Same as stocks. The two terms can be used interchangeably.
Securities: Any or all of the following — stocks (equities), bonds, or money market instruments such as T-bills.

Asset Allocation: The process of determining what mix of money market, bond, and equity funds are suitable for a particular investor.

Cap: Short for "capitalization," which means how big a stock is. "Large-cap" funds invest in the stocks of large companies who issue a lot of stock; "small-cap" funds invest in the stocks of smaller companies who issue smaller amounts of stock.

Let's get started on the most compelling idea in the investment process, an idea which is still a bit of a secret in Canada, even though it's well established in the US: the case for indexing.

1

What Is Indexing?

Indexing is a trend that has been building momentum ever since the 1970s. It started in the pension industry in the United States and spread to the American retail mutual fund market in 1976, only to grow steadily and become the fastest-growing segment of the mutual fund industry today. Your broker or planner may not be excited about this trend, but millions of investors in the US are getting rich by following it, and more Canadians are starting to realize its power.

Indexing is not as technical as it may sound. And it's not a get-rich-quick scheme by any stretch of the imagination. Instead, it's a slow and steady method of building wealth, and it accounts for currently 50 percent of equity mutual fund sales in the US and about 15 percent of Canadian equity mutual fund sales. In the 1999 RRSP season, index funds accounted for 20 percent of equity sales in Canada. Index funds are growing at more than twice the rate of other mutual funds in both countries. Over 30 percent of the US pension industry assets are indexed, compared to 27 percent of the Canadian pension industry assets. This is not a fad or niche trend. It's big and getting bigger.

The best way to define indexing, also called "passive management," is to contrast it to the other, more familiar approach to investing called "active management." The regular mutual fund managers that you have heard of, including the superstar managers whose pictures you see every time you open the business section of the paper, are all *active* managers. They *actively* choose certain stocks or bonds that they believe will generate higher returns than other stocks or bonds. These active managers are often judged against other money managers and against an index that represents a fair comparison to the stocks or bonds that they are picking. For instance, a Canadian stock fund manager will be compared to other Canadian stock fund managers, as well as to the TSE 300 — an index that represents the broad Canadian stock market. Some managers don't mind underperforming the index because they are more focused on reducing the risk to the money they invest. But most managers, and certainly the "winners and losers" that you see reported in the paper every morning, are out to beat the index.

Indexes are created for two principal reasons: they provide investors with a picture of an entire market at any given point in time; and they help investors assess the talent of investment managers. If an active manager cannot generate returns that are better than the index, then she is not adding value with her stock or bond choices. For example, if she produces a return of 10 percent by investing in Canadian stocks, and the TSE 300 index went up only 8 percent over the same time period, then we can assume that she did a great job picking her stocks. (But before we congratulate her and put all our money in her hands, we also want to make sure that she didn't take on much more risk than was inherent in the index itself.)

There are many indexes, even within the same markets. In the Canadian market, there are a few indexes that track stocks traded on the Toronto Stock Exchange. In addition to the TSE 300, there is the S&P/TSE 60, which tracks 60 of the largest stocks traded on the exchange. There is also the Toronto 35, which tracks an even smaller sample — the 35 largest stocks. And there are more. Each market has more than one index because it is useful to see how different *segments* of the market are doing. While the TSE 300 may have generated a very small gain over six months, the large-company stocks that make up the S&P/TSE 60 may have gone up by a larger amount. This distinction is important to fund managers who are constantly assessing the markets, and to investors who are assessing fund managers. If a fund manager specializes in large-company stocks only, his performance should be compared to the S&P/TSE 60 index, rather than the broader TSE 300 index.

Passive managers of index funds do not "pick" in the traditional way of an *active* manager. They do not do research. They do not pore over the financial reports of companies and crunch numbers into the late hours of the night. They do not fly around the world interviewing company executives and visiting exotic countries to see the newest mining technology or to tour a new manufacturing facility. They do not do these things because they are not in a quest to find the best companies to invest in. While the active managers are actively buying and selling securities in an attempt to beat the market index, passive managers simply buy *all* the securities that are included in the index, and they hold onto them. By owning all the securities in the index, the returns of the funds they manage will end up being very close to the returns of the index itself. For instance, if a passive manager is running a Canadian index fund, he simply buys and holds all the stocks in the TSE 300 index, which is the index that is most representative of the entire Canadian stock market. The returns of his fund will therefore be close to the actual returns of the TSE 300.

Passive managers may appear pretty lazy in comparison to the other fund managers, but they're not. They come in every day for a very busy morning, when they can be found staring at their computers and putting in orders for stocks or bonds. Then they sit at their computers, watching the markets carefully, until the end of the day, when things get hectic for an hour. They are actually very talented and under a lot of pressure, because one false move can tarnish their reputations for as long as their funds remain in existence.

What is it that they are doing? They are *passively* investing in the stocks or bonds that make up the index, but this is not as easy as it sounds. That's why I prefer the term "indexing" to "passive management." One mistake on a particular day can lead to a gap between the fund return and the index return. If the index returns 12 percent in a given year, but an index fund only generates 10 percent, the investor will not be pleased. It is very difficult to close a gap in an index fund once one opens up. That's why the index manager is one of the most under-appreciated professionals in the money-management industry.

A manager might replicate either stock or bond market indexes.

(There aren't many money-market indexes. Since the returns of short-term paper fall within such a narrow range, it's not worth tracking them.) As we've seen, within the stock category there are large-company (or "large-cap") stock indexes, small-company (or "small-cap") stock indexes, and "universal" stock indexes that represent the entire stock market. Going to an even deeper level of detail, there are indexes that track certain investing styles. For example, a "value" index buys all the value stocks in a market — these are the "cheap stocks" that can be bought at prices that are lower than their expected long-term values. "Growth" indexes, on the other hand, are made up of growth stocks — the stocks of companies that are expected to grow faster than most other companies. Some indexes, such as the TSE 300, are based on particular countries. Other indexes are based on a *collection* of countries — an example is the Morgan Stanley Capital International Europe, Australasia, Far East Index, which is usually condensed to MSCI EAFE. Although it is a very popular index, I have never heard two people pronounce it the same way! (For the record, I say *ēfa*, but *ēfē* is equally valid; most people pronounce each letter in "MSCI" separately.)

Most of the traditional mutual fund industry is built on the backs of hardworking and very dedicated people who spend their days (and many nights) researching and choosing particular stocks for their funds. The managers are supported by many hardworking and dedicated analysts, working at brokerage companies, who do their own research and recommend stocks that they hope the fund managers will buy. There are also the hardworking and very dedicated people who spend their days researching and choosing particular mutual funds to recommend to their clients. That's a lot of people who are earning a living on the basis of active management. Not to mention the authors and commentators whose claims to fame are the many books that recommend which funds to buy. There are a lot of people making money on the premise that it's possible to pick certain stocks that will outperform most other stocks.

This feeding chain sharply contrasts with the lonely but equally hardworking index fund manager who quietly goes about replicating whatever index she is tracking. She gives no consideration to research and has only the minimal support of a good trader who buys and sells the stocks or bonds that are in the index and invested in the fund.

You can see now why there are a lot of individuals who are not as enthusiastic about the trend toward indexing. Most champions of active management are true professionals who believe in their hearts that they have the talent to outperform their peer group of investment managers and outperform an index. I have interviewed over 100 money managers and I have not met one who was not sincerely devoted to the goal of outperforming. Many of them are more focused on picking the right stocks and beating other mutual funds and the index than they are on getting rich themselves. If they didn't believe they could beat other funds and the index, they simply wouldn't be motivated to spend the time and effort to do what they do.

I am a huge fan of many active managers and believe they have an important role in the investment process. But, I am also an equally big fan of indexing and believe that it *must* have a central role in the process as well. In fact, the purpose of this book is to demonstrate that every investor, no matter what stage of life they have reached and no matter how much they have to invest, should hold index products as the *foundation* of a diversified, long-term investment portfolio. Actively managed funds can be added as a complement. Some advisers may disagree and recommend a minor role for indexing, if they recommend indexing at all.

Indexing was born in academia in the early 1960s at the University of Chicago and was implemented in the early 1970s by some pension funds. Indexing didn't truly become popular with retail investors until the 1980s; now, there are over 150 index mutual funds in the US.

Indexing was first formally implemented in 1971 when Wells Fargo Bank in San Francisco launched the first index mandate for the pension fund of Samsonite Corporation. This original index strategy was not based on a public index, but on a custom-built index using stocks traded on the New York Stock Exchange. In 1974, the American National Bank of Chicago created a trust fund that was based on the Standard and Poor's 500 Composite Stock Price Index (S&P 500), a broad US equity index covering about 75 percent of the value of the entire US market. The S&P 500 index consists of 500 stocks chosen by Standard and Poor's Corporation. Most of these stocks are the stocks of large companies.

John Bogle — the founder of The Vanguard Group — launched the first index fund for the retail investor in May 1976. Based on the S&P 500, it was called First Index Investment Trust. It was originally launched as a "load" fund, which meant that investors had to pay commissions to purchase units in the Trust. The commissions were dropped later and index funds can now be bought directly from Vanguard at no cost. In March 1980, the name of the original fund was changed to the Vanguard Index Trust; it is now the second largest mutual fund in the world.

Unfortunately, the first index mutual fund had a bumpy start. It outperformed only 25 percent of US equity funds between 1977 and 1979. The stocks of smaller companies, which were weighted less heavily in the S&P, did better than the large-company stocks. But between 1980 and 1982, the index beat more than half of all other US equity funds, and went on to beat 75 percent of all US equity funds between 1983 and 1986. The first bond index fund was launched by Vanguard in 1986. Other mutual fund companies, amazed at the success of the Vanguard funds (both in generating superior performance and attracting increasing levels of cash from investors), slowly started to launch index funds as well. Fidelity, the largest mutual fund company in the world, launched its first index funds in 1990. Vanguard began to create more index funds itself, starting with funds that track the indexes of smaller-company stocks and then funds that track the indexes of international stock exchanges.

While the individual investor took a while to embrace the concept of indexing, institutional clients — pension funds, for example — were very quick to implement indexing in their investment mandates. By 1986, 15 percent of US pension assets were indexed. That figure has doubled to about 30 percent today.

So how does it all work? Let me introduce myself to Bob and Brenda as I arrive at their home for a discussion on investing and the power of indexing.

Brenda: Thanks for coming over tonight. I've been told you know something about investing, which is good because we need some help. I have to admit that the mutual funds we've invested in haven't performed as well as many other funds.

Bob: That's right. Brenda does our finances around here and we've both been disappointed with our returns, especially when you compare them with some of the hot funds you always read about. And we hear you're a big fan of something called indexing. I don't know anything about it myself, but I may have read something about index *funds* in the newspaper.

Brenda: I know that index funds just track the index. A Canadian index fund would track the TSE 300. But the problem is you only get average performance because you can't do any better than the TSE 300, so indexing isn't something we're really interested in. We were hoping you could help us choose the best mutual funds — that's where we really need some help. The funds we have don't seem to be doing that well compared to others, even though they come highly recommended.

Ted: I'm happy to help. But you're getting way ahead of me. Let's back up to what an index fund is, because it's true that I am a big fan of indexing. You're right when you say an index fund tracks an index. The manager of an index fund simply buys the securities that are in the index and holds them, so the return that his fund generates is close to the return generated by the index itself.

Indexing is just a name for the broader concept. Index funds are one of the most common methods of indexing. But there are other methods, such as index-linked GICs, and unit investment trusts that trade on the stock exchanges. You're just hearing a lot more about index mutual funds these days because they are being written about in the newspapers and magazines and being discussed on any number of investment television shows.

Bob: How is an index fund different from a regular mutual fund?

Ted: The kind of mutual fund that you may be more familiar with is one where the manager buys stocks or bonds that she thinks will outperform both the indexes and all other fund managers. The manager of this type of fund is constantly buying, and then selling when she thinks the stock or bond has reached its potential and it would be better to hold another one. The index fund manager doesn't engage in that kind of guesswork.

Brenda: You can have bond and stock index funds, right?

Ted: That's right. But I think I'll use stocks for most of my examples just to keep it simple. There are bond index funds and all the principles that apply to the stock index funds apply equally to bond index funds.

Bob: So a regular mutual fund buys stocks and then sells them to buy other stocks when the manager feels he can get a better deal or higher return on another stock? He's basically correcting a mistake, isn't he, by selling and buying another stock?

Ted: Not at all. At some point the original stock that he purchased will rise to a price that he thinks is high enough, and then he will want to replace it to buy another stock that he thinks will do well. Or he may sell because the original stock isn't looking as good as it did when he first bought it. Conditions in the company may have changed and the outlook for the stock may no longer be as favourable.

The key point is that the typical mutual fund buys and sells quite a bit — it is not unusual for a fund to buy and sell nearly all of the stocks in the fund in a given year. These funds are called "active" funds because the manager is *actively* buying and selling in order to generate superior performance. An index fund is called a passive fund because the manager is not actively trying to beat the index. He is passively buying the stocks that are in the index and holding them. His primary activity is to adjust the fund when changes are made to the index itself. He is also concerned about investing the cash deposits made into the fund, and raising cash by selling some of the stocks when investors redeem their units in the fund.

Bob: Sounds like a dream job — where can I apply? I could do that lying in bed and watching TV at the same time.

Ted: It's actually nowhere near that easy. I'll explain later on why it takes a certain skill to manage an index fund. There's nothing very "passive" about it at all.

Bob: What about the other forms of indexing, like those trust things you were talking about?

Ted: I'll get into those a little later too . . .

Bob: This is going to be a long night, isn't it?

Ted: The simplest form of indexing for most investors is index funds since they are so easy to buy. But we will look at the unit trusts such as TIPS, SPDRs, and WEBS because they have their advantages as well.

Just remember one of the main differences between active and passive management: **the active manager buys and sells with the view to generating *better* performance than the index, while a passive manager buys and holds to generate the *same* performance as the index.**

While an index fund aspires to do no better and no worse than the index it's tracking, it will be destined to always do a little worse, since the fee of the fund itself will prevent it from generating the exact returns of the index. The indexes are developed by independent companies that are usually not related to any specific stock exchange. Standard and Poor's, a large company in the US, developed and maintains the S&P 500. They have also done some work with the Toronto Stock Exchange to develop new indexes for it. A stock must meet strict criteria before it's included in an index, such as the number of shares that are publicly traded each day, and the financial health of the company. A committee reviews all eligible stocks before they are chosen. Many of the international indexes are developed and maintained by Morgan Stanley Capital International, abbreviated as MSCI.

Most indexes are market-capitalization weighted. For instance, the 300 stocks in the TSE 300 are *not* equally weighted in the index at one-three-hundredth each, because then the index wouldn't be reflective of the market as a whole. So most indexes use the size of the stock issue that is publicly traded to determine weight. "Size," in this case, means the number of stocks multiplied by their price. This is called their total market value, or their market capitalization. So a high-priced stock with many shares trading in the market has a high market capitalization and will therefore have the heaviest weight in the index. A lower-priced stock with fewer shares trading will have the lightest weighting. This translates into bigger companies having more influence in the index than smaller companies, which makes sense.

Let's have a look at the more common indexes that a manager might try to replicate:

Canada	TSE 300	*300 stocks representing about 85% of the total value of all Canadian stocks*
	S&P/TSE 60	*60 largest stocks trading on the TSE*
	Scotia Capital Markets Universe Bond	*850 bonds representing most of the Canadian bond market*
US	S&P 500	*500 stocks chosen by Standard and Poor's, representing about 75% of the value of the entire US stock market*
	Wilshire 5000	*7,200 stocks representing 99% of the total value of the US stock market*
	Russell 2000	*2,000 small-company stocks representing about 12% of the value of all US stocks*
	Dow Jones Industrial Average	*30 large stocks chosen by Dow Jones*
International	MSCI Europe, Australasia, Far East	*1,500 stocks representing 21 countries in Europe, Australia, and Asia*
	MSCI Europe	*600 stocks of 15 European countries*
	MSCI Emerging Markets	*1,200 stocks of 26 developing countries, mostly in Latin America, Asia, and Eastern Europe*
	J.P. Morgan Global Government Bond	*500 bonds representing 12 countries*
Single International Countries	WEBS	*17 individual country index products trading on the American Stock Exchange*

There are many more indexes out there. The US market in particular, because of its size, has many indexes of small and medium-size companies.

Brenda: But how does a manager track an index with thousands of stocks in it? How can she buy all those stocks?

Ted: There are three ways to index. *First*, the manager can simply buy all the stocks, which is the case with most TSE 300 funds. *Second*, the manager can use what's called a sampling technique, or optimization. This strategy involves picking a sample of securities that, together, move very closely with the index. Instead of owning the thousands of stocks in the Wilshire 5000 index, the manager will just hold 1,000 or 2,000. She has to be very adept at picking the right stocks, though, since her goal is to generate the same performance as the index. She will rely on computer modelling to assist her in the process of determining the right sample of securities. All bond funds are optimized since there are too many bonds in the index to purchase, and many of them do not trade frequently.

Third, the manager can use derivative instruments such as futures to replicate the returns of the index without actually holding the stocks. This sounds more complicated than it actually is. A futures contract is simply an agreement to buy a certain asset for an agreed-upon price at a certain point in the future. So to replicate an index, the manager simply invests in T-bills, and enters into futures contracts representing the stocks that make up that index. Futures are easy to buy and sell in large markets such as the US.

Whatever the method, index managers have the same objective: to generate performance that is as close as possible to the returns of the index that is being tracked.

Bob: Leaving the stuff about futures aside, which mostly went over my head anyway, why wouldn't the manager aim for returns that are better than the index, even just a little bit?

Ted: Don't worry about the futures. To answer your question: Some index funds do try to do a little better, but they are not pure index funds. You can't try to do better without risking that you'll do worse, and the purpose of an index fund is to avoid the risk of doing worse. The objective of a legitimate index fund is to do the same as the index.

The Bottom Line

From a humble beginning in academia, indexing was first employed by pension funds in the early 1970s. Vanguard, headed by John Bogle, led the charge into retail indexing with the launch of the first index mutual fund in 1976. Since then indexing has become the fastest-growing segment of the mutual fund industry in both Canada and the US.

Indexing is simply the investment process of buying and holding the securities that are in the index. The index fund manager's ambition is to come as close as possible to the index returns. There are different ways he can do this, but his goal is always the same. The goal of matching the index contrasts with the goal of the active manager who is attempting to beat the index by buying the stocks or bonds that she thinks will do better than other stocks or bonds. Her goal is to not only beat the index, but also to beat most of the other managers that she is competing against.

2

What's So Special About Index Funds?

The most common method of indexing is by investing in index funds. We will explore other ways to index later on in Chapter 7. For now, we'll use index funds as the product of choice for our analysis. What's so special about index funds? It's simple: **they outperform most actively managed funds**. That's it. There's nothing more mysterious to their popularity than that. What is a little more complicated is understanding why they outperform. But the simple fact is that active managers, in most markets, are hard pressed to beat the market index consistently over time.

Once you see the comparisons of index and active returns, the argument for indexing becomes quite compelling. So let's jump to the facts.

Ted: It's a simple historical fact that most fund managers have great difficulty beating the index.

Brenda: Which index?

Ted: It depends on the market we're talking about. Most Canadian equity managers have difficulty beating the TSE 300, which is the broadest stock index in Canada. Most Canadian bond managers have difficulty beating the Scotia Capital Markets Universe Bond Index, which is the most popular bond index. Most US stock managers can't beat the S&P 500, which is a highly followed stock index in the US. Most European managers can't beat the MSCI Europe index.

The particular index isn't that important. But it's interesting to observe that it is usually a *minority* of active managers that are actually able to beat the index of the market they are managing money in.

Brenda: When you say "minority," how small a number are we talking about?

Ted: Let's look at the facts. You can judge for yourself.

Bob: Facts would be good. I want to see the numbers!

Ted: Oh, you'll get your share of numbers tonight, I can guarantee you that. I'm going to show you returns for various markets. We'll look at both the index returns and the returns of the average active manager. I'm going to show you the most efficient markets first, then move to the less efficient markets.

Bob: What are you talking about?

Ted: Every market has a different form of efficiency. "Efficiency" is simply the degree to which the prices in a market reflect all possible knowledge about the companies that trade in that market. For example, the US market is considered highly efficient, especially the stocks of large companies. This means that the prices of large-cap stocks fully reflect all the information that is available about the stock. In the large-cap stock sector of the US market, there are so many analysts, pension fund managers, mutual fund managers, insurance companies, and individual investors who are constantly valuing and analyzing the stocks that it's very difficult — probably impossible — for one investor to know something that no one else does. It is therefore very difficult for an investor to take advantage of a potential mispricing of a stock, because it is highly unlikely that a stock will ever be mispriced. If thousands of people are watching and analyzing the stocks of large companies every day, how is anyone going to find out something that everyone else doesn't already know?

That's why the US market is considered very efficient: the prices of stocks are rarely — if ever — wrong. An active manager is unlikely — if ever — to get information that would allow him to buy a stock that will rise in price faster and higher than everyone else already thinks. Any new information that comes out about a stock, such as the company's earnings, will be immediately reflected in the price as all investors immediately respond to the news by buying and selling until the stock's price reflects that news.

Brenda: But surely the people that work in a company have a lot more information about that company than outside investors do. The company executives, for instance, would know all about the company's earnings long before the investor would. That would make the stock market inefficient, since inside executives could buy and sell on information that wasn't yet publicly available.

Ted: They can't do that because it's illegal. An insider is not allowed to trade on information that is not public. The securities laws preserve the efficiency of the market. Most inside executives are only allowed to buy and sell their own company stock during certain short periods after the earnings have been announced to the public. I'm not saying it never happens — just that it's illegal, people go to jail for trying it, and it is therefore not a large factor in the operation of the market as a whole.

Bob: Are all markets efficient? Is the US market the only one?

Ted: Actually it's not just the US market. The stocks of large companies in the US tend to be the most efficiently priced of any market in the world. But the Canadian stock market is quite efficient. So are the Canadian and US bond markets. The prices of bonds reflect all investors' views on interest rates and the economy. European markets are fairly efficient. When you get to Asia and especially emerging market countries like Latin America and Eastern Europe, Africa, or India, there are far fewer investors analyzing the stocks of companies. Because the stocks of these countries are less closely followed, there are more opportunities for investors to take advantage of potential mispricing, because information may be available that not everyone has uncovered or knows about.

Bob: So why wouldn't everyone just invest in those less efficient markets and forget about Canada, the US, and Europe?

Ted: Just because the Canadian and US markets are so efficient doesn't mean they are not great places to invest. The factors that drive a country's stock market are interest rates, company earnings, the country's economic conditions, and future projections of all of these factors. If the Canadian economy is expected to be the strongest among many economies around the world, then it makes sense that Canadian stocks are good investments. Let's say an investor decided that the stock of a Malaysian company was undervalued and that it was expected to rise 8 percent instead of the consensus projection of only 5 percent. It would still be better to invest in a Canadian stock if the projected return for the Canadian stock was 10 percent, even if the investor didn't have any special information about that stock that would allow him to get a better return than what the consensus was predicting. You want to invest in the best performing markets with the highest potential returns — not just the ones where you have a better chance of outsmarting all the other stock pickers. Additionally, the less efficient markets are usually riskier to invest in.

Bob: Okay. But does this have anything to do with why index funds are so great?

Ted: You bet. I've brought some charts with me because they capture the benefits of indexing quite effectively. I love charts, as you'll see, so I hope you don't mind that I use them to make my points.

Bob: Charts are cool.

Ted: Here's the first one. It outlines the markets and indexes we'll look at, and below it are the comparisons that we'll make for each market. Each market has an index that represents the stocks or bonds of that particular market, and it is the performance of the index that we're going to compare to the average active manager who is managing a fund in that market.

Market	Index
US stocks:	*S&P 500 and Russell 2000*
European stocks:	*MSCI Europe*
Canadian stocks:	*TSE 300 and TSE 200*
Canadian bonds:	*SCM Universe Bond*
International bonds:	*J.P. Morgan Global Gov't Bond (excluding Canada)*
Asian stocks:	*MSCI Pacific*
Emerging stocks:	*MSCI Emerging Free*

Useful Comparisons

1. Percentage of managers over- and underperforming the index over 1, 5, and 10 years
2. Percentage of managers beating the index in each of the previous calendar years
3. Average active fund compared to its index over 1, 5, and 10 years
4. The amount by which winning funds beat the index and losing funds underperformed it

Bob: No pictures? I don't think words in a box is what most people would call a "chart."

Ted: Don't worry — most of my charts are pictorial. In fact, I'd like to throw you in the deep end if you don't mind so we can get right at it.

Bob: Let's go for it.

Ted: Okay. This will help you see how powerful indexing is right away. Here is a series of charts, or graphs, which show how many managers did better than the index in the markets where they invest. What I'm assessing with these charts is the ability of the active manager to do better than the index. Simple as that. If he can't beat the index, then he hasn't earned his salary and the fund he manages hasn't earned its fees. I recognize that some managers and some funds have different objectives than just beating the index. For instance, some are trying to minimize risk or generate maximum income, rather than maximum overall returns. But it is definitely safe to say that the vast majority of active managers have one objective: to maximize growth and beat the market index.

The charts show the percentage of managers that beat, or outperformed, the index, and the percentage of managers that underperformed the index. The index is different for each comparison because we're looking at a different market in each case. What I've done for all of my comparisons is deduct a fee of 0.9 percent from the index. By deducting the fee, we end up comparing the active funds to what would essentially be an index fund. The index fund is basically the index minus the fees you pay for the fund.

Bob: Why not just keep it simple and compare the index to the active manager? Why complicate things by deducting fees from the index?

Ted: Since you can't actually invest directly in the index itself, it's not really fair to compare it to an active manager. I want to determine if it's better to invest with the active manager, or an alternative. The alternative that I'm using for these comparisons is an index fund, which has fees like any other mutual fund.

We're looking at three different time periods in each case — the returns over one, five, and 10 years. In some cases, where the funds don't have that long a history, we're looking at one, three, and five years. The most striking thing about these charts is how few managers were able to beat the index, even after 0.9 percent fees were deducted from the index to simulate an index fund. We'll start by looking at the percentage of large-cap and diversified US funds that beat the S&P 500:

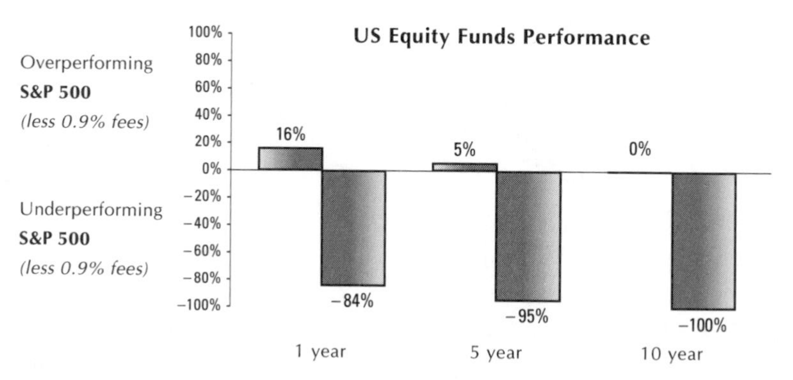

You can see that small-cap managers have greater success beating the Russell 2000, which tracks stocks of smaller US companies:

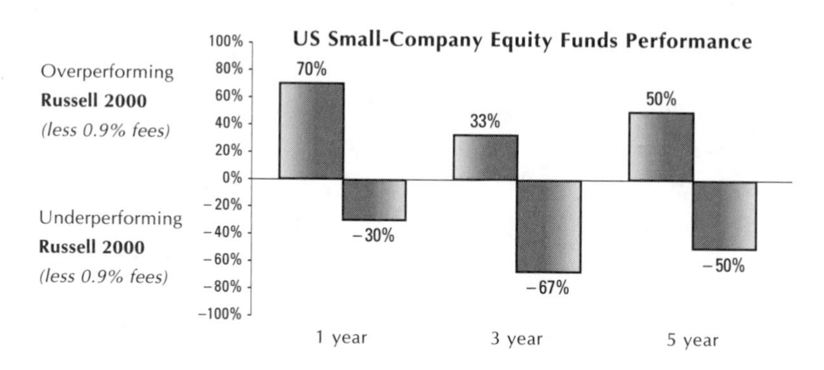

Here are the same charts for Canadian equity and bond managers:

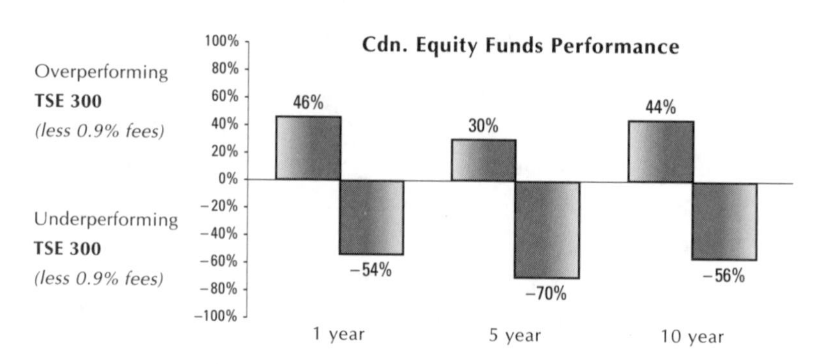

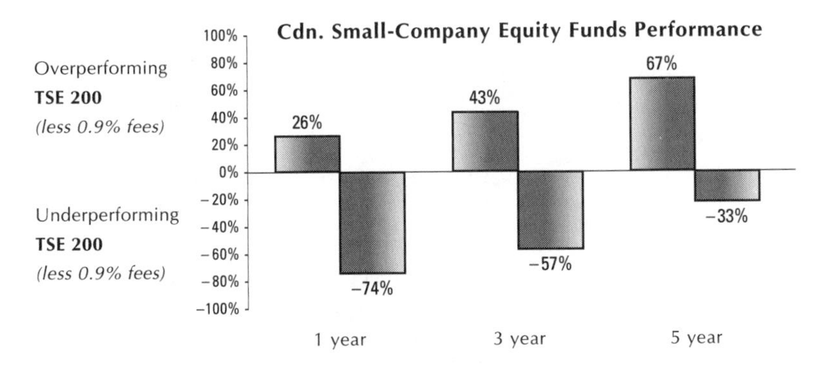

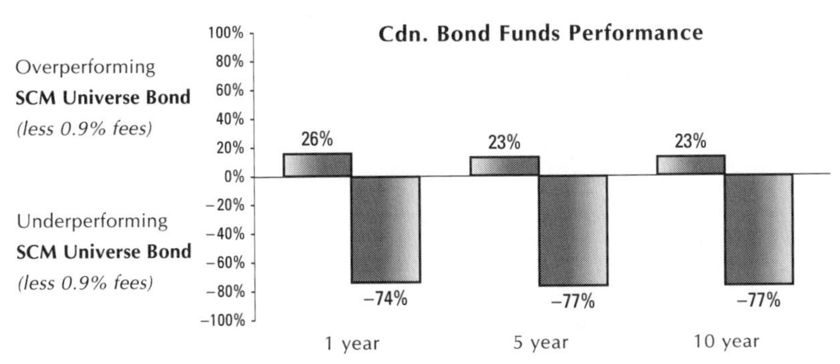

I haven't shown a comparison of active foreign bond managers against the J.P. Morgan Global Government Bond index, because it looks almost identical to the Canadian bond comparison.

If we look internationally, we can see that active European funds don't perform very well against the MSCI Europe index:

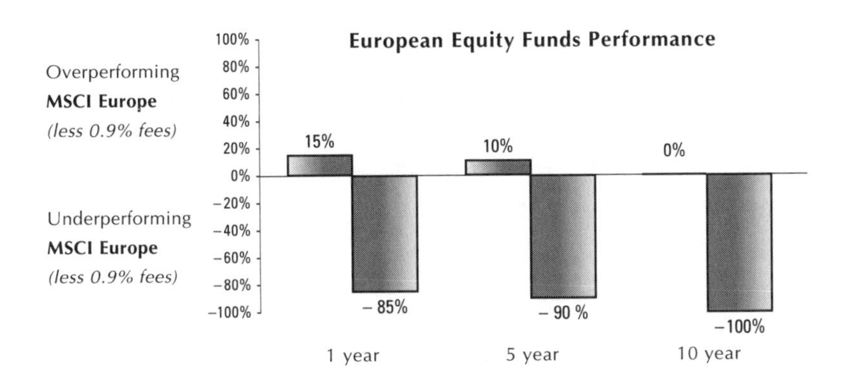

But because the emerging markets are less efficient, a majority of active managers were able to beat the index, just as we saw they did in the less efficient small-cap markets in the US and Canada.

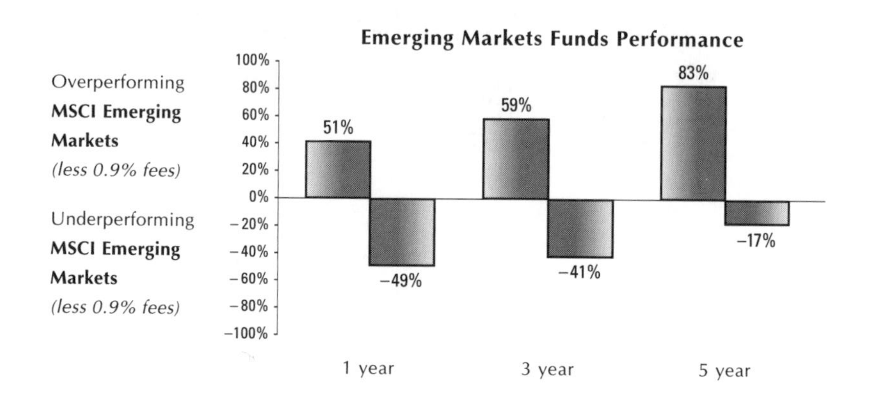

Bob: Those are cool charts.

Brenda: Do the active managers really do that badly against the index?

Ted: The charts tell the story. You can see that the managers do better or worse, depending on the market they are investing in. We'll explore these different markets in a bit more detail. But the essence of indexing — why it is so special — is that most regular mutual fund managers have a hard time beating it. It simply isn't much more complicated than that.

Bob: I have a feeling you're going to make it a little more complicated, judging by all those charts you've got with you.

Ted: Well, I'll be honest. You seem like you really want to understand how to put together an investment plan that works for the long term and doesn't need a lot of tinkering. So I'd rather err on the side of explaining what I believe in so passionately, rather than leaving you with just a few superficial ideas.

Brenda: We definitely want to understand *and* get our investments working better for us. We really appreciate your help.

Ted: It's my pleasure. Let me take you market by market so we can get into a little more depth. All I'm trying to do right now is convince you that indexing is powerful, given its track record. We'll worry about why it's powerful later. And I won't leave without giving you specific advice on how to put together a portfolio that will serve you better than what you're invested in now.

Bob: I sense more charts coming on.

Ted: I'll start with the US market because that's where the case for indexing is most convincing. I'm going to take my time explaining the US charts since I use the same format for all the markets we'll be looking at. If you understand how I'm looking at US stocks, you can follow the same analysis for Canadian, European, and other stock markets.

We're going to assess how active managers did in comparison to the index, for each major asset class. As before, we'll deduct fees from the index so that we're making an apples-to-apples comparison of two potential investment opportunities. I think you'll find it interesting.

Bob: I'm on the edge of my seat.

Ted: I'm going to look at each of these markets in different ways to make sure that we cover all the angles. Be patient with me. It will pay off. The argument for indexing begins with the facts and the facts are reflected in the historical performance of active managers competing against the indexes.

This first chart shows the percentage of US equity funds that beat the index in each of the 16 years from 1983 to 1998. I deducted 0.9 percent from the index before assessing the active managers against it. We're comparing the S&P 500 index with the average active US stock fund.

So what you see depicted here are the US equity funds that are available in Canada and that beat the index-minus-fees, as a percentage of all actively managed US equity funds. Can you believe how few beat the S&P 500 in 1998, even after fees were deducted from the index? Only 16 percent! And 1998 wasn't an unusual year when you look at the other years. There was only one year where more than half the funds beat the index — 1993. Even then, only 56 percent outperformed it. Not much of a majority in the only year where there was a majority. You might think that Canadian managers trying to beat the US index are at a disadvantage compared with the US-based managers, who are attempting the same thing. This isn't on the chart, but only 17 percent of the US equity funds that are managed and available in the US beat the S&P 500.

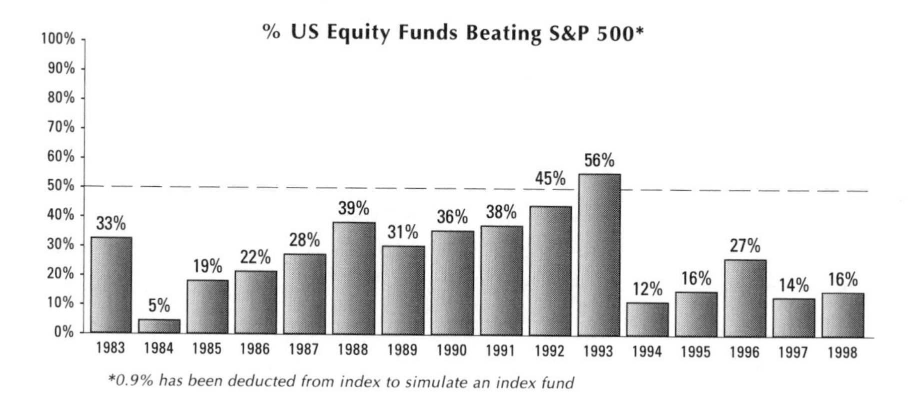

*0.9% has been deducted from index to simulate an index fund

Bob: Unbelievable.

Brenda: Shocking.

Bob: Spellbinding.

Ted: Now let's look at by just how much the average manager beat the index over one, five, and 10 years. I'm going to use the average active fund manager here, although an alternative would have been to compare the index to the median manager in each category. The median is the manager in the middle if you stacked all of the managers from top to bottom in terms of performance. The median is very close to the average, though, for all my analyses. Believe me, I checked it out. So for ease of understanding, I'm just going to use the average since we all know what average means — it's just the blend of the best and worst together.

Bob: Average is cool. My high school statistics is a little rusty.

Ted: The average fund, in this case, is a US large or mixed-sized stock fund that you would buy in Canada. So here's the first comparison, which looks at the index returns against the average active fund returns over three time periods. I've also included the number of years that the index beat the average US equity fund.

% Returns	**1-year**	**5-year**	**10-year**
		(Ending December 31, 1998)	
S&P 500 (less 0.9%)	36.8	26.8	21.3
Average US Equity Fund	26.6	19.7	16.3
Difference	10.2	7.1	5.0

Number of years S&P 500 beat the average fund: 16 out of 16

Isn't that remarkable? The index beat the average US equity fund by more than 10 percent last year and over 5 percent annually over the past 10 years. And if that wasn't convincing, in each of the last 16 years the index, minus fees, beat the average manager. Every single year in the past 16 years!

Brenda: Is the average fund before or after fees?

Ted: It's after fees. But I have not included any commissions or "loads" that might have been paid to purchase the fund.

And again, I've adjusted the index by subtracting the 0.9 percent fee, so that the comparisons are realistic. In fact, the difference between the average active fund and the typical index fund is even larger than it appears here because some index funds only charge 0.3 percent for accounts that are bigger. And there are other ways to invest in the index that we'll talk about later. These alternatives are often even cheaper — sometimes as cheap as 0.05 percent in the case of TSE unit investment trusts. So I'm definitely giving the active managers the best possible advantage — and they still can't pull it off!

Not only that, but all of my comparisons give the active fund another advantage called "survivorship bias." What often happens is that losing funds are merged with winning funds in a mutual fund company, in order to bury their dismal track records. So the history of poorly performing funds gets eliminated, making the average fund appear to perform slightly better than if the entire sample — including all of the old, defunct funds — was available. Studies have indicated that the performance of the average fund would really be 0.6 percent lower than it appears, if all the defunct funds that people invested in were included in the calculation.

I haven't deducted 0.6 percent from the average active fund's performance. So the index funds look even better when you consider a few things: the returns of the active funds are overstated by 0.6 percent; many active funds charge purchasing or selling commissions, which most index funds do not; and I deducted 0.9 percent of fees from the index even though I could have deducted as little as 0.3 percent.

Brenda: Okay. But all those returns are covering periods that end in December 1998. Would the story change if you had done a chart with periods ending in a different month?

Ted: Very clever. You are addressing an issue called "end-date bias," which simply means that the numbers can tell a particular story, depending on which end date you use. So let's have a look at the same chart using December 31, 1997.

% Returns	1-year	5-year	10-year
	(Ending December 31, 1997)		
S&P 500 (less 0.9%)	38.3	22.3	18.3
Average US Equity Fund	28.1	16.6	13.9
Difference	10.2	5.7	4.4

You can see that the story hasn't changed.

Brenda: Fine. But is the index riskier than the so-called average fund?

Ted: What's interesting is that this index is considered a less risky investment than many other active funds because it has a volatility of around 12 percent, whereas the average active US equity fund is around 14 percent. So it achieved better returns, with less risk.

Brenda: But isn't it a little deceiving to show just the average US equity fund? What about all the funds that weren't average, but were above average? The funds that did do better than the index must have cleaned up. Those would be the real winning funds to invest in and those are exactly the ones we want to know about.

Ted: Surprisingly, the so-called "winners" didn't win by much. This next chart shows all the funds above and below the index-minus-fees. I think you'll find this interesting. I've broken down the returns into categories that are based on the size of over- or underperformance against what would be a typical index fund. First let's look at how many active funds beat an index fund over five years and by how much:

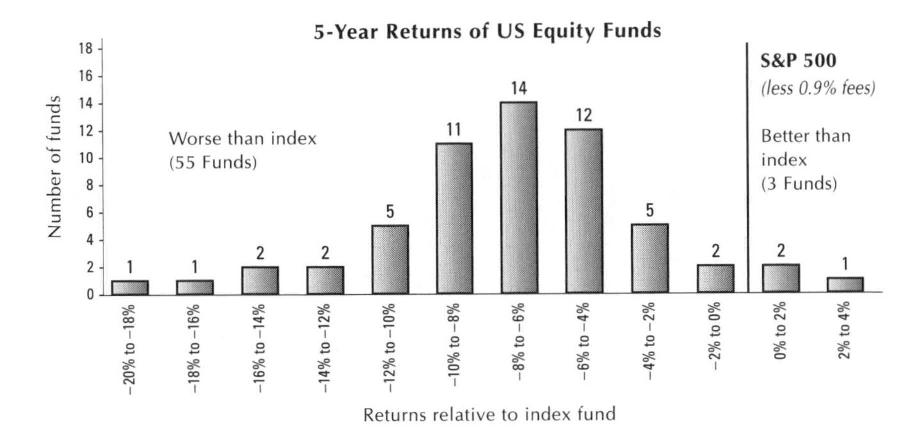

Look how skewed the data is — most managers underperformed by 6 percent or more. And there was only one manager that beat an index fund by more than 2 percent! Let's look at the same graph, but this time we'll look at the returns over 10 years. The story is the same, if not even more exaggerated:

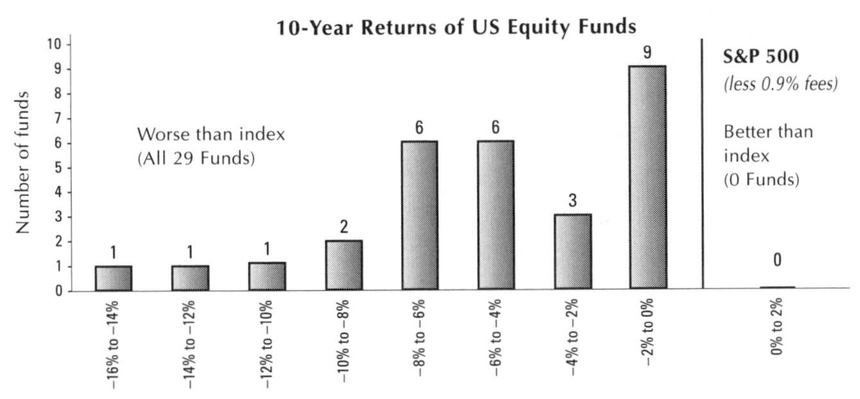

It's clear that it is very difficult for a US equity manager to beat the index. Remember: the S&P 500 index consists mainly of the stocks of large companies. It's a little easier for an active manager to beat an index that is based on the stocks of smaller American companies. The Russell 2000 is the standard US small-company, or "small-cap," index, consisting of 2,000 stocks of smaller companies. There isn't as much performance history on small-cap US stock funds sold in Canada because they haven't been around as long, but the data we do have suggest that an active manager of a US small-cap stock fund has a better shot at beating the Russell 2000 than her counterpart running a large-cap fund has at beating the S&P 500:

	1993	1994	1995	1996	1997	1998
% Managers outperforming the Russell 2000 (less 0.9%)	50%	50%	20%	33%	38%	70%
Number of funds	4	4	5	6	8	10

This is because the market for US small-cap stocks is less efficient than the market for US large-cap stocks. This observation is supported by data from the US mutual fund industry, where funds with longer histories are available. The average manager of US small-cap funds sold in the US has been able to beat the Russell 2000 by about 2.4 percent per year.

Bob: So why wouldn't every manager just focus on small-cap stocks if it's easier to beat the index?

Ted: For the same reason that you wouldn't want to invest all your money in Latin America, even though it's a less efficient market. The returns of larger companies have been higher in many years, and most investors want to have exposure to the bigger companies. Just because it's easier for a manager to beat the Russell 2000 than the S&P 500 doesn't mean she is going to get better returns overall. She may beat the Russell 2000 by 2 to 5 percent, but if the S&P 500 beats the Russell 2000 by 5 to 10 percent, it would be better just to invest in the S&P 500 index fund.

It's important to note that the broadest index to track the US market is not the S&P 500. It is the Wilshire 5000. Where the S&P 500 covers about 75 percent of the entire US market, the Wilshire 5000 covers over 99 percent. The Russell 2000 covers just over 10 percent of the whole market.

Brenda: So managers have trouble beating the US index, except maybe the small-cap index, which is still difficult to beat. What about the Canadian market? How do managers do against the TSE 300?

Ted: The Canadian funds are a little odd and require a little more work to make accurate comparisons. Most Canadian funds have investments in US stocks, so we have to make some adjustments in order to compare. Additionally, our index is less broadly diversified than the US indexes.

Bob: Yeah. It's an odd country we live in.

Ted: As we look at each market to see how compelling the case is for indexing, it's important to make sure we're making proper comparisons. Before getting to Canada, let's look at a market where the case for indexing is almost as compelling as it is in the US market — Europe.

The European Monetary Union has created a large and powerful economy based on a population of over 290 million. In total, the countries of the Union represent an economy and combined stock market that are second only to the US. Let's re-create the comparison charts for European funds. In this case the index we'll use is the Morgan Stanley Capital International Europe Index — the most widely followed European index. Again, I've deducted 0.9 percent in fees from the index so we're actually comparing the active European fund managers to the returns of a typical European stock index fund.

European funds haven't been around as long in Canada as the US funds, so we can't go as far back in our analysis. In 1990 there were only five funds, but there were 14 in 1994 and 40 in 1998. Here's the first chart showing how many funds beat the MSCI Europe index, after fees are deducted:

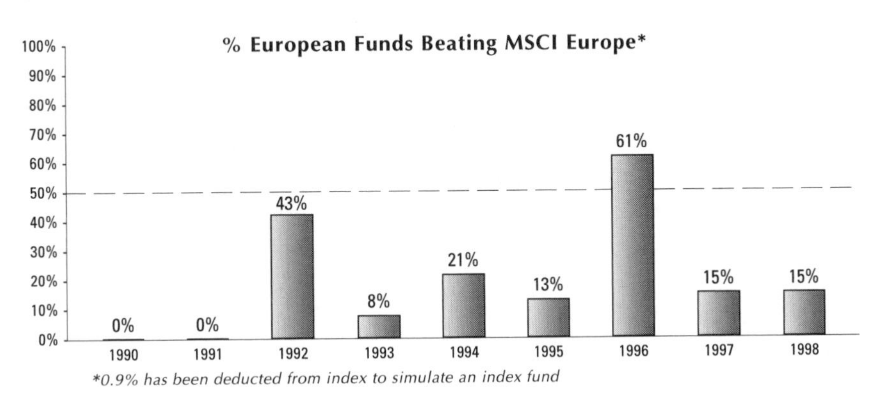

*0.9% has been deducted from index to simulate an index fund

Brenda: You're right. The European index easily beat most active managers.

Ted: Here's how the average fund did over one, three, and five years. We can't generate a 10-year comparison, since there aren't enough European funds that have 10-year returns in Canada.

% Returns	1-year	3-year	5-year
	(Ending December 31, 1998)		
MSCI Europe (less 0.9%)	37.5	29.0	22.2
Average European Equity Fund	25.4	23.9	16.9
Difference	12.1	5.1	5.3

Number of years MSCI Europe beat the average fund: 10 out of 11

The index easily surpassed the average manager. Even though there aren't that many funds with 10-year track records, we can still go back 11 years to discover that the index beat the average manager in 10 of the past 11 years. If we change the end date to December 31, 1997, the difference is not much different: the index-minus-fees beat the average European manager by 7.3 percent over one year, 3.9 percent over three years, and 6 percent over five years.

There's not much evidence that supports the active European manager. The ones that did beat the index didn't beat it by much. Most badly underperformed a typical European index fund:

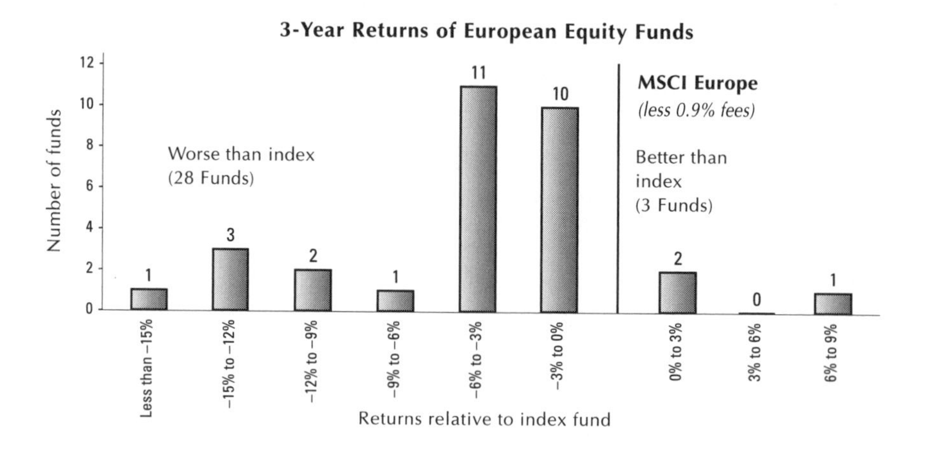

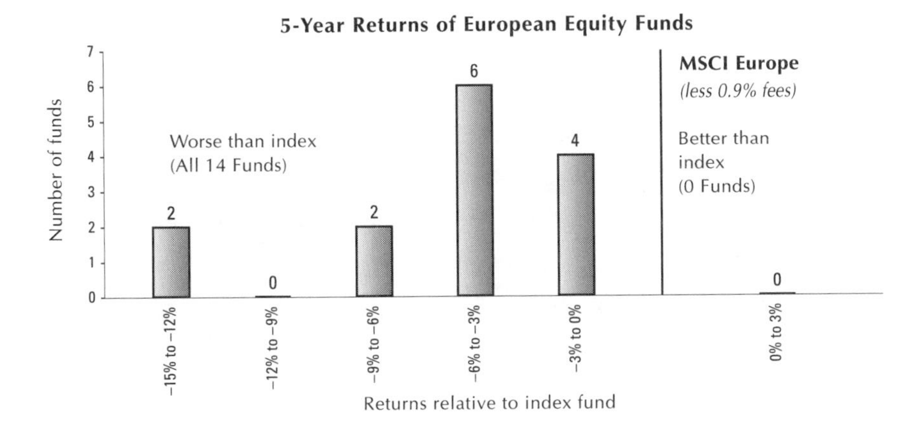

Bob: Too bad you don't have any 10-year comparisons.

Ted: Believe me — the few funds that do have 10-year returns did very poorly against the index-minus-fees: none beat it. This data is corroborated by a lot of research in the UK market, where pension managers have underperformed the British FTSE 100 index by about 1.7 percent on average, although they have been able to beat the FTSE small-cap index by about 2.2 percent.

Bob: Can we look at Canada now? Most of our investments are in Canadian stocks and bonds.

Ted: Sure. Incidentally, that is a problem in itself. Canada represents a very small portion of the entire number of stocks that trade in the world — only about 2 percent. It's hard to justify having most of your investments in Canadian stocks. But we'll get into that later when we talk about using index funds to circumvent the 20 percent foreign content constraint in RRSPs and RRIFs.

Bob: Can't wait.

Brenda: Leave him alone . . . he's trying to help us.

Ted: Let's look at the numbers.

Here is the straight comparison that we've done before, except this time we're comparing active managers investing in large and medium-sized Canadian stocks to the TSE 300 index, after fees:

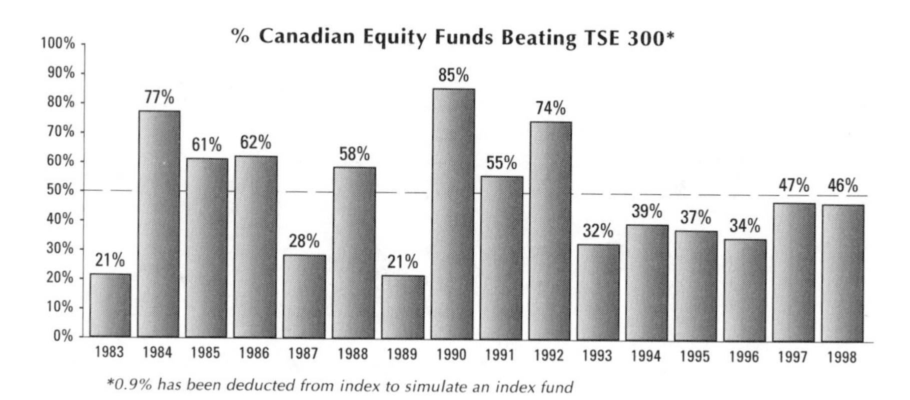

*0.9% has been deducted from index to simulate an index fund

There are seven years where a majority of active managers beat the index.

And here is the comparison against the average active manager, over one, five, and 10 years:

% Returns	1-year	5-year	10-year
		(Ending December 31, 1998)	
TSE 300 (less 0.9%)	(2.5)	9.8	8.8
Average Canadian Equity Fund	(3.6)	8.2	8.7
Difference	1.1	1.6	0.1

Number of years TSE 300 beat the average fund: 10 out of 16

Brenda: So the TSE 300 is apparently not as hard to beat. At least the average manager came a lot closer to beating it. And they were practically tied over the last 10-year period.

Ted: It's true that the index didn't beat the average manager by much. Even if we change the end date to December 31, 1997, the difference between the index and the average manager is still only 0.9 percent, 1.6 percent, and zero percent over one-, five-, and 10-year periods.

But this isn't an entirely fair comparison because most Canadian funds hold 7 percent of their investments in US stocks and another 2 percent in international stocks, on average. Because our government only allows us to hold 20 percent in foreign content in our RRSPs and RRIFs, many Canadian funds buy up to that limit in order to give investors the benefit of some foreign exposure. But that means we're comparing apples to oranges: the TSE 300 is purely Canadian, but the average Canadian stock fund is 91 percent Canadian and 9 percent foreign.

Brenda: But does that really matter?

Ted: Actually it matters a lot because the US and many international markets have done much better than the Canadian market in the past decade. The active managers had the benefit of holding some stocks that were performing much better than the Canadian market as a whole.

For this reason, I'm going to make some adjustments so that we compare the average active Canadian equity fund with a new index — the TSE 300 adjusted for 7 percent US content and 2 percent international content. The adjustment for 7 percent US is based on the S&P 500 index and the international adjustment is made using the MSCI EAFE index, which is a broad international index. These adjustments reflect what the average Canadian equity manager holds in US and international stocks.

Bob: Why do you have a problem with active managers holding US stocks anyway?

Ted: I have no problem at all. It's actually a good strategy, considering most investors hold too much in Canadian stocks anyway. But you have to remember what we're trying to do here. I'm trying to assess the active manager's ability to beat the index. To make a proper assessment, everyone has to be on a level playing field. Here are the same charts where the TSE is adjusted for US and foreign content:

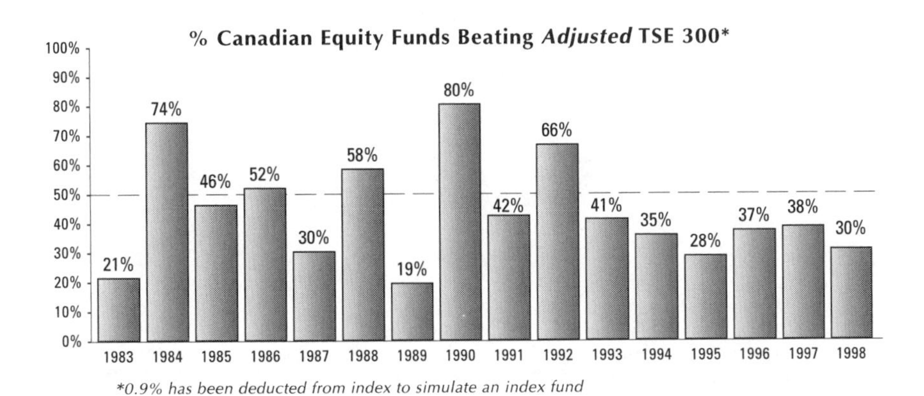

**0.9% has been deducted from index to simulate an index fund*

There are fewer years — five — where a majority of active managers were able to beat the TSE 300, after adjusting for foreign content.

Once we adjust the TSE 300 to reflect the holding of US and

EAFE stocks that the average Canadian equity fund holds, the numbers suggest that the active managers have more of a challenge, since there are only six years where the active managers beat the index-minus-fees.

% Returns	1-year	5-year	10-year
		(Ending December 31, 1998)	
TSE 300 adjusted for foreign content	0.5	11.0	9.6
Average Canadian Equity Fund	(3.6)	8.2	8.7
Difference	4.1	2.8	0.9

Number of years TSE 300 beat the average fund: 10 out of 16

Looking at a different end date, December 31, 1997, the results are the same with the adjusted index-minus-fees, beating the average active manager by 2.3, 2, and 0.5 percent over one, five, and 10 years.

Now let's look at by how much the active managers beat the index over five and 10 years. I'll show you the results both before and after adjusting the TSE 300 for the addition of 9 percent foreign content. As usual, I will deduct fees from the index.

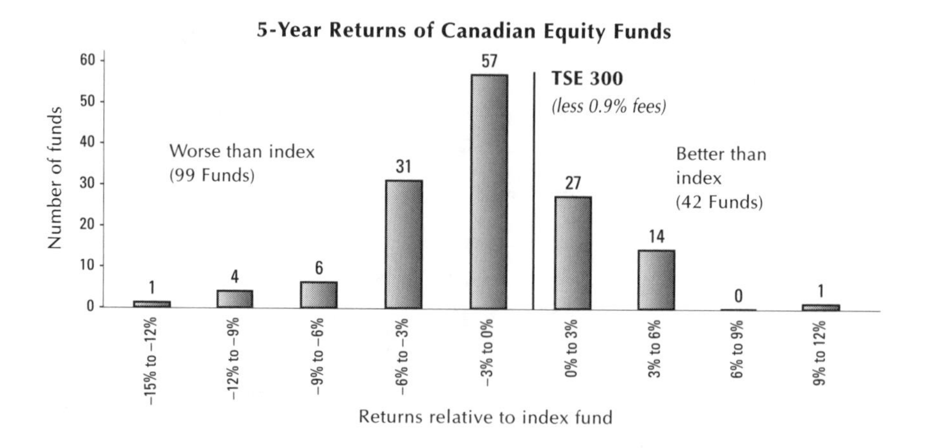

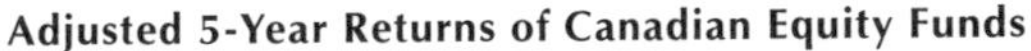

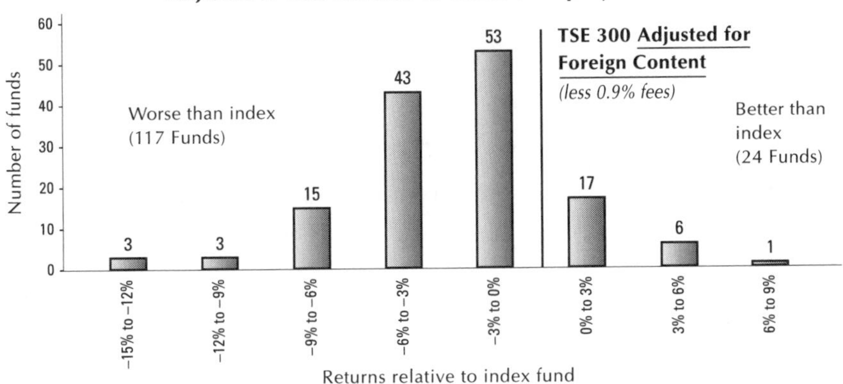

10-Year Returns of Canadian Equity Funds

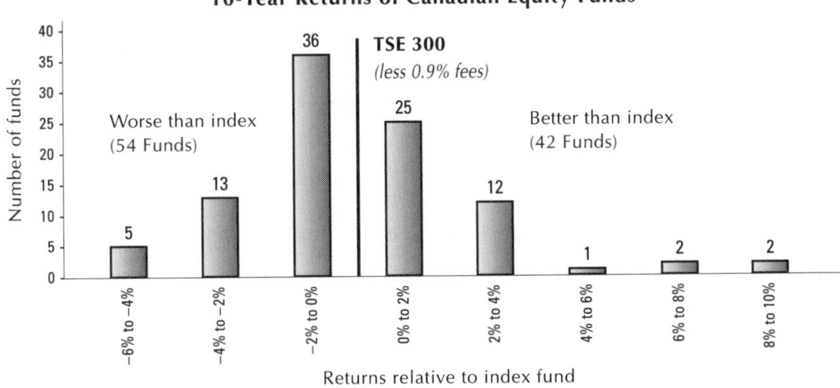

Adjusted 10-Year Returns of Canadian Equity Funds

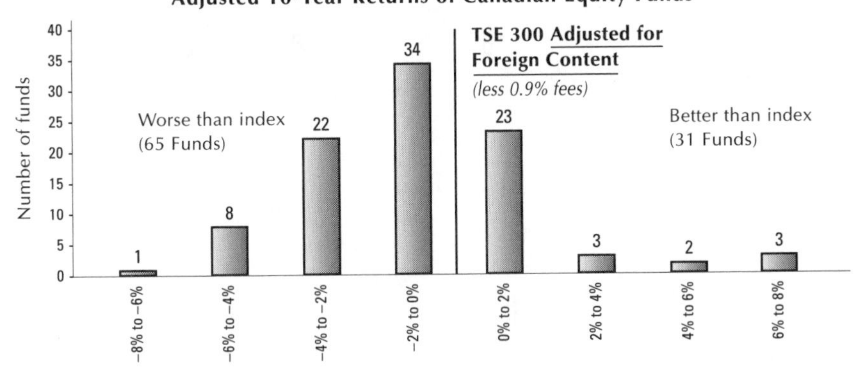

Bob: How about small-cap stocks? Is it the same as the US market so that active managers do better beating the TSE 300?

Ted: It is the same, but don't forget that we're not comparing the small-cap active managers to the TSE 300 since that index is mostly large-cap stocks. This time we compare the active small-cap stock manager to the TSE 200, which excludes the largest 100 stocks in the TSE 300. And just as in the US, we find that active managers of small-cap funds have a better shot at beating the index —

Brenda: Because the small companies are less followed and less actively traded than the larger companies. It's therefore a less efficient market.

Ted: Wow. You learn fast.

Bob: Show off.

Ted: There is more history for Canadian small-cap funds than for US small-cap funds. This time we don't have to adjust for foreign content holding since the average small-cap stock manager doesn't hold much in foreign content — just about 5 percent in US stocks and one percent in other foreign stocks. Here are the charts that compare the active Canadian small-cap funds and the TSE 200 after 0.9 percent fees are deducted:

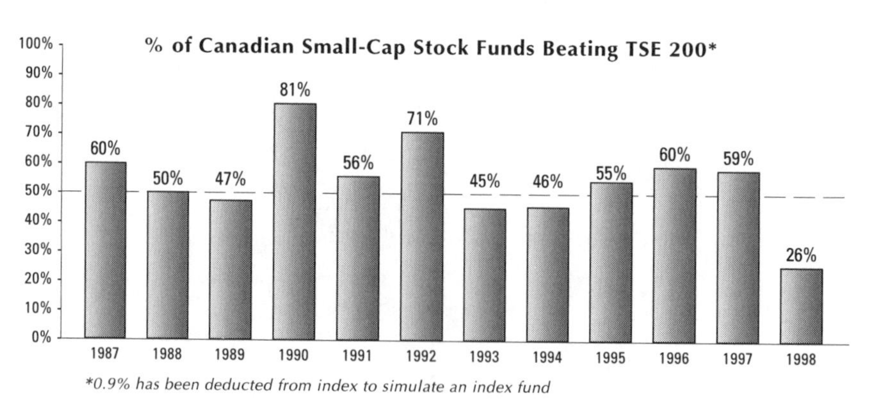

*0.9% has been deducted from index to simulate an index fund

% Returns	1-year	5-year (Ending December 31, 1998)	10-year
TSE 200 (less 0.9% fees)	36.8	26.8	21.3
Average Canadian Small-Cap Fund	26.6	19.7	16.3
Difference	10.2	7.1	5.0

Number of years TSE 200 beat the average fund: 7 out of 16

If we change the end date to December 31, 1997, the gap closes to a 1.2 percent difference over one year, and the average manager actually beats the index after fees by 0.8 and 1.5 percent over five and 10 years.

Here is how many managers beat and how many underperformed the TSE 200, less fees, and by how much. I'm going to look at three and five years since there aren't enough funds that have 10-year histories for a meaningful comparison.

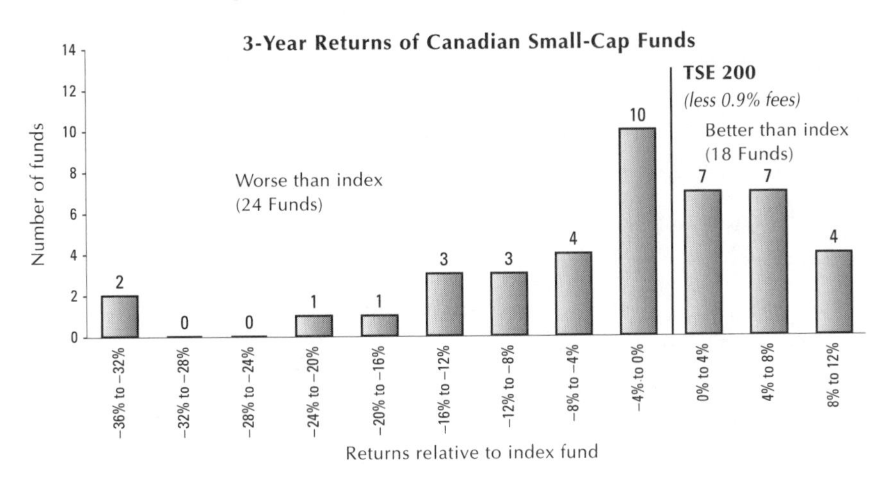

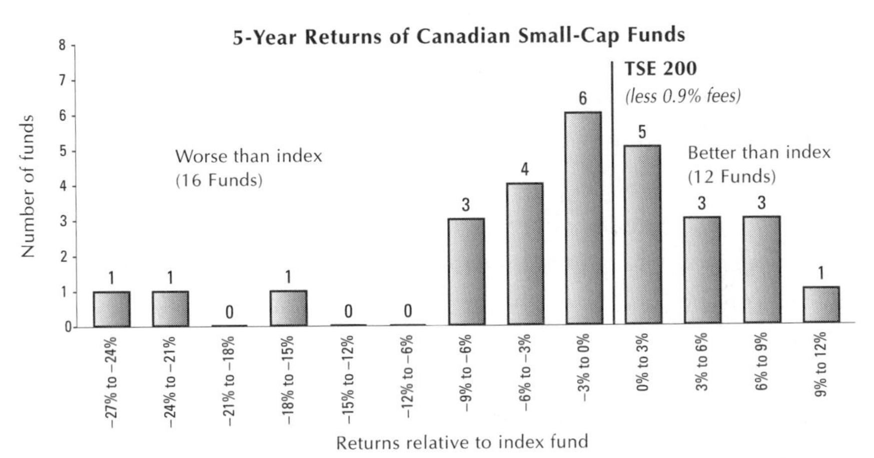

Brenda: Piece of cake to outperform the small-cap index.

Ted: I don't know if it's a piece of cake. Only about one-third did it by 2 percent or more over five years. But it's certainly easier than beating the TSE 300. There is another small-cap index for Canadian stocks called the Nesbitt Burns Small Cap index. It includes stocks of companies that are even smaller than those that make up the TSE 200. If we use it as the index to judge active small-cap Canadian funds, instead of the TSE 200, we get similar results. The average small-cap stock fund beat the Nesbitt index by 2.6 percent, after fees are deducted from the index, over the five years ending in December 1998. The Nesbitt index, less fees, beat the average small-cap fund in only five of the last 16 years. In 10 of the last 16 years, a majority of active small-cap funds beat the index after fees, including 1998 where 79 percent beat the index. Finally, I can tell you that 62 percent of active small-cap managers beat the Nesbitt small-cap index by 5 percent or more in 1998, and 54 percent beat the index by 5 percent or more for the five-year period ending December 31, 1998.

Bob: It's hard to absorb all those numbers. Do you have a chart I can see instead?

Ted: I didn't do charts for the Nesbitt index because it's not the best way to assess most Canadian small-cap funds, which tend to hold a good portion of medium-size companies. Some even hold as much as 30 percent of their funds in large companies. The Nesbitt index is a pure small-cap index, so to compare its returns to those of mutual funds, you have to find small-cap funds that are truly focused on small Canadian companies — not an easy task, because there aren't that many out there.

Brenda: Why would Canadian small-cap funds hold something they are not supposed to?

Ted: Active managers who oversee small-cap stock funds are allowed to hold a portion in larger companies. Most of them hold large companies simply because their funds get too large to be able to hold only small companies. They end up drifting toward other stocks that are not really part of their core mandate. There is a name for this phenomenon. It's called "style drift," and you want to beware of it since you may end up holding a small-cap fund that is only slightly more than half invested in small-cap stocks.

I didn't show you the charts since I don't want you to be taken in by the illusion that the small-cap index doesn't have a chance against the active managers. The numbers are deceiving, so let's just leave it at the fact that small-cap fund managers can add value beyond what the pure small-cap index can do on its own.

Bob: You really like numbers, don't you?

Ted: Yeah, they help make the point. I'm trying to show you the facts, which I think speak very clearly to the point that the index is a formidable opponent. I don't want to leave you with any reason to doubt me, so I'm purposefully erring on the side of showing you the same picture many ways. I don't want you to accuse me of using statistics to suit my purpose.

Brenda: What about bonds?

Ted: Bond funds are an easier story to tell.

Bob: Back to the charts?

Ted: We'll start with the number of funds that beat the index after fees are deducted from the index. In this case we're comparing the active Canadian bond funds with the Scotia Capital Markets Universe Bond Index, less fees:

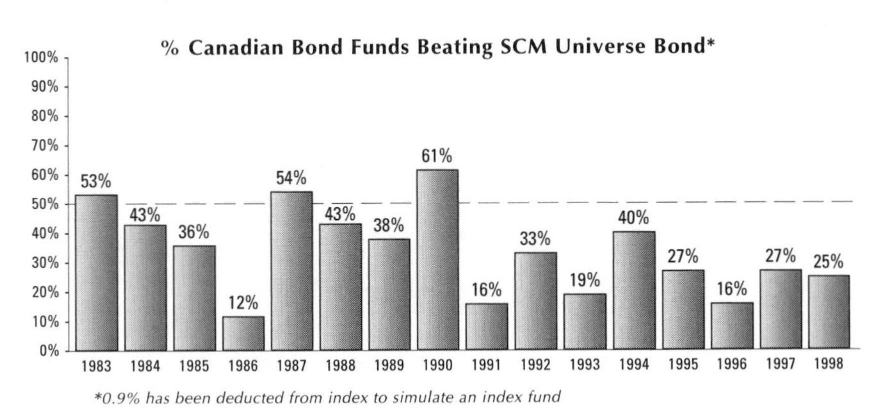

The active Canadian bond manager was obviously hard pressed to beat the index in most years. That goes for the average manager in one-, five-, and 10-year periods as well:

% Returns	1-year	5-year	10-year
		(Ending December 31, 1998)	
SCM Universe Bond Index (less 0.9%)	8.3	8.3	10.6
Average Canadian Bond Fund	6.8	7.3	9.8
Difference	1.5	1.0	0.8

Number of years SCM Bond beat the average fund: 13 out of 16

Brenda: The index wasn't that far ahead.

Ted: Not by a huge margin. Results are the same using a different end date of December 31, 1997: the index beats the average bond manager by 1.4 percent, 1.1 percent, and 0.8 percent over the three different time periods.

But the little bit adds up over time. Don't forget that a one-percent gap between an index fund and an active bond fund represents *10 percent* of the total return you would have received over the last 10 years. And in most years the index beat the average fund.

And the winners didn't win by much, although the losers lost by a fair amount:

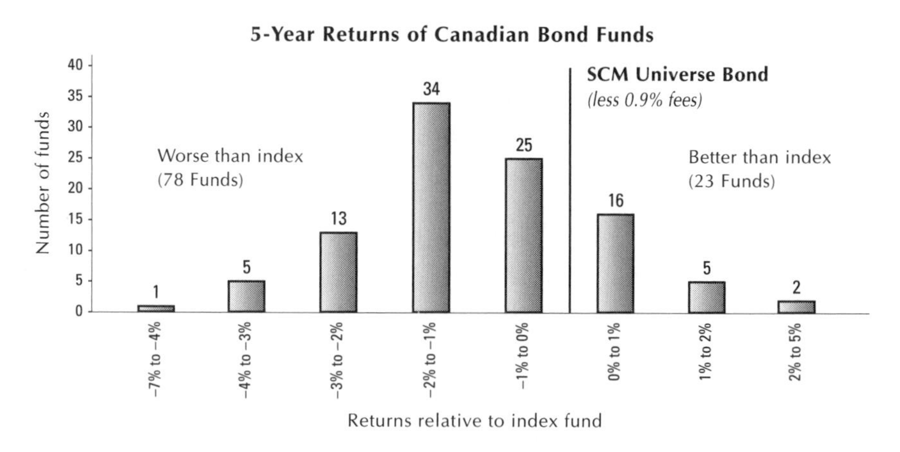

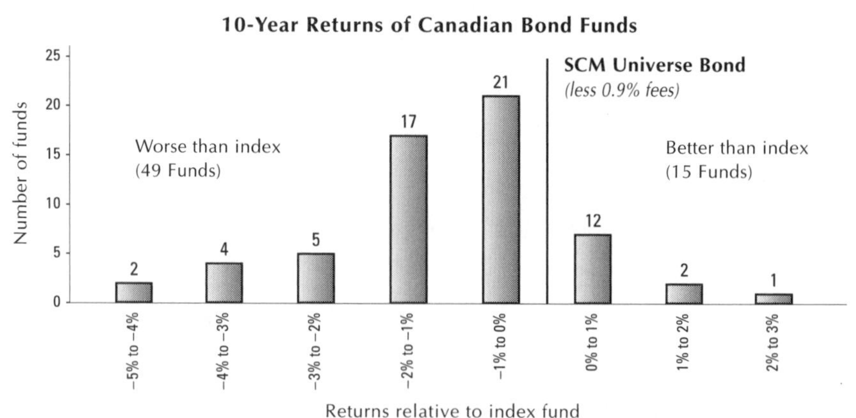

So the bond index is also a difficult benchmark to beat.

Bob: Does that apply to both Canadian bonds and international ones?

Ted: Yes it does. Here is a look at international bond funds compared to the J.P. Morgan Global Government Bond index, excluding Canadian bonds:

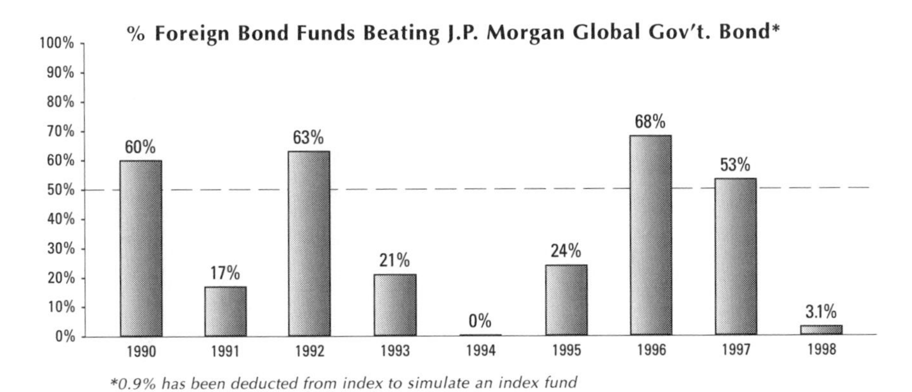

*0.9% has been deducted from index to simulate an index fund

1998 was a year in which international bond funds really did well. Not as well as the index, mind you. Check this out:

% Returns	1-year	5-year	10-year
		(Ending December 31, 1998)	
J.P. Morgan Global Gov't. Bond (less 0.9%)	23.3	10.5	11.0
Average International Bond Fund	11.6	7.1	8.4
Difference	11.7	3.4	2.6

Number of years J.P. Morgan Global Gov't. Bond beat the average fund: 7 out of 12

The index did a nice job beating the average manager. But this is where the end date can bias your perspective a little. If we change the end date to December 31, 1997, then the gap between the index, less fees, and the average active manager shrinks to 0.5 percent, 1.9 percent, and 1.1 percent over one-, five-, and 10-year periods.

Active international bond managers don't appear to be able to beat the index by much, but the ones that underperformed the index certainly bombed:

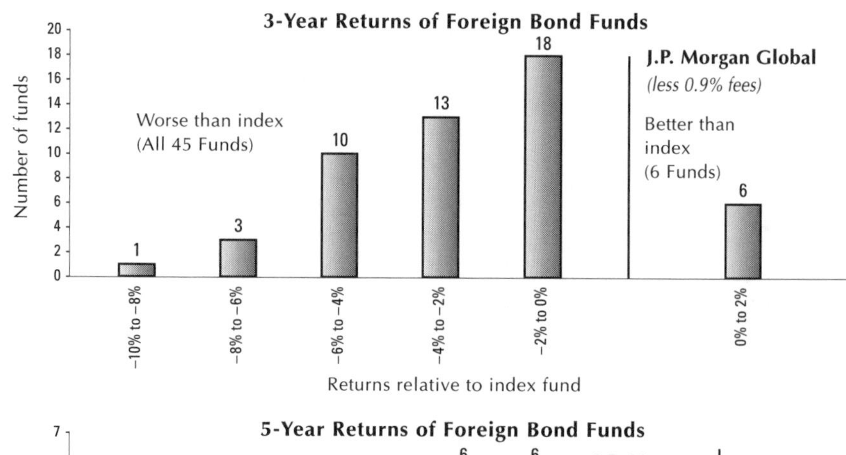

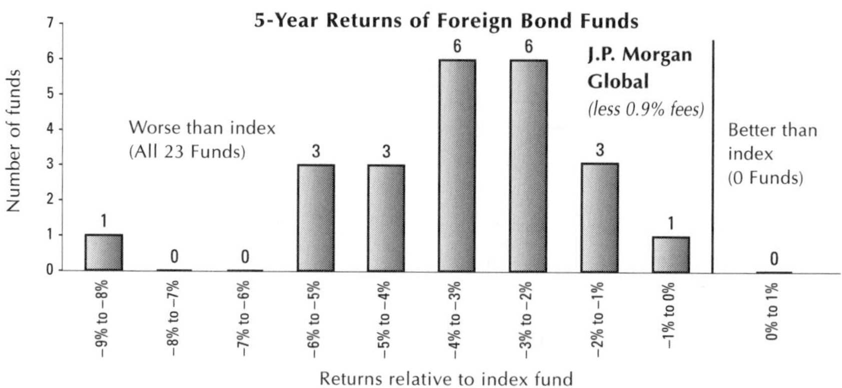

Brenda: Are there any markets where the index isn't so imposing?

Ted: Yes. The less efficient markets such as Asia, and the emerging markets such as Latin America and Eastern Europe. These funds haven't been around that long, but let's look at how active Asian funds stand up against the MSCI Asia Pacific index:

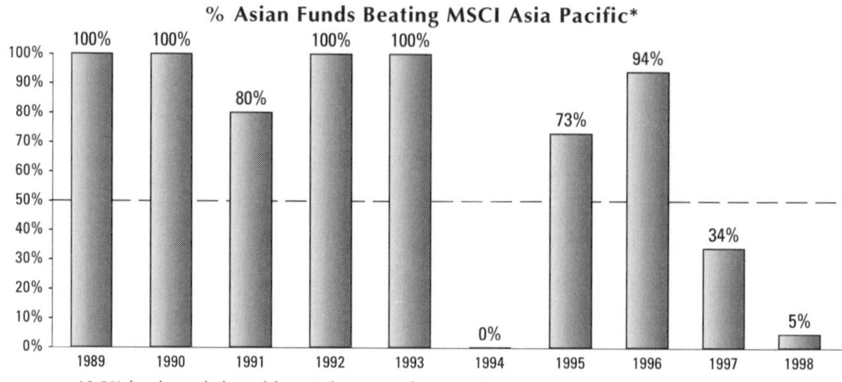

% Returns	1-year	3-year	5-year
	(Ending December 31, 1998)		
MSCI Asia Pacific (less 0.9%)	8.6	(9.0)	(2.9)
Average Asian Fund	(3.3)	(9.1)	(9.7)
Difference	11.9	0.1	6.8

Number of years MSCI Asia Pacific beat the average fund: 4 out of 11

Although the Asian index has a better track record over one, three, and five years than the average fund, it was only able to beat the average in four of the past 11 years. If we change the end date to December 31, 1997, the average active manager would have outperformed the index-minus-fees over three years by 1.6 percent, but would have underperformed the index-minus-fees by 0.3 percent over five years.

Although more managers lost against a typical index fund over three years, the winners did quite well. I'm showing you a three-year comparison since there are more funds to look at over this period; however, I will point out that managers didn't do quite as well against the index over five years:

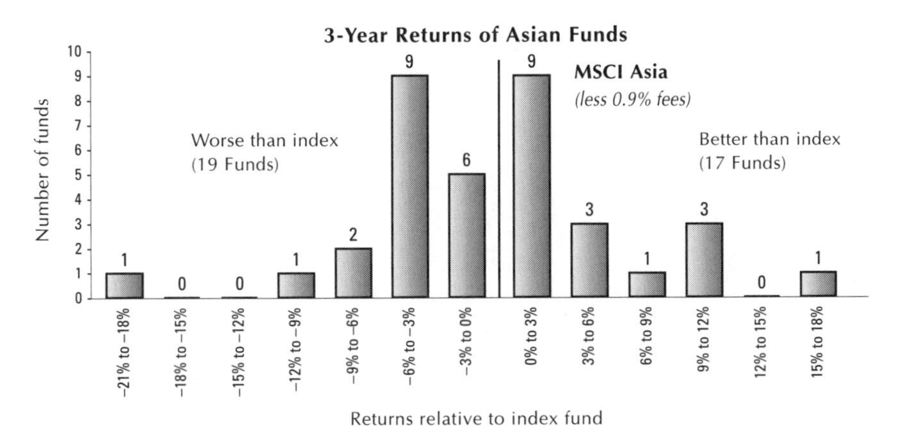

The emerging markets index does even more poorly against the average manager. Let's compare the active emerging markets funds to the MSCI Emerging Markets Free index:

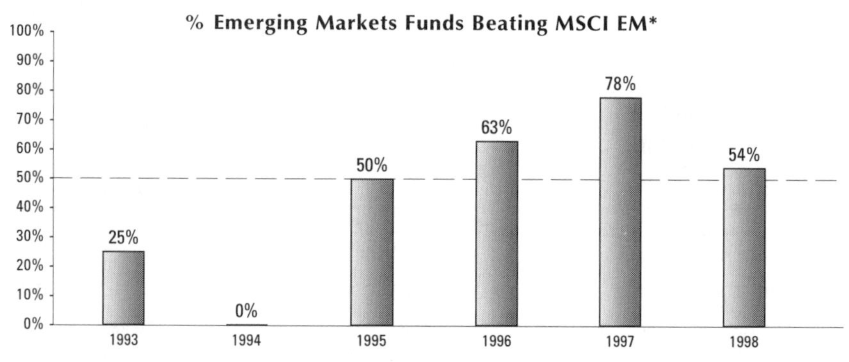

*0.9% has been deducted from index to simulate an index fund

And the average active emerging markets manager did reasonably well over three and five years, against the emerging markets index-minus-fees:

% Returns	1-year	3-year	5-year
		(Ending December 31, 1998)	
MSCI Emerging Markets (less 0.9%)	(20.8)	(8.5)	(7.6)
Average Emerging Market Fund	(19.9)	(5.7)	(4.0)
Difference	(0.9)	(2.8)	(3.6)

Number of years MSCI Emerging beat the average fund: 4 out of 7

Bob: Man. Those emerging markets returns are ugly!

Ted: Yes, the emerging markets have had a rough time of it, although they will come back. Using December 31, 1997, as an end date, the results are similar: the average active manager beats the index over all three periods. If you go back further, to December 31, 1996, when the emerging markets showed positive returns over the periods, index fund returns were more competitive against the average active manager, although not by much. The emerging markets, being less efficient, are clearly a place where an active manager has a better chance of outperforming the index.

When you look at the percentage of managers who were able to beat the emerging markets index by a reasonable margin, you can start to see how the active manager can really add value in these less efficient markets.

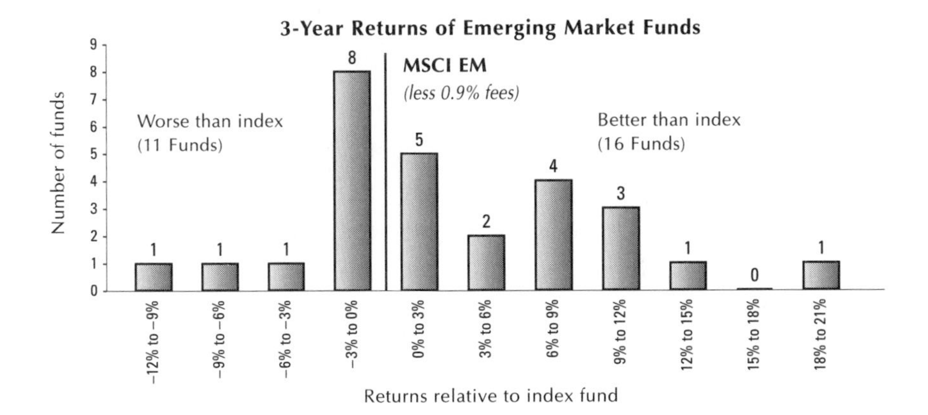

Brenda: These numbers are a little confusing. They suggest that managers of Asian funds tend to beat the index by a healthy margin, but not over five years. Emerging markets managers are able to beat the index each year, but not by as large a margin as Asian-fund managers.

Ted: Yes, this is a case where the numbers can get a little confusing. This is because there is not as much history for Asian and emerging markets funds, so we can't go as far back to make comparisons. And these markets can be so volatile that the returns bounce around a lot. Compared to the other equity markets we've looked at, there is more latitude for managers of Asian funds to make bigger bets in certain countries. For instance, some Asian-fund managers have very little exposure to Japan, which means they can deviate quite significantly from the index because the index is about 65 percent weighted in Japanese stock. Similarly, emerging markets managers can overweight developing Asian economies and underweight Latin American economies — strategies which can also lead to returns that are very different from the index and from other managers. The emerging markets index is weighted about 45 percent in Latin America, for example, so an active manager can generate returns that deviate substantially from the index simply by choosing to increase the percentage of her fund in Asia and reducing the exposure to Latin America.

It's safe to say that beating the index in the Asian and emerging markets is not as challenging as the more developed and efficient markets of North America and Europe.

Brenda: Any other places where active managers always do well?

Ted: Specialty sectors like technology, precious metals, health care, and resources. In these more narrow sectors, there is either no appropriate index, or it just doesn't make sense for a manager to index the sector since a skilled manager can easily do better. There is not enough history for Japanese equity funds to be definitive on whether or not active Japanese managers can beat the Nikkei 225 — the most common Japanese index. A good active manager should be able to beat the Nikkei 225, since he can pick small companies that aren't in the index.

Bob: So what does all this mean? My head is spinning and I'm starting to lose track of what all these charts and numbers are supposed to prove.

Ted: The charts prove how powerful indexing can be as an investment strategy. In most markets, particularly the very efficient ones, the active manager is hard pressed to beat the index.

In most years, and in most markets, most managers are not able to beat the index, even after deducting 0.9 percent from the index.

The average manager tends to underperform the index in most markets. And, in those same markets, a lot more individual managers underperform the index than beat it. Not only do most underperform the index, but **the managers who are able to outperform don't beat the index by much.** Finally, **the managers who underperform the index tend to underperform it by quite a bit.**

Brenda: I can see why you're so keen on this indexing thing.

Ted: You simply can't deny the statistics. They tell a very definite story — the story that indexing is a very powerful investing technique.

Bob: I'm all statisticked out. Can we take a break from numbers? Please?

Ted: Okay. But you have to admit that it's amazing when you consider the millions of dollars that investors put into underperforming funds. *Canadian Business* magazine reported in its February 26, 1999, edition that 82 percent of all money invested in Canadian mutual funds was in funds that didn't beat the index. That means many investors are losing out on a lot of money!

The Bottom Line

The index is a hard benchmark to beat in most markets. The *average* manager has underperformed the index over short and long periods of time. The *majority* of active managers have underperformed the index in most years. The ones that are able to beat the index don't beat it by much. The majority that underperform the index tend to underperform it by a lot.

The case for indexing depends on the market that is being invested in. The US stock market is very efficient and the case for indexing it is simply undeniable. The Canadian market is a little easier to beat but most active managers fail to. In European equity and Canadian bond markets, the index outperforms most managers. It is not until you get to the less efficient markets, such as Asia, and especially emerging markets, such as Latin America and Eastern Europe, that the active manager has a better track record for beating the index.

3

Why Indexing Is So Powerful

It's all well and good to shower you with statistics. The numbers alone tell a very interesting story that should command your attention. But if all these numbers are to have any relevance, then they have to be supported by solid reasons that explain them and show that indexing will continue to be powerful in the future, as it has been in the past. Otherwise, the impressive results of indexing may be just coincidental. The last thing anyone needs is another investment fad that is hot today and disappointing tomorrow.

Are there legitimate and compelling reasons why the index usually beats *most* active managers in *most* markets, *most* of the time? You'd better believe there are. This chapter is the centrepiece of the book in many ways. It outlines why indexing has been and *will continue to be* a successful investment strategy. I will walk Bob and Brenda through the arguments one by one, allowing them to question me along the way. In the chapter that follows this one, I will let Bob and Brenda have their way with me . . . they will shoot their best objections at me and I will attempt to address them one by one. I will leave no stone unturned, and no objection unanswered.

Before we tackle objections in the next chapter, we'll start with the rationale for why indexing works. The power of indexing is multifaceted, combining superior performance with other benefits that are not directly related to performance. I'll address each of the advantages in turn.

Here are the five reasons why indexing — and an index mutual fund in particular — outperforms most actively managed funds:

1. Index fund fees (management expense ratios and commissions) are lower.
2. Trading costs within an index fund are lower.
3. Capital gains taxes are largely deferred in index funds.
4. Cash holdings in index funds are lower (in fact, they're close to zero).
5. The ability of active managers to "beat the market" is limited, over the long term.

Here are three other reasons why indexing is powerful, besides the ones above that explain why your odds of outperforming are better:

1. Index funds are one of the very few ways that you can entirely escape the foreign content constraints that the government places on your RRSPs and RRIFs.
2. Indexing allows you to make pure and therefore more effective asset allocation decisions, since you know exactly what you're investing in.
3. Indexing is one of the most convenient ways to invest.

Let's pick up the conversation where we left off and see if I can convince Bob and Brenda on each of these points.

Bob: So why does the index do so well? Why do the managers underperform it in most markets?

Ted: That's the $100,000 question, isn't it? After all, as we've seen, your savings could be increased by hundreds of thousands of dollars if you had the index returns compared to the average actively managed returns. There are a number of reasons why the index is hard to beat. I'll tell you about all of them since they are each very important on their own.

Fees — how they add up for actively managed funds

Ted: The first reason is as straightforward as it is important. The index funds have lower fees. You rarely have to pay a commission, or "load," as it's called, to purchase an index fund. That's because most index funds are sold at banks and other no-load fund companies.

Many actively managed funds in Canada are sold with an up-front commission or "front-end load." This up-front charge ranges from 2 to 6 percent of your investment. Even more funds are sold with a commission that is paid if you redeem the fund before a certain time period has elapsed, usually between five and seven years. These commissions are called "back-end loads." Back-end commissions vary, but are usually around 2 to 3 percent if you redeem your money five years after you invested it, or as high as 5 to 6 percent if you redeem within the first year. The funds sold at banks and direct marketing companies are called "no-load" funds because there are no commissions to buy or sell them. Index funds are usually no-load.

The brokers and planners that sell index funds can charge a front-end commission on some index funds. They justify this charge on the grounds that they need to get compensated for the advice they are giving you. This is a legitimate argument, but only if you are getting high-quality advice. The fund companies usually pay the brokers and planners an ongoing fee called a "trailer fee." This fee, which is usually around 0.25 to 0.5 percent of your assets for an index fund, is paid to the adviser for servicing an investor. In addition to the trailer fee paid to your adviser by the fund company, *you* are likely to be charged either an upfront commission of up to 4 percent or an annual fee of 0.5 to one percent. As an alternative, many of the major banks are able to offer advice, especially when it comes to putting together a portfolio of index funds. You can also buy index funds without paying a commission at most discount brokerage firms.

More important than the savings on commissions are the lower ongoing fees associated with index funds. Here I'm referring to the management expense ratio (MER), which is the name given to the total fees charged to you on an annual basis. It is a ratio because it is calculated as a percentage of your investment — usually around 2 to 3 percent, for the typical actively managed fund. That's a lot of money every year that comes right out of your returns. When you look at your mutual fund returns in the newspaper or on your statement, the fees have already been deducted, so you might not even be aware of them! The MER fees are the payment that the fund company charges for managing the investment, operating the fund, and administering your account.

Brenda: I know what an MER is.

Bob: Never heard of it before.

Ted: Research has shown that most people — as high as 70 percent of Canadian investors — don't know about MERs. But a higher MER fee can have an enormous impact on your returns. Take a look at this chart. It shows how the higher fees associated with the average active fund fee can really take a bite out of your returns, when compared with lower index fund fees. I'm assuming the average index fee of 0.9 percent and the average active fee of 2.25 percent. It tracks two investments — one of $10,000 and one of $25,000. Both are tracked over 20 years.

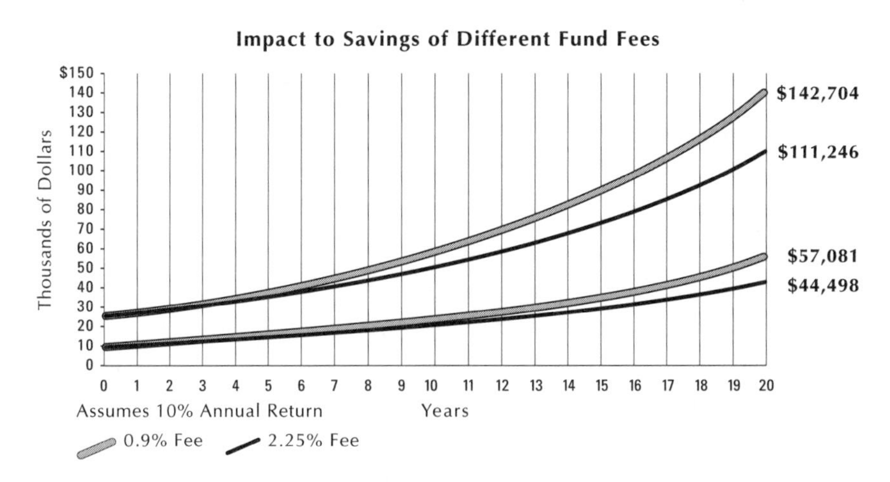

Bob: Those fees really add up over time.

Ted: The effect of compounding year over year can really make innocent-looking fees become real culprits. Look at the difference to your final investment over 10 and 20 years. With a $10,000 investment, you end up being $12,583 richer with the lower fee and with a $25,000 investment, you are $31,458 richer. You can't ignore these kinds of results.

The average fees on index funds are less than half of the average fees on active funds:

	Average Active Fees	Average Index Fees
Canadian Equity Fund	2.25%	0.95%
US Equity Fund	2.20%	1.00%
International Equity Fund	2.50%	1.00%
Canadian Bond Fund	1.60%	0.85%

Bob: So why are the index funds so much cheaper?

Ted: Because of the buy-and-hold nature of indexing. The manager isn't trading a lot in the index fund — he's not researching which stocks or bonds will do better than the rest. He is simply buying the securities in the index and holding them. The cost of management, therefore, is a lot less since the decision on what to buy and hold is already made. No effort, time, or money has to go into choosing which stocks to buy for an equity index fund.

Brenda: In other words, the index manager is just a robot.

Ted: As a matter of fact he is anything but a robot. He has to have a special skill in matching the index. Let's say that there are 50 investors on a particular day that all buy into an index fund. It is likely to be the case that their purchases do not add up to enough cash to buy all the stocks in the index. The manager has to use sophisticated computer modelling and a lot of skill to determine which stocks to buy that will most closely match the index, until he gets enough investors' cash in to buy all the stocks.

That's why there is a cost to managing an index fund. It will never be entirely free. But the lower cost of managing an index fund gives it a huge advantage over an active fund.

Brenda: It's pretty obvious how the difference in fees can add up.

Ted: Not only that. Think of the active manager and the index manager both at the starting line of a 25-year marathon that happens to be your personal investment time horizon. The active manager would have to start far behind the index manager since he has a large fee differential to make up before he's even in the running with the index manager.

So he has to run harder and faster to just catch up to the index manager, before he is even neck and neck. And then he has to continue running harder and faster to get ahead of the index manager. He would have to be a very athletic marathoner to cover as many miles and ultimately get as far as the index manager, over the same 25 years.

Bob: It would be impossible for him to beat the index manager.

Ted: It's not impossible. In fact it has been done. But not by many. The fact that the active manager starts the marathon at such a severe disadvantage makes it difficult for him to add value on a consistent basis, above and beyond the index, since he has to catch up to it first!

Brenda: So the commissions to buy many active funds and their higher MERs give the index fund a significant advantage.

Trading costs — why they're lower for index funds

Ted: Right, but we're still not done with the fee issue. Not only are there the commissions and MERs to think about, but there are other less conspicuous fees that affect your returns. These are the transaction costs for buying and selling the securities for the fund itself. It's interesting — where fees are concerned, we always come back to the comparison between the buy-and-hold strategy of indexing, and the buy-sell-buy-sell strategy of active management. That difference has many implications to an investor.

Don't forget that the index fund is simply buying the stocks in the index, and holding them. A Canadian index fund will buy and hold the stocks in the TSE 300. There are only two reasons for an index manager to buy or sell a stock. *First*, if the index changes, the fund must change. If stocks are taken out of the index, the manager must sell those stocks and purchase any stocks that are added to the index. Or if the weight of certain stocks changes in the index, then the manager must make changes in the fund. Changes occur to an index because of stocks that are replaced because they no longer meet the criteria required to be included in the index. Changes can also occur when mergers or acquisitions change the stock that is publicly available, new stock issues are brought to the market, or a company buys back some of its stock. The dividends that stocks pay will alter the weightings of the stocks in the index as well. When the index changes, the index manager must shift her index fund to match the change. These changes are usually made at the end of each calendar quarter, but can be made immediately to the index if they are big enough. Most big shifts in the index occur once a year when a more thorough review of the index is implemented.

The *second* reason for a manager to buy or sell a security in an index fund occurs when investors make new purchases in the fund or redeem units. The new cash must be invested, or, in the case of redemptions, stocks must be sold to pay out the investor.

These two drivers of activity in an index fund do not generate that much buying and selling. The securities in an index do not change frequently and managers usually use derivative products, such as futures, or trust units, such as TIPS, to manage small cash flows in an index fund.

In an active fund, the manager must also buy to invest cash or sell to meet redemptions. But in addition, she is always on the lookout for securities that she thinks will generate better returns than the market. For example, when she finds a stock that she thinks will outperform the market, she will buy it. But at some point she'll decide to sell it because it has generated a good return and she thinks it will no longer outperform. Or she may revise her opinion of the stock and decide that it is no longer a good hold. Alternatively, she may find a stock that she likes better, in which case she would switch the two stocks by selling the first one and buying the second.

I'm going to show you the "turnover" of an index fund compared to an active fund. A fund that is constantly buying and selling stocks has a very high turnover because it is turning over its portfolio more quickly. A fund with 100 percent turnover is a fund that either sells every stock in a year and buys another to replace it, or buys and sells some stocks so many times that the activity is equivalent to selling every stock in the fund. Turnover measures the percentage of a fund that is bought and sold in a given year.

Percentage of Stocks Bought and Sold in a Year		
	Active Fund	Index Fund
Range of Turnover	30–150%	5–15%
Average Turnover	85%	10%

The typical active fund will buy and sell between 30 percent and 150 percent of its entire holdings in a year. Some funds even have turnover ratios of 200 percent, which means they buy and sell so much that it is equivalent to selling every stock in the whole portfolio, buying new ones, selling the new ones and buying still newer ones — all in the same year! Turnover of 30 percent is considered extremely low for an active fund.

Brenda: Why on earth would a manager buy and sell so much? Do they make that many mistakes?

Ted: No. It's simply a matter of trading for short-term gains. They buy a stock that they think might go up fast over a short period of time, such as within the next month or two. And when it does goes up, they sell it, take the gain, and buy another stock. Or if it doesn't go up, they sell it to buy another one that they think will go up.

Bob: Sounds nuts.

Ted: Some managers have made great names for themselves using this strategy, so it can't be that crazy. But a manager has to be pretty skilled to be able to keep trading in and out and make good returns for his clients.

Brenda: So why is turnover important?

Ted: Turnover is extremely important. Turnover can have as much impact on your returns as the lower fees can. All that buying and selling has two effects: it generates more trading costs that are charged to the fund, and it increases the present value of the capital gains tax you have to pay.

Bob: Okay, I'm lost. Time for a break.

Brenda: Shush.

Ted: It's actually not as complicated as I just made it sound. Let's leave the tax issue aside for the moment, and come back to it. Trading costs are the costs that the fund pays as the manager buys and sells securities for the fund. The most obvious of these costs are brokerage commissions, which are paid to brokers for buying and selling the stocks in the mutual fund.

Brenda: I thought you said that index funds usually don't charge load commissions for purchases or redemptions?

Ted: That was for the investor buying or selling the fund. But now I'm talking about the fund manager buying and selling the stocks that are in the fund itself. When the fund manager buys or sells a stock, he has to pay a commission just like anybody else.

Bob: Same for a bond?

Ted: Actually, the bond commission is built into the difference between the buy and sell price of the bond, which is known as the "spread." But it's still there, just less visible.

Let's look at what happens when a manager buys a stock for a fund. The fund manager usually trades through an institutional equity trader at one of the big brokerage firms. The flow of the transaction looks like this:

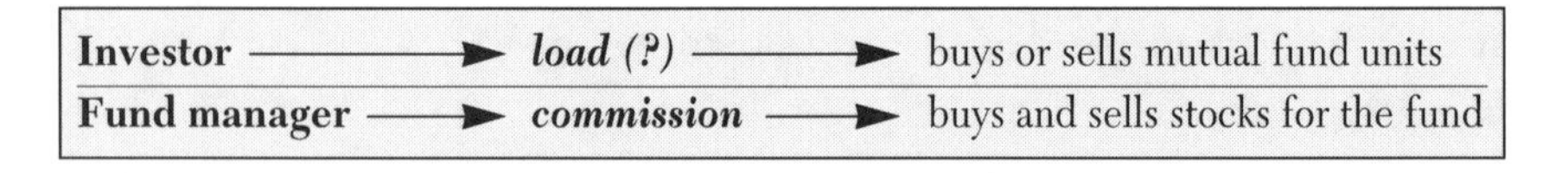

Investor →	***load (?)*** →	buys or sells mutual fund units
Fund manager →	***commission*** →	buys and sells stocks for the fund

Although I've written *load*, which is what you pay to buy or sell your mutual fund, you may not necessarily pay one, depending on whether it's a no-load fund or not; hence the question mark in my diagram. Most index funds are no-load. Where I've written *commission* you can see where the fund manager pays the institutional broker a fee for buying and selling the stock that goes into the fund.

Bob: So there are two commissions — one to buy the fund and another to buy the stocks for the fund?

Brenda: Well, the commissions that the fund manager pays would already be in the MER fees that are charged to the fund anyway, so they have already been taken into account.

Ted: And that's exactly the point — they're not!

Brenda: They're not in the MERs?

Ted: No. There are two fees that do not appear in the MERs, and one is the commission on buying and selling stocks for the fund. Many people who know a lot about mutual funds don't know this tidy little fact.

Bob: We'll be sure to share it at the next cocktail party we're invited to.

Brenda: You said there were two fees that aren't in the MERs. What's the other one?

Ted: Can you guess?

Bob: Someone's salary or bonus?

Ted: Not quite. It's GST.

Bob: Brother.

Ted: But the point worth noting is that because there is so much buying and selling in an active fund, there are a lot more brokerage commissions paid out of the fund. And you probably aren't even aware of them since they are virtually invisible to you, unless you go through the annual financial statements of the funds very carefully. You will find them listed in dollar amounts. The annual financial statements are mailed to you once a year by the fund companies.

Not only do active fund managers pay more brokerage commissions, because they do more buying and selling, but the commission *rates* they pay are higher than they are for index funds. Whereas an active manager might pay around five cents a share, an index manager would pay around three cents. This is because the fund manager has to reward the institutional equity broker for the research and stock tips that are passed on to her as she is managing the fund. Some of the fund manager's ideas are generated from the research departments of the institutional equity brokers. In the case of an index fund, there is no research, so no payment has to be made for this service. Additionally, the index manager often buys the index stocks in baskets, all at once. This enables her to pay a reduced commission since she is, in effect, buying in bulk. Nearly 80 percent of her purchases can be made in bulk by ordering a customized basket of the stocks she needs. So not only is the actual commission rate lower for an index fund, but commissions are paid less frequently since there's less turnover. *The active manager pays a higher commission, and pays it more frequently.*

Here's a comparison between the commissions a typical actively managed equity fund pays in a year for buying and selling stocks, and the same for an index fund. The commissions are expressed as a percentage of assets managed:

	Active Fund	Index Fund
Annual Trading Commissions	0.3–1.1%	0.03–0.25%

The active fund pays a higher commission and pays it more often, resulting in an annual trading commission that is around five times as large. Those commissions come right out of your return because they are charged to the fund. You can see how that gives the index fund another fee advantage. The disadvantage that the active manager has to overcome is quite significant. We'll add all these fee differences up when I'm done.

Bob: You mean there are more fee differences?

Ted: You bet. I told you there were solid reasons underpinning the outperformance of the index fund. It's not just coincidence or bad luck on the part of active managers.

The higher turnover of the active funds generates additional costs that go beyond just the brokerage commissions. When a manager buys a stock there are actually four costs associated with the trade. Brokerage commissions are only one of them. The other three costs are market-related costs.

The first is the bid-ask spread, which simply means the difference between the price that a buyer is willing to pay to purchase the stock, and the price that the stock is being offered at by a seller. Every time a fund manager buys and sells a stock, he can lose the spread. If he buys a stock one week at the asking price of $5.00 and then decides to sell it one week later, he might only be able to get $4.95 even if the stock itself hasn't gone up or down. The reason is that on the particular day he wants to sell the stock, there simply might not be that many interested buyers. With fewer buyers bidding for the stock, the bid price might be firm at $4.95 and no higher. In order to sell the stock, he has to "step across the bid-ask spread." That's five cents he lost, on every share traded.

Brenda: Why wouldn't he just wait for there to be more buyers so he can get $5.00?

Ted: He may want to buy another stock with the money — a stock he thinks will do better. Or he may be worried that the stock he wants to sell is going to go down, so he wants to unload it as quickly as possible. Bid-ask spread costs range from 0.3 percent for funds investing in large-cap stocks that are actively traded, to as high as 3 percent for funds with small companies that don't trade very often.

There are two other costs associated with trading. There is a market impact cost and an opportunity cost.

Bob: You know I'm not planning to be a mutual fund manager, in case there's any confusion in your mind.

Ted: Hang in there, I'm almost done explaining costs. It's important to understand how much of an advantage the index funds have.

Market impact is the effect that buying has on a stock's price. It's just like quantum mechanics, where you affect the speed of an electron as you attempt to locate it with a beam of light, so you can never know both the speed and location of the electron at the same time.

Bob: You're not making this any easier, you know.

Ted: Sorry. It's simple, actually. If everyone is trying to buy a stock, then the price will be pushed up, just as prices always go up for things that are in high demand. If an active manager decides that she wants to add a particular stock to her portfolio, then she puts in an order to buy it at a certain price. But if the order she puts in is large enough, the sellers of the stock might decide that they can get a better price, and so the asking price jumps up. The impact of buying on a stock price depends on how many shares the manager wants to buy and how many shares are available for sale. Small companies have fewer shares available on the market and are therefore subject to greater market impact than larger companies with many available shares. The cost of market impact is more relevant to an actively managed fund, especially one that has smaller-company stocks in it, because active managers trade more frequently and are therefore much more subject to their own undesirable influence on the prices of the stocks they are buying and selling.

Bob: Let's get to the last cost and finish up this fee thing. I get the point already.

Ted: The last cost is called the opportunity cost because it measures the cost of lost opportunities to the manager. Let's say a manager decides to buy a stock and places a buy order at a certain price. But before all of the stock he wants is purchased, the price goes up and he decides it's too expensive so he cancels the rest of his outstanding order. He has lost the opportunity to own the stock that he wanted.

Brenda: That sounds like the same as market impact cost.

Ted: Not quite since the cost of market impact makes the purchase more expensive whereas the opportunity cost represents a failure to make the purchase at all. Opportunity cost is not an issue with indexing since the stocks are always bought at or near the closing day prices, no matter what those prices are. It's impossible to quantify opportunity cost for an active manager, so I'm not going to include it in any comparisons, but it's there nonetheless and simply represents the failed attempts of an active manager to buy a stock at a price that he thinks is reasonable. He ends up not owning a stock he wanted to own.

Here's an indication of how the different costs add up for active and index funds. Most people just focus on the commissions and management expense ratios, but the other costs should not be ignored. The load commissions paid by an investor for buying or selling the fund are one-time costs, not ongoing ones. But they can take a large bite out of an investor's returns, so I've included them, but not added them in as specific amounts. Many studies have been done to measure the average costs of bid-ask spread and market impact. These two costs are related to the turnover of the fund since they both relate to the buying and selling frequency of the securities.

	Active	Index	Difference
Load Commissions	Often	Rarely	0–5% one-time fee
MERs	2.25%	0.90%	1.35%
Turnover Costs:			
Brokerage commissions	0.40%	0.05%	0.35%
Bid-ask spread	0.40%	0.10%	0.30%
Market impact	0.50%	0.05%	0.45%
Total Fees/Costs	**3.55% + loads**	**1.10%**	**2.45% + loads**

Every study and every manager will estimate commissions, bid-ask spread, and market impact differently, and these costs will vary from fund to fund, depending on whether the fund is focused on small-cap stocks or large-cap stocks. However, every study and almost every manager I've talked to estimates the difference between active and index costs to be between 1.5 and 4 percent. On the low end of the difference, an active fund may have a low MER and very little turnover, in which case the difference could be just over one percent. On the high end of the difference, an active fund may have a high MER, high turnover, and be buying and selling small-cap stocks which are less liquid and therefore have bigger bid-ask spreads and market impact costs. In the latter case, the difference could easily be close to 4 percent. In between the two extremes is the basic fact that there is usually about a 2.5 percent difference in costs between the active and index fund. *The point is that there is more to the index fund cost advantage than just MERs.*

Cash drag

Part of the reason index funds do so well is the difference in management expense fees and trading costs. But there are other factors that contribute to the stellar returns of the index, including the fact that index funds hold little or no cash. Because they are attempting to generate the same returns as the index they track, they can't hold cash because they must hold the same securities, in the same proportions, as the index. In order to meet redemptions or handle small inflows of cash from investors who purchase, for example, a Canadian equity index fund, the fund manager will put the cash in derivatives or unit trusts such as TIPS. These products can be easily bought and sold and they allow an index manager to quickly invest cash or meet redemptions without actually buying individual stocks. The benefit of TIPS is that they are trusts that represent a basket of stocks on the TSE, so they generate the same performance as the index, but they are easier to buy and sell than all of the stocks at once.

Active managers have to hold some cash or else they wouldn't be able to meet redemptions — unless they sold some of their stocks, which they don't want to do since they might not be able to get the price they want on any given day. Most active managers also hold cash so that they can buy stocks if their prices go down to levels where they are deemed to be attractive.

Bob: Why wouldn't an index fund manager just hold TIPS and nothing else in the fund, if they're so great?

Ted: First of all there are no TIPS for the TSE 300 index — only for the Toronto 35 index. But even if there were, or if the index fund was tracking the Toronto 35, the manager would be reluctant to invest a lot in TIPS because the dividends are not paid out until the end of each calendar quarter. That delay would generate a tracking error for the manager since the actual index assumes automatic reinvestment of stock dividends as they are paid by companies. The TSE withholds dividends until quarter end in order to cover the costs of administering the TIPS.

Brenda: Why does holding cash affect returns?

Ted: If markets go up then cash is a drag on performance. If markets go down, then cash is a cushion against falling returns. But what direction do you think markets go in the long term?

Brenda: Up. So cash is a drag in the long run.

Ted: You got it. The average manager of an active Canadian equity fund holds as much as 10 percent of the fund in cash. That's a lot of money to not have invested in the stock market over the long term. While the stock portion of the fund can be expected to generate around 9 to 11 percent in returns over the long run, the cash portion will only generate 3 percent. The cash holdings of the active fund put it at a disadvantage of around 0.7 percent or more per year. That may not sound like much, but over 10 years a $10,000 investment could easily earn an extra $1,500 or more by not holding cash.

The Canadian and US stock markets have been negative only once over a 10-year period and that was during the Depression. It has been estimated that over a 10-year period, the odds of stock markets generating a negative return is between one and 2 percent. Over a five-year period it's somewhere around 5 percent. The TSE 300 index was established in 1956. Since then, there have been over 400 10-year periods that began and ended on each month since its inception. Of those hundreds of 10-year periods, there has not been one period that was negative. And of the 500 periods that are five years in length, there have been only three that were negative. These three occurred in the last few months of 1974 and were minus 2.2 percent, minus 1.5 percent, and minus 0.6 percent, respectively.

The odds of the stock markets going down over a five-year period are low. They are extremely low over 10 years, and practically nonexistent over 20 years — not impossible, mind you, just unlikely. As a long-term investor, you can count on the probabilities of the market going up, and so you want your mutual fund to hold as little cash as possible.

Bob: What's long term?

Ted: I would say that if your time horizon is less than five years you're not really investing, just saving. You shouldn't be invested in the stock market for less than a five-year period, unless you have money that you are prepared to risk losing. Most of the volatility that occurs in a stock's price is driven by changes in a company's earning expectations within the next five years. So long term in my mind is anything longer than five years.

Brenda: So index funds win out because the all-in fees are lower and because they don't hold cash, which drags down performance in the long term.

Ted: And there's more. The performance comparison tables I showed you earlier all demonstrate how the returns of index funds have done against their actively managed counterparts. But we've only compared returns as they are reported in the newspapers, on the Internet, and by the fund companies themselves. They aren't the actual returns that you get at the end of the day.

Bob: Because the brokerage commissions haven't been taken off.

Ted: No, those have been taken off. The brokerage commissions are not part of a fund's MER so they are harder to see and assess, but they are deducted before returns are published. By regulation, fund companies must deduct all expenses that are directly charged to the funds before publishing the returns. But the returns you *read about* aren't the returns you *get*.

Bob: Oh, yeah. It's the load commissions that you might pay that aren't reflected in the reported returns.

Ted: I wasn't thinking of those but you're absolutely right. Sales commissions to buy and sell the funds are not reported in the published returns. But even for no-load funds where there are no sales commissions, the reported returns are not the ones you actually earn.

Bob: What is this — a trick question? How could the reported returns not be the ones we earn if all the fees have been deducted?

Brenda: I know. It's because most investors aren't invested for the exact period that the returns are calculated for. Just because the newspaper reports that a fund had a 14 percent return for the year ending December 31 doesn't mean that's the return most investors got. Only the ones that invested on December 31 the year before got that exact return.

Ted: That's true, and a very good point. But even the investors who put their money in on December 31 the year before didn't earn the reported return.

Bob: So what's the big mystery?

Ted: The fee that isn't as obvious is the biggest fee of all. But it doesn't go to the fund company or the person advising you on your portfolio. This fee goes to Ottawa every April.

Bob: Tax. Of course.

Capital gains tax — to defer or not to defer

Ted: The return you earn is a lot less than the reported return, and it will depend on what your marginal tax rate is.

Brenda: But the active and index funds are both taxed the same, so I don't see why the index fund is advantaged.

Ted: You're right — they are taxed the same way. But the amount of tax you pay is different.

Bob: You must be a big Lewis Carroll fan. I keep feeling like I'm in *Alice in Wonderland*.

Ted: Let me explain. The index fund benefits from a larger deferral of capital gains tax. Before you say anything, don't worry, you don't have to be an accountant to understand this.

It goes back once again to the fact that the active fund does much more trading. That higher trading has many implications to an investor's ultimate return. The result of higher trading is that there are more stocks sold during the year. Many of these stocks are sold at a gain. That's the intent of the manager, of course, to sell stocks at a gain and buy other stocks that she thinks will go up even more.

The problem is that every time a stock is sold at a gain, a capital gains distribution is made, which appears on the T3 tax slip sent to you in late February or early March by the fund company. You have to report the capital gains on your tax return and pay tax on it. The more gains that are generated from buying and selling, the more tax you have to pay. A fund with a very high turnover, one that is constantly buying and selling stocks all year, will distribute large capital gains to you and your tax liability will be higher.

The index fund, as we've seen, does not do a lot of buying and selling. It simply buys and holds the securities in the index. So there is much less capital gains distribution. The only reason for a capital gains distribution to occur is . . .

Brenda: When the index changes so the manager has to change the stocks he's holding, or if he sells stocks to meet redemptions.

Ted: Exactly.

Bob: Why don't you two lovebirds carry on while I grab a beer and watch some TV?

Brenda: Oh, come on, Bob. Admit it, you're learning a lot. So Ted, we're paying a lot less tax on the index funds and that never shows up in the return comparisons.

Ted: It never shows up. But it's not exactly that you're paying less tax. You're postponing paying tax. You're deferring it. You actually end up paying the tax when you sell your fund units at the end of your investment time horizon. In the active fund, the adjusted cost base of your investment increases with every capital gains distribution, so your capital gains tax is less when you eventually sell the fund. It's not important to understand all of the accounting intricacies, but it *is* important to understand that although you pay roughly the same amount of tax with both types of funds, the postponement — or deferral — of capital gains tax is a benefit. By deferring the payment of tax, you keep your money working for you over a longer period of time and that can add up to a lot of extra returns.

Let's say I gave you the choice of giving me $100 now or in 10 years. Which would you choose?

Bob: I'd choose 10 years since it would probably be worth less than it is worth now.

Brenda: We could invest the $100 for 10 years, and keep the interest we earned, after paying back the original $100 to you in 10 years' time.

Ted: That's precisely right and the exact same principle applies to the deferral of tax. By postponing the payment of it until you sell the fund, you keep the money earning returns on itself and therefore you generate higher returns overall.

There will always be some capital gains distributed in an index fund, since the stocks or the weighting of the stocks in the index can be changed. But the capital gains generated from these changes are much less significant than the gains you'd have to pay tax on in an active fund. Most studies suggest that the deferred-capital-gains benefit of low turnover funds generates an additional one to 3 percent in returns each year, depending on how long you keep the investment. Over a 10-year period, an active fund with turnover of 80 percent could generate about one percent less in annual after-tax returns than an index fund. Over a 20-year period, the difference would be around 1.8 percent. For a fund with very high turnover, greater than 100 percent, the tax impact can be as high as a 2 percent annual penalty against your returns. Whatever you pay as tax on the distributions that are made from the fund is money you don't have working for you to earn more returns.

Adding up all the fees and costs

I can add this difference to the chart I showed you earlier — the one that compares the fees of active and index funds. I'll be conservative and estimate a tax fee of one percent from the higher turnover that occurs in the active fund. While I'm at it, I'll add in the cost of cash drag as well.

	Active	Index	Difference
Load Commissions	0–5% one-time fee	Rarely	0–5% one-time fee
MERs	2.25%	0.90%	1.35%
Turnover Costs:			
Brokerage commissions	0.40%	0.05%	0.35%
Bid-ask spread	0.40%	0.10%	0.30%
Market impact	0.50%	0.05%	0.45%
Cash Drag	0.70%	n/a	0.70%
Taxable Capital Gains	1.00%	0.10%	0.90%
Total Fees/Costs	**5.25% + loads**	**1.20%**	**4.05% + loads**

See how the difference in costs is much higher than you might think if you only compare MERs.

Bob: Okay. I think I've got it. Index funds win out because the fees are lower, the hidden costs are lower, the lack of cash provides more return in the long run, and most capital gains taxes are deferred.

That's all well and good, but what about those managers that did beat the index? They were able to overcome all the disadvantages.

The winners — how do they do it?

Ted: Here's an important question to ask if a manager has had spectacular returns: How much risk did he take to get those returns? The problem with some funds is that they post eye-popping returns and so investors flood the fund with their money in the expectation that a brilliant manager will make them rich. The problem is that if you don't look behind the numbers you don't know what's lingering there. It is often the case that the driver behind unusual performance is unusual risk. And the problem with unusual risk is that it can come back to haunt you in the form of unusually bad performance. Here are the returns of an actual fund compared to the TSE. The fund is classified as having higher-than-average risk by all the books and newspapers that rate it.

	Returns (%)									
	1991	1992	1993	1994	1995	1996	1997	1998	5-year	10-year
Fund	34.5	30.2	46.7	1.7	14.8	17.0	4.1	-9.0	5.3	17.1
TSE	12.0	-1.4	32.5	-0.2	14.5	28.3	15.0	-1.6	10.7	9.7

Look at the spectacular returns from 1991 to 1995, when the manager easily beat the index. But then everything fell apart in the next three years. You can see that the five-year returns have badly underperformed the index but the early great years helped the fund show a great 10-year return. The higher-than-average risk didn't pay off in the last few years. Do you think many people who invested in the fund I've shown knew they were in a risky fund? Or do you think they just thought the manager was brilliant and could do no wrong?

Bob: They probably thought he could do no wrong.

Ted: I think so too. And the fact that many of them redeemed their investments over the past few years suggests they lost faith.

Bob: So maybe this manager will come back with a vengeance in 1999 and 2000.

Ted: He can't. He no longer manages the fund. And the fund is now classified as average risk, since it's taken on a new style with a new manager.

Bob: Why is it that a manager who is skilled enough to use risk to his advantage in the early years ends up stumbling later on?

Ted: That's a really important question. Why is it that most managers underperform the index over longer periods of time? Why is it that even the ones that seem to be doing so well appear to stumble eventually?

Brenda: Well, you already told us. The fees and trading costs are higher in active funds, and the long-term holding of cash drags performance down, too.

Bob: But that still doesn't explain why a great manager who has beaten the index year after year can't sustain his performance. Why, for that matter, do so few managers overcome the disadvantages like higher fees?

Ted: I'll tell you why — it's because they're human. Being human has its drawbacks. We're emotional and often irrational. In fact, much of our irrationality comes from our emotions. While emotions can be great survival mechanisms, since they trigger us to action in the face of danger or challenge, they can often interfere with our ability to sustain cold, detached logical thinking. Ever notice that other people's problems seem so easy to solve, while your own often paralyze you? That's because *the emotional interference that our own problems generate gets in the way of rational thinking.*

Unfortunately, investment managers are subject to the same human limitations that all of us are. They can become emotionally affected by the investment choices they make. For example, they often hold on to losing stocks too long in the hopes that they will recover. Alternatively, they might sell stocks that have risen a fair amount, even if there is good reason to think there is still more upside to the stock. They will drift from the strategies that worked for them if they run into market movements that aren't as familiar to them. They will get overly excited about a particular story on one stock and underweight the risks of that stock in their mind.

Simply put, fund managers are vulnerable to the influence of emotion. They are not cold, calculating machines that constantly apply rigorous methodologies in a detached and computer-like way.

Brenda: Although some do use computers, right?

Ted: They all use computers to assess potential investments. And a few managers use nothing but mathematical formulae to pick stocks. But the problem is that the algorithms or rules that are programmed into the computer to buy and sell are often changed, based on the manager's changing view of the markets.

Brenda: But the market itself is equally emotional, isn't it? It gyrates unpredictably in what appears to be a very emotional way. Overreacting to some news, underreacting to other news. Falling 3 percent one day and rising 3 percent the next.

Ted: Well, that's an interesting and debatable point. I think we need to take a moment to talk about the markets themselves. After all, it is the markets that the active managers are attempting to outsmart.

What's so special about the stock markets?

Markets are a little mysterious. The trading prices of securities in the market represent the totality of all investors' views. The buying and selling that occurs determines the trading prices. Every bit of news that comes out, at every minute of the day, can affect the market in some way because the market is always digesting information and revaluing the prices that stocks trade at, on the basis of news. That's why we see swings up and down as information comes out relating to inflation, unemployment, the currencies of other countries, or anything else that might have an impact on prices.

Stock prices simply reflect the expected earnings of companies in the future and the value of those earnings today. Stock prices are affected by changes in those projections. For example, if economic statistics are released that suggest inflation is rising, the market gets nervous that the Bank of Canada might raise interest rates to slow the economy down, and therefore control inflation. But higher interest rates are bad news for future corporate earnings, since the cost of debt increases for companies, consumer demand for their products falls, and higher rates reduce the current value of dividends that will be paid in the future.

Bob: Doesn't sound so mysterious to me — the part I understood, anyway. A little complicated. But not mysterious.

Ted: You're right, that part is not. The mysterious part is in the emotional side of the market. The emotional or less rational part of the market causes exaggerations in the way prices reflect news. It's not that the price movements themselves are irrational, but sometimes the extent of the price changes can be more extreme than the facts would warrant. For example, the market hates uncertainty. Remember that stock prices reflect the estimated value of future earnings. New information about a company or the economy might affect those estimations and, therefore, the prices that are based on them. Any kind of uncertainty makes earnings estimations more difficult. Uncertainty can come in many forms, such as an overseas war, political scandal, or unexpected economic statistics. Because estimations of future earnings become less reliable, the market can react swiftly and viciously to increased uncertainty.

Bob: You're giving me the creeps. You make the market sound like some living, breathing monster.

Ted: In a way it can be seen as a living organism. The market is always assessing the value of future earnings and making "best guess" estimates of future earnings. But these estimates may appear way off when new information is released. A massive reevaluation of pricing can occur as a result. This reevaluation can sometimes get a little carried away as the market reacts, almost emotionally, to the news and gyrates up and down attempting to find a price level that reflects the newest "best guess" of future earnings.

Bob: So what's the bottom line on whether the market is rational or not?

Ted: There are two schools of thought on the question of how rational the market is as a whole. Some academics believe the market is purely rational, and only reflects the consensus of all investors' views, at any given moment. Others believe that the market is largely rational but can be driven from time to time by irrational overreactions to news.

The first view holds that every market move is simply driven by news that causes all investors to reevaluate the prices of every stock. If Russia defaults on its debt, stock prices will fall to account for the increased possibility of a global recession, which will drive down earnings expectations.

The second view insists that the market is as emotional as any one person is. The market will overreact to news because investors tend to overreact. That's why many managers view market dips as "buying opportunities" — when the market corrects its initial overreaction, the prices will rebound to a "less emotional" level. Projecting the earnings of companies is a difficult task that is based on estimates of economic growth, demand for products, and corporate balance sheets. To these inputs you have to factor in the risk of the projections being wrong. In summary, *some people view the price gyrations as the rational reevaluation of prices responding to news. Others see the gyrations as both the rational readjustments to earnings expectations, and irrational overreactions to the news inherent in these readjustments.*

Bob: What do you believe?

Ted: I subscribe to the more common view — that the market moves in reaction to both rational and emotional drivers. Over *shorter* time periods, the irrational elements that drive the market — the ones that exaggerate the ups and downs — can outweigh the rational fundamentals that dominate in the *longer run*. A stock's price reflects the value that investors place on expected future dividends, which are generated from the company's earnings. About half of the value of a typical stock can be attributed to the earnings that the company is expected to generate *after* five years. The other half of its value is driven by the projected earnings in the shorter term — *within* five years. It is this half — the one driven by shorter-term earnings projections — that can cause a stock's price to be very volatile. With every change in earnings projections or interest rate forecasts comes a change in the stock price, which can often be exaggerated by fears or euphoria, depending on what the news is. *It's very difficult, probably impossible, to consistently anticipate the irrational side of the market.*

Bob: Just as you can't anticipate the emotional side of some people I know.

Brenda: Don't get me started, buddy.

Ted: In the long run, the rational side of the market dominates. That's because in the long term, the dividends and the earnings that generate the dividends have the greatest impact on the price of a stock. In the short run, the value that investors put on future earnings can have a large impact on the price of a stock, especially if there is a lot of uncertainty that affects the valuations. But over the long term, the market does reflect an accurate picture of the economy and earnings and that's why it goes up in the long run: because over the long term the economy keeps expanding. If the economy didn't keep expanding, we'd eventually all lose our jobs, unless the world's population stopped growing, which isn't happening.

Brenda: So, the market moves in a rational way most of the time, and always in the long run, by reflecting the long-term earnings of companies. But in the short term, the market can gyrate with price movements that are exaggerated by irrational drivers that alter the valuations that investors put on future earnings.

Ted: Perfect.

Bob: So she gets an "A" in comprehension, but what does all this mean to a fund manager?

The active manager and the market

Ted: The active manager must not only overcome all the starting disadvantages that we've discussed, but he must also overcome the emotional and irrational parts of himself that can interfere with his ability to apply a rigorous technique in choosing securities. Finally, he must be able to understand the wild beast called the market. He must have a solid view on how and why the market moves. Only then does he have a chance of applying his talent to the task of beating the market.

Bob: That sounds doable.

Ted: It is. But to do it consistently over a long period of time is something that only a minority of managers are capable of. Don't forget that the market represents the consensus view of prices. The market is simply the representation of every single investor's opinion on what the prices should be at any given moment in time. All of the investors from all over the world — the small retail players and the huge pension fund managers — are buying and selling and their actions all contribute to the price of every stock and bond that ultimately make up the markets that the stocks and bonds trade in.

In order for an active manager to beat the market, she has to know something that the majority of investors don't know. That's the challenge — if she doesn't possess special information, then she can't outwit everyone else. The consensus view of stock prices is the one that dominates at all times. Over 80 percent of all trading is done by sophisticated institutional investors such as pension funds and mutual fund managers. They spend a lot of time and a lot of money researching stocks and following the markets so one active manager has to either know something that they don't know, or she has to be smarter than everyone else. She has to digest and intellectualize all of the information that is available to everyone, but in a way that is different and enables her to beat the consensus view of prices. Investing is a zero-sum game in the sense that if one investor is right about a stock going up higher or faster than everyone else believes it will, she has to have bought it from someone who didn't believe that and was willing to sell the stock. They can't both be right.

Bob: Getting inside information wouldn't be that hard, I wouldn't think. That would allow her to know something that no one else does.

Ted: But remember, just as company executives can't use inside information for their own benefit, fund managers can't trade on important information that is not public. That kind of activity is illegal and the punishments are very severe. No manager wants to suffer the humiliation and financial impact of having his trading registration revoked. All reputable investment firms have many compliance systems in place to prevent managers from trading on inside information.

Brenda: So it comes down to the talent of an individual manager and her ability to overcome all of the advantages of an index fund. She has to be smarter than other investors. She has to have a solid and rational system for outsmarting the consensus view of prices.

Ted: That's the trick. You can see how hard it is to beat the index. It takes a very unique skill set to beat the market, since the market has a lot going for it: lower fees, lower trading costs, lower cash levels, tax advantages, the consensus view of what the prices should be. The buy-and-hold strategy that index managers employ on stocks works equally well for investors on their mutual fund investments. The concept of indexing is designed to give investors the benefit of long-term growth without sacrificing the returns that are often lost when investors jump from one fund to another, looking for the best short-term returns. Studies have proven that the buy-and-hold strategy almost always beats the buy-sell-buy-sell strategy. In fact, over the decade ending in 1995, the average American stock fund returned 12 percent on average. But the average American investor only enjoyed a return of 7 percent. Do you know why? Simply because the average investor bought the so-called "winning" funds at their peak and sold them long after their returns became disappointing, and then bought another "winning" fund at its peak, sold it after it declined, and so on. It's a proven fact that most investors undermine their own investment returns by trying to time the market, and by trying to jump from previously "winning" funds to the newest crop of "winning" funds. The beauty of indexing is that it is the quintessential buy-and-hold investment strategy. The manager buys and holds the stocks, and the investor buys and holds the fund. Long-term investing that stays the course is the principle upon which indexing is based.

There are other advantages to indexing, and index funds in particular, that are worth mentioning.

Other benefits of indexing — more foreign content, please

Ted: Actually there are at least three more benefits. All relate to performance, but less directly. The first relates to registered accounts only — RRSPs and RRIFs.

As you know, the government limits the amount of foreign content that investors can put into their RRSPs and RRIFs. The maximum foreign content you can have in your registered account is 20 percent of the book value of your investment. Beyond 20 percent you are penalized one percent per month on the amount that exceeds the limit.

Bob: Why do they do that?

Ted: Mostly political reasons. It relates to the perception that it is better for Canadians to invest in Canadian companies to help support our economy. And they fear that by increasing the foreign content that you can hold in your RRSP, demand for Canadian stocks might go down.

Bob: Is that true?

Ted: Not likely. It's highly improbable that every retail investor would dump their Canadian holdings in favour of foreign equities. Besides, the government has recently allowed the Canadian Pension Plan to invest in Canadian equities for the first time, so this will create new demand for Canadian stocks. Up until recently, the CPP only held bonds. But the important point is that an investor's returns can be severely penalized by restricting foreign content to only 20 percent. In 1998, the TSE 300 went down 1.6 percent, whereas both the S&P 500 and the European markets went up by 38 percent. Your RRSP didn't fare so well if you had 80 percent in Canadian stocks.

Bob: So I guess you wouldn't call yourself a patriot.

Ted: It's not that. I love this country. But as much as I love it, and as big and beautiful as it is, it only represents 2 percent of the value of the entire world stock market. That's pretty small in the grand scheme of things. I love Canada, but if I have to choose between being entirely loyal to it and retiring comfortably, it's not a difficult decision to make. Why in the world would anyone want to put so much investment in only one place, especially one as small as Canada? What's more, the Canadian economy is not celebrated for its productivity. We have high taxes . . .

Bob: Tell me about it.

Ted: . . . and our markets are very dependent upon the resource sector and the price of commodities, which explains why 1998 was such a bad year for the TSE — commodity prices declined so resource companies didn't make much profit.

You are already quite heavily invested in Canada if you think about it. Your job is here, so your income is dependent to an extent on the Canadian economy. You buy most of the things you consume in Canada, so you are subject to Canadian inflation. It only makes sense to diversify your investments outside of Canada. In fact, you could make the argument that most of your investments should not be in Canadian stocks. I'll talk about asset allocation and how to diversify your holdings later on. But for now I want you to understand that *most Canadians are far too heavily invested in one small market called "home."* There will be years when the Canadian market does better than many other markets, especially when commodity prices are rising. But for the long term, I'd strongly suggest that 20 percent foreign content is far too low if you are attempting to maximize your returns.

Brenda: So what can we do besides writing our MP to get the foreign content limit raised? What's all of this got to do with indexing?

Ted: Index funds are one of the few ways, and certainly the easiest way, to get around the foreign content constraint. Not just any index fund, mind you. It has to be a derivatives-based index fund. Usually these funds have "RRSP" right in their names to distinguish them as derivatives-based funds that are suited for RRSPs. You don't want to use these funds outside of your RRSP or RRIF because the capital gains on derivatives are treated by Revenue Canada as income, so you don't get the benefit of the favourable way in which capital gains are taxed. Only 75 percent of capital gains are taxable, but 100 percent of income is taxable.

The derivatives-based funds use futures contracts to replicate the returns of an index. But they invest predominantly in treasury bills. Because they invest in T-bills, they are considered domestic content, even though the returns they generate are the same as foreign indexes. The two most common index RRSP funds track the S&P 500 and the MSCI EAFE index.

Here is a chart to help explain the difference between a regular index fund, which invests in the stocks of the index, and a derivatives-based fund, which invests in T-bills and futures contracts. The common index fund, which invests in index stocks, is called a "physical" index fund because it invests in the physical stocks themselves. The derivatives-based index fund invests in futures contracts, which are considered to be derivative financial instruments because the value of the futures contract *derives* from the underlying security that it is based on.

Physical Index Fund		Derivatives Index Fund
500 stocks of the S&P 500	=	Cdn. T-bills in US dollars + S&P futures contracts

In this example I've used the S&P 500 index but we could have shown another example which uses the MSCI EAFE index. The T-bills that the derivatives-based fund invests in are Canadian issued, meaning they are issued from Canadian governments. But they pay interest in US dollars. Because the T-bills are issued by Canadian governments, the fund is considered domestic content. Although both index funds generate the same returns, the derivatives one is not considered foreign content, where the physical one is. You could, in theory, hold 100 percent of your entire portfolio in the derivatives index fund so that your entire RRSP portfolio would generate the same returns as the US market or the EAFE market. I don't recommend that as an investing strategy. But the point is that by using derivatives-based index funds, you are not constrained by the 20 percent foreign content limit, which is an artificial constraint and one that is likely to penalize your returns over the long term. Most people should have a lot more exposure in their RRSPs and RRIFs to foreign equities than they do. Index funds are one of the best ways to diversify outside of Canada beyond 20 percent. And I do strongly recommend diversifying outside of Canada because your returns are affected by the geographic mix of your investments.

Why index funds are better for asset allocations

Here's another benefit of index funds. It relates to the mix of your assets. One of the most important investment decisions you have to make is how much of each asset class you should have in your portfolio and how to diversify your investments geographically. That's why I said earlier that the most important part of a financial adviser's job is helping you construct a portfolio by determining how much you should put into each asset class. We will be putting some portfolios together later on, but for now it is important to stress one point as it relates to indexing.

One of the largest determinants of an investor's overall returns is the mix in his portfolio of cash, bonds, and Canadian and foreign equities. The percentage that each of these assets is allocated — that is, the asset mix — has a crucial impact on the portfolio's returns.

The problem is that because most active mutual funds hold some cash as well as other assets, you aren't able to accurately and effectively manage your asset mix. You can't possibly make your asset mix decisions work for you if you don't know what you're holding.

The beauty of index funds is their purity. Remember how we adjusted the TSE 300 to account for the 9 percent of foreign stocks that are in most Canadian equity funds?

Bob: Yes.

Ted: And remember how we looked at the percentage of cash held in most Canadian equity funds? It averaged around 10 percent.

Bob: Yes.

Ted: Well, those are two examples of how impure most active funds are. They hold all kinds of surprises in them. All Canadian equity funds hold some cash in order to meet client redemptions when they occur. Some funds hold large amounts of cash simply because the managers can't find any stocks that they think are good investments. Most hold US stocks in order to take advantage of the RRSP rules that allow funds to hold up to 20 percent in foreign content. As we saw earlier, this can help boost the returns of a Canadian equity fund.

Bob: So what? That sounds like a good thing.

Ted: In and of itself it's not bad. But the problem is that if portfolio returns vary based on the asset mix decision, how do you know what your actual asset mix is if most of your equity funds are holding some cash, some foreign equities, and even some bonds? Let's say, for example, that the best asset mix for you is 25 percent bonds, 15 percent Canadian stocks, 35 percent US stocks, and 25 percent international stocks. This is the mix that you need to maximize your long-term returns. I'm going to use real, existing mutual funds to demonstrate my point. Say you use a leading active bond fund for the bond allocation, one of Canada's most well-known Canadian equity funds for the Canadian part, a strong-performing US equity fund, and a five-star international fund.

Bob: Sounds like a great mix of funds.

Ted: Sure. But the active funds aren't pure. The bond fund has 10 percent cash. The Canadian fund has 10 percent cash and 15 percent US stocks. The US fund holds 5 percent cash and 5 percent in European stocks. The international fund holds 5 percent cash and 45 percent US equity, but no exposure to Japanese stocks.

Here's the comparison:

	Recommended Asset Mix	Actual Asset Mix
Cash	0%	7%
Bonds	25%	23%
Canadian Equities	15%	11%
US Equities	35%	45%
International Equities	25%	14%

Do you see what's happened here? Because the active funds hold a lot of things that you might not even be aware of, your asset mix gets way out of whack. Don't forget I used the holding of actual star mutual funds, so this is not just an exaggerated example. If you were holding this portfolio of winning funds, you'd better hope that Japan isn't a hot market, since there is none in your international fund. And you'd better hope that the US market is better than any other market, since you unknowingly hold 10 percent more than you are supposed to in US stocks.

Bob: What a mess.

Ted: This problem — and it's a big one — is completely avoided with index funds, since *index funds hold only what they are supposed to.* Indexing allows you to manage your asset mix properly, which is critical given the enormous role that asset mix plays in determining your ultimate returns. An index fund — at least the kind of index fund you should be investing in — is pure. A Canadian equity index fund holds 100 percent TSE 300 stocks, and very little, if any, cash. Same for all other index funds. They are the perfect vehicle for ensuring you have the asset mix working properly for you.

I can't overemphasize this benefit. It is so important because there are so many active funds that are celebrated for their spectacular performance, when in reality the manager was simply lucky. There are "superstar" Asian funds that you discover, after digging a little, were great just because the manager wasn't allowed to hold any Japanese stocks, which went down over a certain period. I know of a celebrated emerging markets fund that simply outperformed because it was holding over 40 percent in cash in 1998 when Latin America and the emerging economies of Asia did poorly. I wouldn't trust a manager's ability to time the market in the short run, so I wouldn't want to invest money in a stock fund, only to discover that I was paying a large fee when half my money was sitting in cash. Risk should be controlled by the asset mix decisions you make, not by the fund manager making a market call. What if all the managers in your portfolio decided to raise cash in their funds? Would you want to have half your portfolio sitting in cash when the markets turn up? With index funds, you know what you're getting. That's the only way to properly manage a portfolio's asset mix.

Brenda: You said there were three other benefits that didn't relate directly to performance. Aside from getting around the 20 percent foreign content limit in registered accounts, and the purity of indexing, which allows for better asset allocation decisions, what's the third benefit?

Making it easy

Ted: The third benefit is the most basic of all — the convenience of index funds. They are so easy to buy. Most banks offer them, so you can walk into your local branch and ask about their selection of index funds. You can buy them over the phone through most banks. And you can certainly buy them over the phone or online through any discount broker. And new services are springing up that are designed especially for index funds — they're called rebalancing programs, or asset allocation services. Both CIBC and TD offer such services. Here's how they work: An investor can choose from many portfolios that consist of index funds only. Each portfolio has a different asset allocation, designed to meet the needs of different investor types. Both the TD and CIBC services can be accessed through monthly investment plans, whereby a specified amount can be withdrawn from your savings account each month and deposited to the service.

Brenda: Okay. I'm convinced that index funds are wonderful. But I certainly don't believe it's all just good news. For instance, I'm worried that if the index fund merely tracks the index, it will plummet when the market goes down. At least the active manager can increase cash holdings to protect my investment from going down too much in a bear market.

Bob: Not only that, your arguments don't necessarily prove that indexing is the best way for us to go. I can see that active management has enough disadvantages to make beating the index very difficult. But why wouldn't I invest in the funds that are managed by the few that do beat the index? Who cares about lower fees and higher taxes? I'd rather own a fund that charges 2.5 percent in fees and has a 20 percent return that I have to pay a little more tax on, than own a fund with 0.5 percent fees but only a 10 percent return.

Brenda: Bob is right. There are some very important points that you haven't addressed. For instance, why would we invest in an average Canadian equity fund anyway? I read the paper and I've bought all the mutual fund guru books. You make a great case for *not* investing in average funds, but who would pick an average fund anyway? We pick winners.

We're better off sticking to the winners who can protect us in down markets and generate superior returns in the long run for us. Who wants to own an "average" fund? I don't aspire to be average in any aspect of my life!

Ted: Tough crowd. Let me address all of these concerns and more. I want you to be entirely convinced of the power of indexing.

The Bottom Line

Indexing outperforms most active managers for sound reasons that will persist in the future. The reasons are: the lower fees and brokerage commissions that are charged by indexed products; the lower trading costs of the buy-and-hold strategy inherent in indexing; the deferred capital gains tax that results from less portfolio trading; the lower cash holdings (which otherwise drag down performance over the long term) in index funds; and the difficulties active managers face in trying to rationally keep ahead of the consensus view of market prices.

There are three other benefits to indexing that don't relate directly to performance, although they do have an indirect impact. There is the ability — offered by derivatives-based indexing — to circumvent the 20 percent foreign content constraint in RRSPs and RRIFs. There is the purity of indexing, which allows a more effective management of asset mix, which is the most important part of the investment process. Finally, there is the convenience of index funds — they can be purchased at most banks, some of which also offer easy-to-use rebalancing programs.

4

Common Objections to Indexing

Well, Bob and Brenda are certainly a hard sell! But that's good. An informed consumer is the most satisfying kind to win over. This chapter is where I really have to earn my credibility. Brenda has done her homework — more than I expected. I've listed below the objections to indexing that you may have heard or come across in the media. I'll focus on index funds, although these objections apply to all index products. Here's what you might hear or read:

1. Index funds underperform in down markets. They only do well in up markets.
2. Index funds are skewed to "large-caps" (stocks of large companies), so when "small-caps" (stocks of small companies) do well, index funds will underperform.
3. Index funds are, by definition, average performers. Investing in an index fund is simply guaranteeing mediocrity. It is far better to invest in a "star" or "winner" fund so that you can do better than the index.
4. Index funds do not suit the risk profile of every investor. Not everyone should own the same portfolio and therefore only some investors are suited to indexing. Indexing is best suited to "beginners."

So let's get at it. You be the judge of whether Bob and Brenda are legitimately and fairly convinced. Would you be?

Ted: You raise some good points — objections you may hear, based on misunderstandings about indexing. Let's start with one of the most common objections — that indexing doesn't protect you in down markets. In the same way as we began our conversation, let's look at the facts first. Then we can explore the underlying rationale.

Do index funds underperform in bad markets?

I've taken the absolute worst market downturns in recent history and compared the TSE 300 to the average Canadian equity fund during those periods. I've also made the same comparison for the S&P 500 and the average US equity fund. This analysis gives as much benefit to active management as possible because if I extend the periods to 12 months or more, the index starts to outshine the average managers. But I've chosen only the very worst period where the two stock markets went down — no shorter and no longer. As usual, I've deducted 0.9 percent from the index so we're actually comparing a typical index fund to the average active fund.

	1984 Jan–May	1987 Aug–Nov	1990 Jan–Oct	1998 July–Aug
TSE 300	(12.3)	(26.3)	(21.0)	(25.7)
Avg. Cdn. Equity Fund	(9.1)	(23.8)	(16.8)	(22.2)
Difference	*(3.2)*	*(2.5)*	*(4.2)*	*(3.5)*
S&P 500	(4.1)	(28.8)	(11.7)	(10.5)
Avg. US Equity Fund	(8.2)	(27.8)	(15.7)	(13.7)
Difference	*4.1*	*(1.0)*	*4.0*	3.2

The numbers tell the story. The TSE 300 *did* underperform the average Canadian equity fund, *but* not by much. And don't forget that the average fund has the advantage of holding about 9 percent foreign equity, which didn't go down by nearly as much in three of the four cases. So the gap between the TSE 300 and the average Canadian equity fund that is purely invested in Canadian equities is smaller than what I've illustrated.

As for the US equity index fund, it did quite nicely by easily beating the average US equity manager — even in these extreme periods! In fact, the index, even after deducting fees, beat the average active fund by a significant margin in all periods, except 1987, when the gap was only one percent.

Bob: Never mind the average fund. I'll bet there were a lot of managers who did beat the index in those periods.

Ted: I just so happen to have a chart that shows you're partially right. In Canada, the managers did very well, whereas in the US, they didn't avoid the down market at all.

	1984 Jan–May	1987 Aug–Nov	1990 Jan–Oct	1998 July–Aug
Cdn. managers beating the TSE 300 (less 0.9%)	75%	67%	81%	81%
US managers beating the S&P 500 (less 0.9%)	4%	53%	29%	19%

Don't forget: the active managers had the benefit of holding some foreign equities. Nonetheless, most were able to beat the index in the extreme periods I've chosen.

What's the bottom line for Canadian equity funds in down markets? If you were looking for your active manager to protect you from the worst possible down periods in the Canadian market, you would have been very disappointed. It's true that the average active manager did better, but not by much. Nothing to boast about. And don't forget that these were the *absolute* worst periods that assume an investor bought at the beginning and sold at the end of the short downturn. This is a completely unrealistic time frame that I used only to force the index to compete in the extreme situation of a severe market correction. As the time period is extended beyond the worst months, the gap closes and eventually, the index fund does better than the average manager.

If we look at US equity funds in a down market, it would appear that it's actually safer to be invested in the index than in the average fund.

Down markets are often contained within periods that allow the index to outperform, whether or not it outperforms in the exact months during which the market moves down. This fact is obvious for US stocks, and a little less clear-cut for Canadian stocks. But if you remove the advantage that active managers have by holding foreign equities, it's evident that they are not that adept at avoiding market downturns.

How can this be? Surely an astute manager can predict a down market and increase her cash holdings in the fund so that it falls much less than a fully invested fund?

The odds are strongly on the side of the index for the simple reason that the active manager has to get two decisions right to avoid a downturn: the timing of the market downturn *and* the timing of the market recovery. *It's not good enough for the manager to accurately predict a downturn by increasing cash and lowering stock holdings. She must also decrease cash by quickly investing in stocks, before the market recovers.* If she only gets the timing of the first decision right, she will miss all of the gains as the market rises, leaving her far behind the index. The probability of getting both decisions right is not that high. And over a period of time that includes a few market ups and downs, it is extremely unlikely that a manager can get both the "out" and the "in again" decisions right.

Bob: It's worth a try, though, don't you think? Might as well give it a shot since the rewards are huge if you can avoid a downturn and invest just as the market begins to recover.

Ted: It's dangerous for anyone, no matter how expert they are at investment management, to attempt to time the market. If you get the decisions wrong and miss just a small percentage of the investment period, your returns can be cut in half or less! Get this: Over the past few decades, 99 *percent of the gains in the stock market occurred during only 4 percent of the trading days. Fifty percent of the gains occurred during only one percent of the trading days.* So the window of opportunity for making the right "out" and "in again" decisions is extremely limited.

This is exactly why most managers don't make large bets on when the market will go down or when it will recover. They know that if they're wrong their performance track record can be destroyed. They also know that they are likely to get it wrong! The market is far too skittish to predict over short periods of time, because it can be motivated by irrational factors, as we discussed.

We can actually see just how unlikely managers are to predict market downturns if we look at the change in cash holdings over a bad period. If managers are actually trying to avoid downturns by predicting them, they would increase cash and reduce their stock holdings. Let's take the summer of 1998 when every headline announced that we had begun a global bear market. How did the cash holdings of managers compare before, during, and after that period, when the TSE dropped a whopping 25 percent?

Percentage of Cash in Average Canadian Equity Mutual Fund			
January 31, 1998	June 30, 1998	August 30, 1998	December 30, 1998
(everything looks rosy)	(still looking optimistic)	(TSE is down 25% since July 1)	(market has recovered from summer lows)
10.2%	9.5%	10.2%	10.4%

Barely a difference from the beginning to the end! In fact, the average manager went into the so-called bear market with a *lower* level of cash — 9.5 percent — than he started the year off with. Let's see how many managers actually raised cash in anticipation of the decline:

Percentage of Canadian Equity Managers Holding 15% Cash or More			
January 31, 1998	June 30, 1998	August 30, 1998	December 30, 1998
19.4%	18.2%	20.8%	18.5%

Before the nasty summer hit, the percentage of managers holding 15 percent or more in cash actually decreased! It is clear that most Canadian equity managers did not time the market downturn.

Either managers are *unwilling* to predict downturns, or they are *unable* to. You'd better believe that if they could predict the downturns and the subsequent upturns, they would surely take action by raising cash before and lowering it after. Imagine what heroes they'd be if they could protect investors on the way down and jump in to reap the rewards on the way up. It just doesn't seem to be the case that they can consistently time the market. So actively managed funds will not protect you from downturns, and you might be safer, believe it or not, in an index fund. That certainly seems to be the case with US equity funds.

Bob and Brenda: Wow!

Ted: Yeah. Wow.

Brenda: So what about the other objections? Like the one that indexing is skewed toward large-company stocks, so when small-company stocks go up, index funds will underperform.

Aren't index funds skewed toward large-cap stocks?

Ted: That is a simple objection to refute: Not all indexes are based on large-cap stocks.

The TSE 300 consists of almost 20 percent smaller companies and the broadest US index — the Wilshire 5000 — has about 10 percent in smaller companies and another 20 percent in medium-size companies, so only 70 percent of the stocks in it can be considered true large-cap stocks. Now the critics have a point when they are talking about the Toronto 35 index in Canada or the S&P 500 in the US, both of which are focused on the stocks of large companies. But so what? Don't index them. Problem solved.

Brenda: But the S&P 500 is the index that most US equity funds track. It's the one you used in all your examples. And I know some funds and GICs that track the Toronto 35. And with 70 percent of the Wilshire and 80 percent of the TSE 300 tracking large companies, the indexes are still very biased in favour of large-cap stocks.

Ted: True enough. But an investor has to have some sort of split between large companies and small companies in her portfolio. She could arbitrarily split them 50/50. But who's to say that's a good mix? The broad market is made up of between 70 and 80 percent large-cap stocks weighted by their stock market values, or "capitalizations," as they're called. In the absence of a better split, it only makes sense to index what the whole market is based on, doesn't it?

I don't think you need to be at all concerned about the naturally heavier weighting of large-company stocks in the broad market indexes. But if you are holding an index fund that is based on the S&P 500 — for example, a derivatives-based US RRSP index fund — and you want more small-cap stocks in your portfolio, you can simply use actively managed small-cap funds to complement your core holding of index funds. I'll get into the use of active funds later on, but it's worth pointing out that active funds are often a good way to add more small-cap stocks to your portfolio, since the small-cap market is less efficient.

The heavier weighting of large-company stocks in the broad market indexes is not likely to detract from your long-term performance for two reasons:

1. The correlation between the Toronto 35 and the TSE 300 is very high — in fact, they move very closely together. Same with the S&P 500 and the Wilshire 5000. It is highly unlikely (but not impossible, mind you) that one will go up and the other down. In fact, their long-term returns are close to each other. But that's not to say the small-cap indexes won't do differently than the indexes that are dominated by large companies. Here's a comparison of the large-cap, small-cap, and broad market indexes in both Canada and the US. For the small-cap stocks, I'm using the Nesbitt Burns Small Cap index in Canada and the Russell 2000 index in the US.

Returns in Canadian Dollars

	Canadian Stocks			US Stocks		
	Large	*Small*	*Broad*	*Large*	*Small*	*Broad*
	Tor. 35	**NB Small Cap**	**TSE 300**	**S&P 500**	**Russell 2000**	**Wilshire 5000**
1984	(5)	(2)	(2)	13	(1)	10
1985	22	39	25	40	40	40
1986	6	12	9	17	4	15
1987	11	(6)	6	(1)	(14)	(4)
1988	11	6	11	7	15	8
1989	22	11	21	28	13	25
1990	(12)	(27)	(15)	(3)	(19)	(6)
1991	11	19	12	30	46	34
1992	(4)	13	(1)	18	30	20
1993	24	52	33	15	24	16
1994	6	(9)	0	7	4	6
1995	15	13	15	34	25	33
1996	30	28	28	24	17	22
1997	16	3	15	39	28	37
1998	0	(22)	(2)	38	5	32
10-yr compound	10	6	10	22	16	21
15-yr compound	10	7	10	16	13	18

You can see how the broad indexes can be influenced by the smaller stock indexes, which tend to be more volatile. With the broad indexes, you get the benefit of both the large- and small-cap stocks.

2. The other argument for choosing a fund with a heavy weighting in large-cap stocks is that large companies seem to have commanded a premium in the market over the past five years and may well continue to do so, for at least three legitimate reasons.

   First, the stock of large companies is highly liquid, meaning that it trades a lot — in greater volumes and with greater frequency than small-cap stock. Because it's more liquid, foreign investors and many institutional money managers, such as pension fund managers, prefer to hold the stock of large companies so that they can trade without much difficulty. For example, if you are a German pension manager and you want to add a bit of Canada or US to your portfolio, you're not likely to be interested in buying a small company's stock since it is hard to get in and out of quickly. Besides, you probably won't have heard or know much about the small companies in Canada or the US since you and your analysts don't have time to research the smaller companies. But you'll definitely know about BCE, Coke, and IBM. Greater demand for the more liquid stock of large companies translates into higher prices.

   Second, larger companies have deep pockets — they can fund huge marketing programs that bolster their brand image and generate increased awareness and sales for them over time and around the world. They can therefore command a price premium on the basis that they have staying power and strength, even when economic conditions worsen. Smaller companies cannot weather economic storms as easily. But when economic conditions become more favourable, smaller companies can really shine. From the chart I just showed you can see the years when smaller companies have outperformed larger companies by a wide margin.

   The *third* reason why large-cap stock tends to command a premium is that governments are starting to use stock indexes as part of their efforts to invest their pension plan assets more aggressively. In February of 1999, the government decided to allow the Canada Pension Plan to invest some of its assets in equities instead of exclusively in bonds. The expectation is that equity investments will yield better returns, which will help the CPP fund the pensions of the huge number of baby boomers that are approaching retirement. The government has required that the stock investments be indexed at least until 2002, and may extend the requirement beyond that date. Government investment on this scale means that the stocks that make up the TSE 300, which are 80 percent large-cap stocks, will continue to get substantial support. Similar changes in the pension system of the US may occur in the future as well.

Bob: So what are you getting at? What's the bottom line on the large-cap stock thing?

Ted: Over the long term, it's debatable whether large- or small-cap stocks do better. Most early studies concluded that smaller companies outperformed over long periods. This observation was supported by the rationale that since smaller companies are riskier investments, they should command higher returns over time. However, recent studies have challenged these findings on the basis that the original studies did not account for all the small companies that went bankrupt and dropped out of the picture! This is called "survivorship bias" because only the companies that survive get included in the studies, so the ones that investors lost money on are forgotten. We saw this problem when we compared the performance history of active funds with index funds; I pointed out that the active funds' performance was overstated, because many losing funds were merged into winning funds so that their underperformance was hidden.

It has also been observed that the early studies did not account for the higher trading costs associated with buying small-cap stock — higher bid-ask spreads, for example. When these factors are considered — both survivorship bias and the higher costs of buying and selling small stocks — the larger companies' performance track record is about the same as smaller companies'. Most of the outperformance in small-cap stocks occurred between 1975 and 1983, when their returns were double those of larger-company stocks. Since 1983, small companies have generally underperformed large-company stocks. The bottom line is that the large-cap bias is not a fatal objection to indexing. Small-cap stocks can easily be weighted more heavily in an investor's portfolio by adding an actively managed small-companies fund to an index fund. So far there are no small-cap index funds in Canada, but that's probably just a matter of time. For those indexes that are dominated by large companies, such as the S&P 500 and the TSE 300, there is reason to be confident that large-cap stocks will not underperform smaller-company stocks over longer time periods.

Bob: Okay, I've got it, but let's tackle another objection. Brenda is right — we don't want just average performance for our portfolio. We want superior returns. Why would we limit ourselves to doing no better or no worse than the market as a whole?

Does indexing just guarantee mediocre returns?

Ted: What if I told you that indexing does not generate average performance?

Bob: Of course it does . . . you said yourself that indexing ensures you do no better and no worse than the market index. You can't get much more average than that!

Ted: Well, let's look at the facts. We can split all mutual funds into top-half performers and bottom-half performers. We can also take the top half and bottom half and split each of those categories up. So we get four categories now: the top quarter, the second quarter, the third quarter, and the bottom quarter. Each of these categories is called a quartile and we can designate them Q1, Q2, Q3, and Q4.

Bob: Is this a trick question?

Ted: No . . . it's easy. Just like a score on a test. A Q1 fund ranks with a score in the 76 to 100 percent range, Q2 ranks between 51 and 75 percent, Q3 is 26 to 50 percent, and Q4 is zero to 25 percent.

Bob: I hope you're going somewhere with this!

Ted: The surprising fact, one that we've already explored, is that index funds are more often than not in the top half, and often in Q1 over many time periods. The index funds are not average when compared to all other active funds. They are top-half performers, and often top-quartile performers. We saw this at the beginning of our talk.

Brenda: But we lose the opportunity to be in the star performing funds if we invest in the index. That's what I'm getting at. It's doubtful that we'll always be in the top quartile if we just stick with the index funds.

Bob: Yeah. She's got you there. It's fine if the index fund does quite well and stays in the top half. But imagine how much richer we'd be by investing in the funds that are the best ones, the ones that outperform the indexes. So what if there aren't many of them? All it takes is a few really good ones and we're in the money.

Ted: So you want to invest in the winning funds? The stars?

Bob: Well, yeah. That's why we asked for your help. We know we're in some crummy funds. We want help in picking the good ones.

Brenda: You're telling us to settle for the index when we want something better. Are you not capable of choosing the winning funds?

Bob: That must be the problem. If you had the ability to pick winners, you wouldn't be such a champion of indexing. With all due respect, and not to sound ungrateful, I think we're better off consulting with someone who can tell us which funds to invest in. Not that this hasn't been very educational. It's been very interesting and enlightening.

Brenda: Yes, it has, and thanks so much for coming over tonight. We really did learn a lot and we'll make sure that whatever funds we choose do better than the index.

Ted: Hold on a minute! There's something you have to understand . . .

Bob: I think we've got it by now. Honestly. I hope you're not offended. We just need —

Ted: No, wait — can you hang in there for just a little longer? I want to make sure you understand something before you go off trying to pick the best funds, or rely on books or advice on what the best funds are.

Bob: It is getting a little late . . .

Brenda: No. We can certainly do you the courtesy of hearing you out. You've been more than generous with your time this evening.

Ted: Thank you. I promise I won't waste your time.

Are the "winning" funds predictable?

Ted: You want to invest in the best funds so you can optimize your returns, right?

Bob: Isn't that everyone's objective?

Ted: Pretty much. But I want to show you how difficult that is.

Bob: We never said it would be easy. You already made the point that not many funds beat the index over extended periods of time.

Ted: It's not only difficult. It's close to impossible to be sure you are consistently invested in the winning funds all the time. That's the problem. If you could be sure that you were investing in the winning funds, that's where you should put your money. But the odds are against it. And, the odds are more in favour of outperforming if you index.

It's as simple as this: Do you want to play the small odds of investing in a fund that is consistently in the top quartile, or the larger odds of investing in a fund that is consistently in the top half? What is the better tradeoff?

Bob: It depends on your personal preference, I guess.

Ted: Does it? Does the maximization of long-term performance depend on the personal preference of the investor?

Bob: Well, we all want the best returns. But I still think we can invest in the best funds. After all, there are books that . . .

Brenda: Yes. I've read a few books that recommend funds. And these books are written by people who make a living by picking funds. Besides, it's pretty easy to see which funds to avoid when you look at the returns in the paper. We just need someone with expertise to help us make the right decisions.

Ted: Okay. I'm going to prove to you that you can't pick the winning funds with much certainty. That's my challenge and I'm up for it.

Bob: Go for it.

Ted: I want to analyze the probability of picking a winning fund. I want to show you that the probability of choosing what will be a winning fund, after you've invested in it, is very low. It's not zero percent. But it's low.

One of the principal reasons why most people cannot pick a winning fund is that they focus exclusively on past performance.

Bob: Well, what else would they look at?

Ted: I'm going to tell you what factors are important to consider when assessing an actively managed fund. But first I want to focus on the mistake that most investors and fund pickers make. The problem with looking at past performance only is that it doesn't allow you to confidently predict future results because statistics get in the way.

Bob: If we're going to hang in there with you, you're going to have to talk normal talk.

Ted: Sorry. I'll try it again. *Looking only at past performance does not allow you to adequately differentiate luck from skill.* The numbers by themselves can play tricks on you. Imagine this:

There is a room with 1,000 people in it. There is a competition that each individual is participating in. It is a very simple competition. Each person is given a coin to toss and the winner is the one who can flip the most tails in a row.

On the first flip, half of the crowd flips a tail, which is what we'd expect since there's a 50/50 chance that the coin will be a tail. The 500 tail flippers are asked to remain standing, and the rest, who are now disqualified, are asked to sit down.

The 500 standing participants who flipped one tail are asked to flip again. Since the odds of flipping a tail are still 50 percent, we'd expect about 250 people to flip a second tail. They are asked to remain standing and the others, who flipped heads, are asked to sit down.

A third toss is done and again about half, or 125, flip a third tail, so they remain standing while the others sit. A fourth toss is requested and 62 flip a fourth tail and remain standing. Thirty-one flip a fifth tail. Fifteen flip a sixth tail. Seven flip a seventh tail. Four flip an eighth tail. Two flip a ninth tail. The tension builds at this point. The suspense in the room is almost too much to bear.

The two finalists square off as all eyes are fixated on their hands and their coins. Up go the coins. Down they come into the palms of each contestant. The coins are turned over and smacked on the back of each flipper's hand. A huge smile and gentle squeal emanates from one, while the other, looking dejected, shakes his head and sits down.

The victor throws her hands up in the air and jumps with pride, as the other 999 contestants jump to their feet in admiration and excitement, chanting her name and elevating her on their shoulders. She is truly a coin-tossing champion, having flipped 10 tails in a row. This is truly a feat worth documenting since the odds of flipping 10 tails in a row is only 0.01 percent! Far less than one percent!

Can you imagine someone beating those odds? Can you imagine how hard someone would have to study and train, day in and day out, in order to overcome those incredible odds? Good coin tossers come and go, but for someone to demonstrate the talent and skill of tossing 10 tails in a row, suggests an aptitude far beyond what most mortals are capable of.

Bob: Cute story, but I hope there's a point to it.

Ted: Why don't you tell me what's cute about it first.

Bob: It's dumb of course. There's no skill required to flip 10 tails in a row.

Ted: Could you do it? Would you even wager that you could flip five tails in a row?

Bob: Of course not. It's just pure luck, assuming it's an authentic coin.

Ted: So how did she manage to do this? Or do you think it's impossible for anyone to flip 10 tails in a row?

Bob: It's pretty much impossible for just *anyone* to flip 10 in a row. But it's not impossible in a crowd for *someone* to do it. You said yourself that since the odds are 50 percent of flipping a tail, with a big enough crowd, someone is going to ultimately flip a bunch of tails in a row. The bigger the crowd, the more tails someone will flip. If you had only 10 people, you'd be lucky to get someone flipping three tails. With a thousand people, 10 tails is possible, I guess.

Brenda: With 10,000 people, you could get close to 15 tails out of someone. But you wouldn't know who the person was in advance.

Bob: That's right. Just because someone flipped that many tails doesn't mean she is skilled. It means she was the one person in a large crowd that ended up being the lucky one.

Ted: That's exactly my point. That you can't differentiate luck from skill when you look at the behaviour of numbers in a large enough sample size.

What if I told you that the thousand contestants were actually mutual fund managers? And that each time they flipped a tail, it actually symbolized a year where their performance was above average. After 10 years, someone will have an extraordinary run of great performance, year after year.

Bob: But that doesn't prove they're *not* skilled.

Ted: You're right. It doesn't prove they're not skilled. But that's not the point. The point is that it doesn't prove they *are* skilled!

Bob: What do you mean?

Ted: I mean that if 1,000 managers are out there competing against each other and against the index, it is inevitable, statistically speaking, that at least one of them will generate superior performance every year for 10 years. In fact, with a large enough group of fund managers, there might be a couple who will have stellar 15-year track records.

Guess what? There are around 1,000 money managers and analysts in Canada. That means, statistically speaking, you would expect some to have great 10-year track records, and even more will have great five-year track records. And even more than that will have unbelievable three-year track records.

But how do you know whether they earned their track records, or were just lucky coin tossers? Do you see what I'm getting at?

Bob: Yeah. But . . .

Ted: Statistics get in the way, don't they? The behaviour of a large sample size, including a large number of managers, will exhibit predictable patterns. Looking at past performance numbers *alone* will not properly let you differentiate luck from talent.

Brenda: But there must be a period of time over which it is statistically unlikely that someone would have superior returns, given a fixed number of managers.

Ted: Yes, you're right. But there is not any agreement in the academic community on what the period is. Given a sample size of 1,000, there is some consensus that it would take around 25 years to be able to conclude that a manager is likely to be talented, rather than just lucky. Even then, we are talking about a higher probability — not a certainty. It has been estimated by some academics that at least 10 percent of all stock funds will beat the average fund for three consecutive years, as a normal statistical event. In other words, we can expect that 10 percent of funds will have better-than-average three-year returns, based on nothing more than mathematical probabilities. The problem is how to differentiate the three-year stars that are based on managerial skill from the three-year stars that are based on pure luck.

Bob: So what are you saying? Past performance is useless?

Ted: No, I wouldn't go that far at all. Past performance is an indicator of possible skill. It helps weed out the losers. Although it is a necessary criterion, it is not sufficient. A review of past performance helps you pick out the funds that have underperformed and point you in the direction of possible winners. But it doesn't let you determine who the real winners are, since it can't help you differentiate the skilled managers from the lucky ones.

Brenda: You mentioned earlier that when you analyze past performance, you should only do it in the context of analyzing risk. So performance is only relevant if you also look at the risk that a manager took to get the performance.

Ted: Yes. That is what I was demonstrating earlier when I showed you how some managers have been able to rack up spectacular numbers only because they took on extra risk. It is important to consider risk when you assess past performance numbers. But even so, it doesn't eliminate the challenge of separating the lucky from the talented.

If a manager achieved superior performance over a 10-year period, while assuming average or below-average risk, it does suggest that she may be quite talented. But she could also be just plain lucky, as we would expect some managers to be.

The bottom line then is that looking at past performance and risk characteristics is useful in screening out underperformers and pointing you in the direction of possible talent. But it cannot come close to assuring you that you've found talent, especially if you are looking at track records that are only five or 10 years in duration. That is simply not a long enough period of time to determine skill in picking outperforming stocks.

Bob: So why are there so many books written on which funds to buy? It must not be as hard as you say to pick winners. Or else you're not telling us the whole story. What do the so-called mutual fund experts consider when they make their recommendations?

Ted: There are other things to consider when picking a fund, and I will tell you what they are. But let's talk about the fund experts first, since they represent a superb example of how hard it is to pick winners.

I took the seven bestselling mutual fund books that recommended top picks for 1999. I tabulated their recommendations for core Canadian equity funds.

If the winning mutual funds are easily predictable, then we would expect to see a fair amount of overlap between the funds, right? If the star funds can be identified, then we wouldn't expect to see too much deviation between each of the seven authors.

Brenda: No, I suppose not.

Ted: If the winners are discernable, then surely the so-called gurus would be able to pick them out of the over 2,000 funds available in the Canadian market. Among the seven experts, I tabulated 74 funds that constituted the list of recommended core Canadian equity funds. All together there were 74 funds. How many funds do you think appeared on all of their lists, or at least most of their lists? If the winning funds were truly identifiable, then we'd expect there to be quite a bit of agreement. And predictable winners should get multiple votes, since these funds would be recognized by most, if not all, of the experts. The results were very interesting:

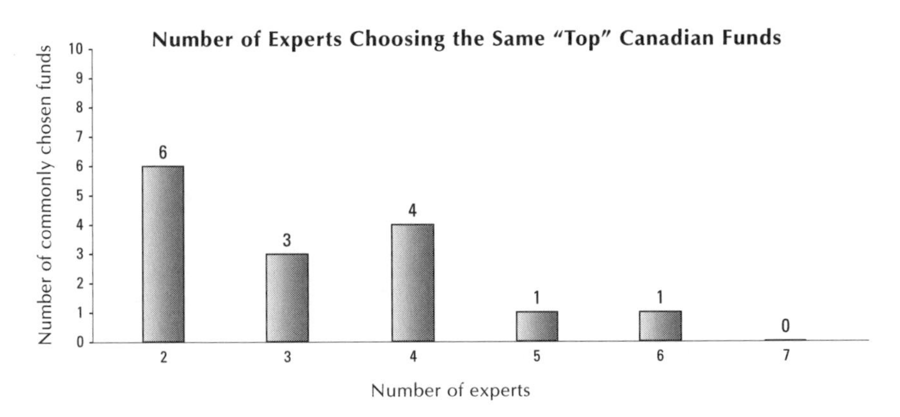

Along the bottom of this chart is the number of experts, to a maximum of seven. Along the vertical axis is the number of multiple votes that the most popular funds got. For instance, at the far left, there were six funds, of the 74, that got votes from two experts.

Aren't the results amazing? There was hardly any agreement among the experts. There was only one fund that six of the seven agreed on. To be fair, this fund was a close runner-up with the seventh expert. The one fund that garnered an almost unanimous endorsement was the Bissett Canadian Equity Fund. That was the only top pick to secure general agreement.

Bob: You've got to be kidding.

Ted: No sir. After all the work the experts put into their recommendations, they all ended up with very different final picks. The conclusion that I draw, therefore, is that it is not easy to pick a winning mutual fund. Plain and simple. The experts don't agree on what a winner is.

Brenda: Maybe it's just the Canadian equity funds that they can't agree on.

Ted: Let's look at their US equity picks, which constituted a list of 41 top fund choices:

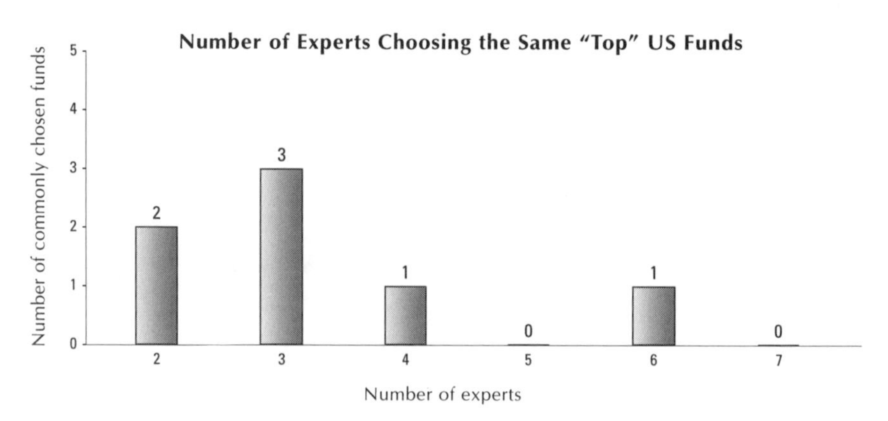

Bob: Wow. Even less agreement.

Brenda: And that's even from a smaller group of selected funds!

Ted: I think it's safe to conclude that picking a winning fund is a lot more complicated than just reading what the experts say. If you go back to their recommendations in prior years, you'll be equally surprised to discover what their picks were — or maybe by now you won't be surprised.

Bob: What were their picks a year or two ago?

Ted: Suffice it to say that the gurus were definitely enthusiastic about some of the bigger Canadian equity funds which are commonly known as poor performers today. In fact, some previously celebrated managers even ended up leaving their funds because of persistent poor performance.

Brenda: Well, I'm sure that some fund experts are more competent than others.

Ted: Some definitely are. But no one stands out as really having the foresight to pick in advance what the winning funds will be. One of the most popular studies ever done on rating the performance of recommended funds was done by John Bogle, the founder of Vanguard, which is the biggest index fund company in the world. He showed that if an investor had invested in the top funds chosen by *Forbes* magazine in the US for the 18 years between 1974 and 1992, the investor would have underperformed the index by 1.9 percent on average every year. This gap added up to a difference of $28,600 on an original $10,000 investment.

Brenda: So why in the world is the track record of expert fund pickers so bad?

Ted: Two reasons. First, many of them rely exclusively on an analysis of past performance and past risk characteristics. As we've seen, if all you do is crunch the numbers that relate to past performance, you can't properly differentiate luck from skill. Not only that, but looking at past performance and risk numbers doesn't alert you to important factors that help differentiate luck from talent. For instance, one manager may not be able to invest in Japan, whereas another manager may be forced to have a minimum holding of 10 percent in Japan at all times. The second manager will obviously underperform when Japanese stocks go down, but that doesn't demonstrate anything about skill, let alone which manager is likely to outperform in the future. An even more common example is how much cash a manager is allowed to hold: some can hold up to 50 percent of the fund in cash, whereas others are limited to 10 percent. As you can see, you really have to dig deep to come up with a useful analysis, and unfortunately, not all mutual fund analysts do. Many experts can be irrationally influenced by short-term results; otherwise, how can you explain why the top fund picks change so much each year? The best fund experts rely on a combination of both numbers and more qualitative factors, such as interviewing the fund managers about their strategies for managing money, and assessing the constraints that are placed on them as they manage. I found one popular fund that was recommended by five of the seven experts, but only two were aware that the manager had been changed the year before. How relevant are past performance numbers when they belong to someone else? Not very!

A second explanation for fund pickers' poor track records is that in addition to an overemphasis on the numbers, the funds themselves, as we've seen, are often not able to sustain consistently superior performance. Let's look at the deviation over time of some of the funds that started as winners and ended up as losers. This demonstration will really convince you that relying only on past performance is, at best, a way to weed out losing funds, and at worst, totally irrelevant and even misleading.

Picking winners — the track record of winning and losing funds

I took 88 Canadian equity funds and looked at their most recent five-year returns ending December 31, 1998. So we're looking at how the funds did over five years from January 1, 1994, through to December 31, 1998. I broke all the funds into four categories: funds with five-year performance in the top quartile, which means they ranked in the top 25 percent of all 88 funds; funds with five-year performance in the second quartile; funds with third-quartile performance; and funds with fourth-quartile performance. Obviously, there were 22 funds in each category, ranging from the best 22 funds in the top quartile to the worst 22 funds in the bottom quartile.

I then took the same 88 funds and broke them into one of the four quartile categories for their five-year performance over the five years ending December 31, 1993 — that is, the five years between January 1, 1989, and December 31, 1993.

Finally, I compared each fund's 1989–93 ranking with its 1994–98 ranking. I wanted the answer to this simple question: *Were the funds that were "stars" — ranking in the top quartile from 1989 to 1993 — able to maintain their top-quartile status from 1994–98?* If a fund had superior performance for five years, would it be expected to continue having superior performance over the next five years? *Can you predict, on the basis of what is a star today, which funds will be stars tomorrow?*

Bob: Are you asking us?

Ted: I'm asking rhetorically. The results were, I thought, astounding.

Of the 22 funds that were stars over 1989 to 1993, only five of them were stars over 1994 to 1998. In fact, 10 of the 22 stars fell to become third- or fourth-quartile funds over 1994 to 1998. Not only that, more than half of the losers became winners: funds that were in the fourth quartile for the first five years shot up to the first or second quartile in the next five years.

Tracking a Canadian Equity Fund's 10-Year Performance 1989–93 ranking compared with 1994–98 ranking	
% of first-quartile funds that moved into third or fourth quartile:	67
% of fourth-quartile funds that moved into first or second quartile:	55

Bob: That's amazing. That means two-thirds of the winning funds with stellar performance between 1989 and 1993 became the losers over 1994 to 1998.

Brenda: And more than half of the losers became winners!

Ted: Let's look at a pie chart that shows the changes. This chart shows exactly what happened to the winning funds that were in the first quartile over 1989 to 1993:

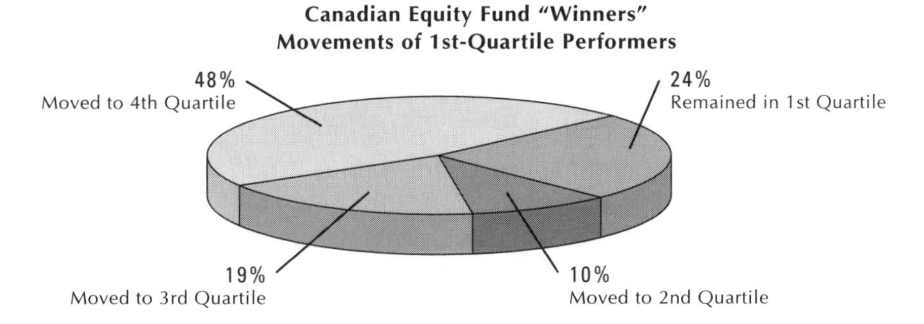

Isn't that amazing? Most of the winning funds fell to the bottom of the pack. And we're not talking about just one-year performance. We're looking at five-year returns.

Brenda: Well, maybe the second-quartile funds did better at maintaining their status. Maybe the best funds are not the first-quartile ones, but the second-quartile ones.

Ted: Wish I could say it was so. Thirty-seven percent of the second-quartile funds dropped to the third or fourth quartile. They may appear to hang on better than the big winners, but second-quartile funds still show no reliable predictability in performance.

Now let's look at what happened to the losing funds that were in the fourth quartile over 1989 to 1993:

Canadian Equity Fund "Losers"
Movements of 4th-Quartile Performers

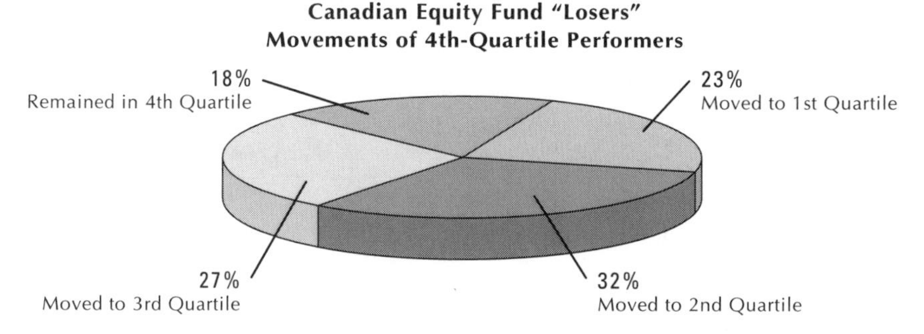

Equally amazing! Most of the losing funds moved up into either first- or second-quartile rankings for the five years that followed their five-year losing streaks.

Bob: An investor would have been better off investing in the loser funds, since they had a better chance of generating superior performance in the next five years!

Brenda: But is this demonstration dependent upon the dates and periods you are using? Not that I want to appear skeptical. But honestly, this seems a bit extreme.

Ted: I have analyzed many periods and I always come up with similar results. If I used only one-year returns, the numbers are even more scattered. But I don't think it's reasonable to judge a fund's performance on just one year. Even the experts base their judgements on at least three years, and longer where possible. For example, there are just a few — I could find 43 — Canadian equity funds that have 15-year histories made up of a 10-year record followed by a five-year record. Of these, I looked at the winning funds that had first-quartile performance rankings over the 10 years from 1984 to 1993, and compared their 10-year rankings to their rankings over the five years between 1994 and 1998. I also looked at what happened to the 10-year losing funds — those with fourth-quartile rankings between 1984 and 1993 — over the subsequent five years from 1994 to 1998.

Tracking a Canadian Equity Fund's 15-Year Performance 1984–93 ranking compared with 1994–98 ranking	
% of first-quartile funds that moved into third or fourth quartile:	70
% of fourth-quartile funds that moved into first or second quartile:	55

Isn't that astounding? What's more, of the 70 percent of funds that dropped from first quartile to the bottom half, 40 percent dropped right to the fourth quartile.

Brenda: Yes, it certainly is surprising. Were the second-quartile funds better?

Ted: Not much: 54 percent dropped to the bottom half — either third or fourth quartile. Do you see what conclusions you can draw from this?

Brenda: Well, it appears, as you've been saying, that it is very hard to pick a fund that is likely to outperform, if you base your prediction on the past performance of the fund.

Bob: What about other funds, like US funds?

Ted: There are only 20 US equity funds that have 15-year histories. But there are 33 with 10-year histories that allow us to track performance over the period 1989 to 1993 and then compare it with performance over 1994 to 1998.

The results are not quite as clear for US equity funds, but you can still draw the same conclusion that a winning fund is not necessarily going to continue being a winning fund.

Tracking a US Equity Fund's 15-Year Performance 1984–93 ranking compared with 1994–98 ranking	
% of first-quartile funds that moved into third or fourth quartile:	40
% of fourth-quartile funds that moved into first or second quartile:	60

Tracking a US Equity Fund's 10-Year Performance 1989–93 ranking compared with 1994–98 ranking	
% of first-quartile funds that moved into third or fourth quartile:	25
% of fourth-quartile funds that moved into first or second quartile:	22

The 10-year track record of US equity funds is clearly not a good indicator of future performance. Almost half of the winners dropped to the bottom half and more than half of the losers became winners. The five-year track record of US equity funds is a better predictor of future performance, but still not convincing. One-quarter of the winners dropped to the bottom half — and these happened to all drop right into the fourth quartile. Almost one-quarter of the losers became winners. For the record, 63 percent of the second-quartile funds dropped to either the third or fourth quartile, so the second-quartile funds were even worse at sustaining superior performance.

Bob: Well, that's certainly surprising. Looks like you might have a slightly better chance of picking winning US equity funds, but not if you were judging a fund based on its 10-year record.

Ted: International funds suffer from the same lack of predictability:

Tracking an International Equity Fund's 15-Year Performance 1984–93 ranking compared with 1994–98 ranking	
% of first-quartile funds that moved into third or fourth quartile:	25
% of fourth-quartile funds that moved into first or second quartile:	40

Tracking an International Equity Fund's 10-Year Performance 1989–93 ranking compared with 1994–98 ranking	
% of first-quartile funds that moved into third or fourth quartile:	60
% of fourth-quartile funds that moved into first or second quartile:	36

Most of the international funds that did well over 10 years managed to stay in the top half over the next five years, but most that did well over only five years fell into the bottom half in the next five years.

It's more interesting when you note the persistency of the indexes for the same markets. Let's look at the quartile ranking of the TSE 300,

S&P 500, and MSCI EAFE over the same periods. I'll even deduct 0.9 percent from the indexes, before I show their quartile ranking.

	15-year 1984–98 ranking	10-year 1989–98 ranking	5-year 1994–98 ranking
TSE 300	2nd Q	2nd Q	2nd Q
S&P 500	1st Q	1st Q	1st Q
MSCI EAFE	Not enough funds to compare	3rd Q	2nd Q

Ted: Gotta love that US index. The MSCI EAFE was a little less reliable, but that's because of the volatility of the Japanese market over different periods. The TSE 300 was consistently in the second quartile.

So where are we? It seems that great mutual fund managers have a hard time staying great. The majority falls from grace. And the mutual fund experts don't seem to be able to agree on which managers will outperform. Here are two insights, the truthfulness of which I hope you are now convinced:

1. Not only do active managers have difficulty picking winning stocks on a consistent basis, but the mutual fund experts also have difficulty picking winning funds.
2. We've seen that the index funds do tend to outperform and do tend to remain winners.

Put those two observations together, and what do you get?

> **Successful investing, based on indexing, depends on trading off the *low possibility* of doing better than the index, for the *high probability* of doing better than most other funds.**

Successful investing is based on playing favourable odds

Investing, as with all of life, is a game of tradeoffs and probabilities. We are constantly making choices based on our assessments of the odds of certain events occurring. And we are always making tradeoffs between certain benefits and their probabilities. For example, when I get in my car I know that there is a risk that I'll get in a bad accident, maybe even die. But the odds are reasonably low. I'm willing to "play the odds" because the payoff, for example getting to work or to the grocery store, outweighs the small risk of getting hurt. I could play it safe and lie in bed watching TV and eating cornchips all day, but the tradeoff is that I wouldn't earn any money or feel self-fulfilled. So I trade off the comfort and safety of my bed for the benefit of something more interesting, albeit more risky, in the outside world.

Bob: I think I prefer the cornchips routine. But I get your point.

Ted: Investing is the exact same game. It's no different. You can choose to play it safe, or take some risk for greater upside. It's all about odds and probabilities. No one can be sure that the stock market will go up in the long term, although that's what it has always done, and the odds are pretty good that it will continue to rise. But you have to choose. On the one hand there is the 4-percent GIC that carries a very low risk of financial loss (it could be a loss if, for example, the banking system collapsed). On the other hand, there is the stock portfolio with a likely long-term return of around 10 percent, but a higher possibility (although still quite low) of being negative over a long period of time.

The tradeoff is straightforward: safety traded off for higher return potential. But the only way anyone can intelligently assess the tradeoff is by understanding the odds — or probabilities — of the best- and worst-case scenarios actually happening. We know that the odds of generating 10 percent or better in the stock market over 10 years or more are quite high — in fact, they're about 90 percent, based on historical performance. But we also know that there's a risk of losing money in the stock market over 10 years — about one to 3 percent. We know that the risk of losing money on a GIC is very low — less than one percent under most circumstances. But the return from the GIC is set when you buy it, and can go no higher. These numbers are just approximate, based on a 10-year holding period:

	Over 10 years	
	GIC	Stock
Probability of Loss	0.5%	2%
Probable Return	5%	10%

The key is to make an *informed* decision on the tradeoff by logically assessing the probabilities attached to the possible outcomes. Most people with long-term investment periods should be invested in stocks because the odds are high that they will do better in stocks, despite the higher risk.

Brenda: So what has all this cognitive psychology and elementary investment theory got to do with indexing?

Indexing — tradeoffs and probabilities

Ted: Indexing is an investment approach that is based on an intelligent playing of the odds. The probability that the index will outperform a majority of active managers in many markets is very high. An investor can choose to trade off the risk of underperforming the market for the potential of doing better than the market. But the probabilities are not in his favour. What you might initially consider "average" performance is not average at all because index funds tend to outperform most other funds over time. Yes, it's true that you are giving up the possibility of investing with a great manager who consistently beats the market. And a manager who can beat the market by as little as 2 percent a year can add a lot to your overall returns.

But if you want to increase the odds of investing in a "winner," and more importantly *reduce* the odds of investing in a loser, then indexing is the way to go. Here's a quote from the March 15, 1999, edition of *Fortune*: ". . . building a portfolio around index funds isn't really settling for average (or a little better). It's just refusing to believe in magic."

Brenda: But indexing is surely not for everyone. You already said that investors can be categorized by their risk tolerances and investment objectives, and that each category or investor type will need a different portfolio.

What kind of investor should use indexing?

Ted: The type of investor you are determines how much of each asset class you hold. For instance, investors with a higher risk tolerance and longer time horizon should have a larger portion of their investments in stocks. But I do think that everyone should have some indexing in their portfolios, no matter what type of investor they are, with very few exceptions.

Brenda: But surely indexing is not appropriate for certain types of investors, such as very aggressive ones. Wouldn't they need both a higher percentage in stocks, and riskier stocks that may not be in an index?

Ted: Well, this issue is debatable. There are those who believe that everyone should have the same portfolio holdings and only the mix of the holdings should change. So the more aggressive investor should simply hold a higher proportion of stocks and a lower proportion in bonds and cash than a more conservative investor would. This approach assumes that every investor should hold the *same* stocks to begin with, just in different proportions. But there are others who believe that the more aggressive investor should hold a higher percentage in stocks and should also invest in more aggressive stocks.

Bob: So which is right?

Ted: The most technically accurate approach is the first one, where everyone holds the same stocks and bonds, but in different proportions. But there isn't really a problem with aggressive investors taking on additional risk by choosing some riskier stocks or stock funds, as long as the riskier stocks are a small part of the extra risk they take overall. Aggressive investors should increase their risk mainly by holding more stocks and less cash. If they were to load up their higher percentage of stock holdings with very risky stocks of little-known small companies, then they would be taking on an excessive amount of risk. That kind of strategy is more like gambling than investing.

Brenda: So how does this relate to my question about whether everyone should index?

Ted: The basic determinant of risk in a portfolio should be the asset allocation between stocks, bonds, and cash. The *types* of stocks or bonds is a secondary consideration that can be standardized across all portfolios, or modified slightly so that aggressive investors hold some riskier stocks, in addition to a core holding of more commonly held stocks. *The core holding, which is the dominant part of both an* *aggressive and conservative investor's portfolio, should be indexed.* For aggressive investors, the complementary active funds that are added to the core index holding can vary slightly to hold riskier stocks. The stock indexes are naturally diversified so they are protected from any single company going bankrupt. And they provide the best method of investing in stocks, no matter what your risk tolerance is. An aggressive investor should hold *more* of the stock index, compared to his cash and bond holdings. The important difference between the aggressive and conservative investor is the *proportion* of stocks she holds, not *which* stocks she holds.

Brenda: But sophisticated investors wouldn't want to index, right? Indexing is just for beginners. If you or your broker or planner know how the market works, it would be senseless to waste all that talent on just buying the index. You'd be giving up the opportunity to own some great stocks that aren't in the index, or to hold a higher percentage of the great stocks that are in the index but given little weight.

Ted: Not the case. I thought we established much earlier that no matter how "expert" someone is at picking stocks, or bonds for that matter, it is very hard for anyone to overcome the probability that the market will outperform over the long run, and often in the short run. In fact, it is the truly sophisticated investor who really understands how markets work and how difficult it is to outsmart the market. *Sophisticated investors should be the greatest champions of indexing, if they truly understand its benefits.* It is the beginner, who often doesn't have all the information, that believes his broker, planner, or even he himself can consistently pick securities that will do better than the market as a whole.

Bob: So you're literally saying that everyone should index their portfolios. Without exception.

Ted: That's what the logic dictates, my friend.

Brenda: But what about all those fund managers out there? Are you trying to put them out of business? What about all the brokers picking stocks for their clients? What will happen to them if everyone puts everything into an index?

Ted: Who said anything about *everything*?

Brenda: You said everyone should index their portfolios!

Ted: They should. But not *everything*. Not the *whole* portfolio. There are some managers out there whose track records suggest they are probably capable of beating the index. And in certain markets, such as the Asian or emerging markets, it's easier to beat the index. The job of a financial adviser is first and foremost to determine a suitable portfolio for each investor, depending on the investor's personal objectives and risk tolerance. That's where the adviser adds the most value of all — in determining the percentage that should go into stocks, bonds, and cash.

Secondarily, she adds value by buying the securities that make up the portfolio, and this is where she should make ample use of indexing. But I am not suggesting that indexing should be the *exclusive* investment vehicle for the entire portfolio. Rather, it should make up a *significant* portion of the portfolio. The odds simply favour it. So why wouldn't you want to index a good portion of your portfolio? Why play against the odds?

Let's say you were faced with two ways of getting across a lake to a warm and cozy cottage on the other side, where a delicious seven-course meal awaits you. One method of transportation is to take a small but very reliable fishing boat with a 10-horsepower engine that would get you across in 30 minutes. The other method is a huge inboard powerboat with a 160-horsepower engine that can get you across in five minutes, but isn't nearly as reliable. In fact, the powerboat has been known to break down just as it reaches full speed and half the time gets completely stalled along the way. Which would you choose?

Bob: The powerboat.

Brenda: No. The small boat.

Ted: Because?

Brenda: Because, just like the index fund, we're more certain of getting across and enjoying the meal.

Ted: And you're prepared to trade off the speed of the powerboat because the odds favour your getting across in the fishing boat.

Bob: I'd still take the powerboat for the thrill of it.

Brenda: Good. More food for Ted and me to enjoy.

So it's that basic then. The argument for indexing is based on the higher probability that the index will outperform.

Ted: It really isn't more complicated than that. The power of indexing lies in its slow and steady ability to outperform most managers. And because it is so difficult to predict the few active managers that will beat the index, it only makes sense to place most of your bet with the index.

Brenda: Just one nagging concern . . . if everyone indexes their investments, won't that hurt the efficiency of the market? And what would happen to the smaller companies that aren't in the index? Don't we have an obligation to help small companies get started and grow by investing in their stock even if they are not part of the index?

How indexing affects the market

Ted: Indexing is unlikely to ever be so big that it will affect the efficiency of the market as a whole. There will always be active managers out there making a living by picking stocks and bonds that they think will outperform. And some managers will do quite well at outperforming, so there will always be demand for them. It appears that indexing levels off at about 25 to 30 percent of invested assets when we look at more mature markets such as the US and UK pension industries, which have been indexing for almost two decades. Some people like to claim that indexing has just become a self-fulfilling trend since the more popular indexing gets, the more the price of index stocks get pushed up. This is a faulty observation. Only a minority of stocks in the TSE 300 and the S&P 500 have enjoyed huge gains in the last few years. In fact, in 1998 only 50 stocks — or 10 percent of all the stocks in the S&P 500 — generated 90 percent of the index's gain. If indexing were self-fulfilling, the other stocks in the index would have done very well too. It won't ever be the case that indexing simply creates its own success, as long as active managers continue to play a significant role in capital markets by buying and selling stocks inside and outside the index. This is exactly what active managers will be doing for the foreseeable future.

As for smaller companies that are not in the index, but need capital to get started and grow, the same observation applies. Active managers will always be interested in small-cap stocks because they are less efficiently traded and priced, so a manager has the opportunity to do much better than the small-cap index. The opportunity for managers to invest in new smaller companies that might enjoy much higher growth than the indexes will keep the capital market for small stocks alive and well.

One of the best things about indexing is that it keeps the active management business honest. Over time, the fees of actively managed funds cannot get too far away from index fund fees, and more importantly, investors in active funds whose returns consistently underperform the index will be able to determine whether they are better off investing somewhere else.

The Bottom Line

I have yet to be convinced by any objection to indexing — and I've covered every one I've ever heard. The strongest objection is that by picking winning mutual funds, you can do much better than the index. While this is partially true (although as we saw in Chapter 2, even the winners don't outperform by that much), it assumes that picking winning mutual funds is feasible. The probability of predicting a winner is quite low. Even the experts are not unanimous on what a great fund is. (For a real test of predictability, keep your eye on the performance of the Bissett Canadian Equity Fund — it has great managers based in Calgary, but I'll bet their recent publicity will result in their attracting more cash than they can invest wisely. It will be interesting to see if the one fund that most experts agree on continues to be a winner.) *In my view, the only legitimate concern when it comes to indexing is that you shouldn't index **all** of your investments.* I don't think it's wrong or imprudent to hold only indexed securities. But for most investors, there is good reason to try for the extra 2 percent that good active management can generate. Active management should be used very selectively, though. And that is the topic of the next chapter.

5

Active Management: Going for an Extra 2 Percent

I hope by now you are becoming convinced of the power of indexing. I hope you're *so* convinced, in fact, that you now need to be persuaded to consider using active management at all. That's what this chapter is about. After alerting you to the potential pitfalls of actively managed mutual funds for four chapters in a row, it's time to give them some credit, and show you how a limited use of them makes sense. As we've seen, certain markets are better suited than others to active management, and even within the more efficient markets, active management can add some extra horsepower to a portfolio.

The challenge is to find a skilled active manager, one that you believe can add value above the returns of the index. When considering the addition of an active manager to your portfolio, the odds that she will outperform the index have to be comfortably over 50 percent. It is not easy to determine that a manager is likely to outperform, but in order to eliminate luck as a factor in a manager's track record, it is crucial that you look beyond past performance. The amount you allocate to active management is different for each market. It is determined by a particular market's efficiency.

Ted: You may be wondering why I would dare recommend active management, after spending so much time demonstrating how difficult it is to beat the index, never mind predict which manager is going to do it.

Bob: Yeah . . . the thought did cross my mind.

Brenda: I can't see how in the world you can possibly argue for active management at this point. You already showed that indexing beats most active managers.

Ted: It comes down to the word "most." Guess what . . . we're into probabilities again.

Bob: My favourite subject.

Ted: The fact is that the index has a very solid chance of beating the active manager in *most* but not *all* markets. There are some markets where the possibility of beating the index is higher. As we saw from the "facts" at the beginning of our conversation, the less efficient markets such as Asia, Latin America, Eastern Europe, and Africa offer the active manager a better shot at beating the index. There are fewer analysts and investors scouring these markets looking for undervalued stocks, so less research is produced on the stocks of these countries. A career in investment management is not held up as the glorified and wonderful job that it is in North America, so fewer talented individuals are attracted to this type of work. Equity markets in Continental Europe are less developed than they are in North America, since the pension plans of European countries are still largely oriented toward investing in bonds. All of this is changing, though. And over time, the active managers' opportunities will shrink, but we're a long way from giving up on active management altogether.

Bob: I believe you mentioned something about probabilities . . . ?

Ted: Yes. The probabilities are higher in the developing countries that an active manager can add value. But even in Canada there's room for an active manager to boost returns, more room than in the US market, anyway. The tradeoff in this case is between the possibility of getting higher returns, and the probability of the index outperforming. Having said that, a little extra value above the index can add up to a lot of extra returns! So if there's a reasonable chance of the active manager outperforming, it's only sensible to allocate some money to her.

We're not aiming for an extra 5 percent, because an extra 5 percent above the index each year suggests that the manager is taking a lot of risk. Bigger bets or riskier investments could easily turn your extra 5 percent into minus 5 percent in future years. However, generating an extra 2 percent above the index over a period of time does not necessarily involve an excessive amount of risk. And an extra 2 percent adds up fast.

If a manager outperforms an index by 2 percent, the impact can be quite substantial to your savings. Let's assume that we're looking at the difference between a 10 percent return and a 12 percent return, over three time periods, with a starting investment of either $10,000, $25,000, or $50,000. The bigger return adds up to a significantly higher ending value for your portfolio.

An extra 2% of returns over the following time periods adds up to these additional amounts:

	5 years	10 years	25 years
$10,000	$1,518	$5,121	$61,654
$25,000	$3,796	$12,803	$154,134
$50,000	$7,592	$25,605	$308,268

Brenda: I can see why you would shoot for the extra 2 percent in some markets, like Latin America or Asia, but why would you attempt it in more efficient markets? Why not just index entirely in efficient countries like Canada or the US?

Ted: There is use for active management in most markets, although the extent of its use depends on the market itself. Just as indexing doesn't make sense for markets that are less efficient, but does make sense for markets that are extremely efficient, a more limited use of indexing makes sense for all the markets in between. We've seen in Canada that the active manager has a better shot at beating the index than in the US, so it makes sense to allocate more to active management in the Canadian portion of your portfolio than in the US portion.

There's nothing complicated or mysterious about it. Our decisions should always be driven by the same premise: *Intelligent investing is based on putting odds in your favour, by making appropriate tradeoffs.* And the tradeoffs we make will depend on the market we're investing in.

The probability of a talented active manager beating the TSE 300 is greater than the probability of a talented active manager beating the S&P 500. Therefore, we should invest more heavily in the index for our US investments than we do for our Canadian investments. In the part of our portfolio that is dedicated to Canadian equities, we invest more in active management than we do in the part that is dedicated to US equities.

Bob: So how do you know how much to index in each market?

Ted: There is a simple criterion for determining this: the likelihood of a manager outperforming the index. The higher the probability that a manager can beat the market of a given index, the more, in percentage terms, we should allocate to active management. If the probability is low, because the market is too efficient, we allocate a smaller percentage to active management.

Brenda: But how do you quantify the probability?

Ted: I'll be honest — there's no scientific formula for that decision, even though it is a very important one. There is no entirely reliable mathematical way to measure a market's efficiency. The best we can do is to look at how active managers have done in the past against the index. If many of them beat the index over a number of time periods, did they beat it by enough to suggest that they're likely to continue beating it? That's why I started with all of those charts at the beginning. They were a crucial starting point in our determination of how much money to allocate to index funds in each market.

Let me show you what I do in my own portfolio so we can talk about the split between actively and passively managed funds. I'll show you the range within which you should index, and the allocation I've chosen for myself, which I've identified as the "target" allocation:

Market	Probability of beating the index	Passive Allocation		Active Allocation	
		Range	Target	Range	Target
Canadian Bonds	Low	80–100%	80%	0–20%	20%
International Bonds	Low	80–100%	100%	0–20%	0%
Canadian Equities	Medium	50–100%	70%	0–50%	30%
US Equities	Low	80–100%	85%	0–20%	15%
European Equities	Low	80–100%	100%	0–20%	0%
Asian Equities	High (excl. Japan) Med. (Japan only)	0% 0–100%	0% 0%	100% 0–100%	100% 100%
Emerging Markets Equities	High	0%	0%	100%	100%
Specialty Sectors	High	0%	0%	100%	100%

Bob: I guess there are a lot of active managers out there who are relieved they still have a job!

Ted: I frankly don't think they're losing too much sleep over the issue of indexing — *yet*. But it is a fact that indexing is the fastest-growing segment of the investment industry and there is increasing pressure on active managers to generate value for their clients. This is especially true as more and more investors become aware of the power of indexing. Anyway, as you can see from my recommendations, active management has an important role to play.

Brenda: Seems kind of arbitrary to me — the way you've split each market into active or passive.

Ted: It's based on judgements drawn from the return comparisons I showed you and the underlying rationale that supports those comparisons. It's not mathematically unchallengeable. But it's not arbitrary. I'll explain how I came up with each split by walking you through each market.

Cash

There's just no point in indexing cash. Invest in T-bills or a money market fund and you'll do just fine.

Canadian Bonds (80 percent indexed)

The historical returns clearly demonstrate that the SCM Universe Bond Index is hard to beat. But that's not to say it can't be done. Active managers have two principal ways of beating the index. First, they can make bets on changes in interest rates. They know that the index has an average term-to-maturity — meaning time before the average bond in the index matures — of just over nine years. A manager can build a fund of bonds with shorter or longer terms, so that changes in interest rates will affect his fund differently than they affect the index. For instance, if an active manager believes that interest rates are going to fall, he can load up on longer-term bonds such as 30-year Government of Canada bonds. Because longer-term bonds rise more when interest rates fall, the active manager can generate more gains than the index, with its shorter, nine-year average term.

The second way to beat the index is to make bets on the yields between different types of bonds. Perhaps the active manager believes that the bonds issued by corporations are yielding very high interest payments compared to government bonds and that the corporate bond yields are likely to fall more than the government bond yields. This situation can arise when an economy is slowing down, but less quickly than everyone thought it would. If the economy is stronger than expected, the risk of companies defaulting on their bonds is also not that high, and the credit quality of corporate bonds looks better than originally thought. This means companies can pay less interest while still being able to sell their bonds. In this example, the manager will increase his allocation of corporate bonds and lower his holding of government bonds. He will therefore be overweight in corporate bonds, relative to the index, and if he is right and corporate yields fall relative to government yields, he will earn more gains on his portfolio than the index.

Bob: Sounds straightforward — the part I understood, anyway. I think I recognized a few words.

Ted: Let me try it another way. The manager can choose to hold more in corporate bonds, especially high-yield bonds. While the index has about a 17 percent weighting in corporate bonds, it doesn't hold any high-yield bonds, which are sometimes unfairly called "junk bonds," but are more properly classified as "non-investment grade bonds." The corporate bonds, of which the high yields are a part, are riskier since their credit quality is lower than government bonds. The index has about a 60 percent weighting in federal government bonds, and a 20 percent weighting in provincial government bonds. So the manager can increase his returns by holding a bigger percentage in corporate bonds, including some high-yield issues.

Bob: I'll take your word for it. Anyway, why don't you put more money with the active manager?

Ted: Because beating the index only sounds easy. It's actually not that easy to do, at least not that easy to get right. Just as we've seen with stocks, the theory often doesn't translate into practice because it's hard to accurately predict all of the elements of bond yields: when interest rates are going to change, in what direction, by what magnitude, which part of the yield curve — short-term or long-term rates — and for what issuers — governments or corporations. The active manager doesn't have to get all of those bets right, but she has to get her biggest bet right — the one she is planning to use to generate extra returns. There are great active bond managers who appear to have added value to the index over long periods. But they are few and far between.

Brenda: Why do you say "appear"? Are they cheating?

Ted: No, they're not cheating. I use the word "appear" because, as we've seen, it's very hard to be definitive when we say that a manager adds value. It's hard to separate out what we would expect to happen statistically from what is attributable to talent. Remember, you need a long period of time before you can say that a manager added value beyond what was statistically possible from randomness, like the coin tosses.

So the bottom line with bonds is that most of it should be indexed. The only way to effectively index is to buy an index bond fund. But I still like to add some juice to a portfolio by allocating some money to an active manager who I think has a good chance of beating the index. Notice that I'm deciding to add an active manager on the basis of probabilities, not guarantees. Because it's hard to beat the bond index, and because I can't be certain that the active manager will beat the index, I allocate 20 percent to the active manager. This 20 percent should go to a bond manager who makes bigger bets in either interest rate predictions, corporate bond spreads, or both. If I were *certain* that the manager would beat the index, there would be no point in indexing at all. *But because it is probabilities that determine a portfolio, not mathematical certainties, I recommend no less than 80 percent in the index.*

International Bonds (100 percent indexed)

This one is perhaps more debatable than straight Canadian bonds. The numbers suggest that indexing this asset class can make sense. But the history is quite short since there aren't a lot of international bond funds with track records, so it's harder to make a comparison between them and the index.

The active international bond manager focuses mostly on choosing the bonds in a currency that she thinks will do better than others. She can also manage the currency exposure of the bond fund. For instance, she may decide that British bonds look like attractive investments since interest rates in the United Kingdom appear to be on the verge of coming down, which means that UK bond prices will go up. But the manager might be worried that the British pound is going to fall heavily at the same time, so she might convert her pound holdings back to Canadian dollars while holding on to the British bonds. By doing so, she is "hedging" her currency risk.

Whether or not an active manager can add value over time by making currency decisions is a hotly debated subject. On the one hand, some managers have demonstrated an aptitude in this area; on the other, hedging eliminates one of the diversification benefits of holding foreign bonds. I am personally skeptical about a manager's ability to consistently make currency calls that add value beyond what you get in an index fund — a simple unhedged exposure to foreign currencies.

Either way, a good portion in an index fund makes sense, since the probabilities favour the index over any one particular fund manager, given that there aren't many managers with long track records. Unless you have a large portfolio in excess of one million dollars, there's no point in splitting off 20 percent into an active international bond fund. Might as well put it all in the index fund. When I get to recommending funds, I'll point out an active international bond fund that could be considered for that small allocation; however, the portfolios that I'm going to show you later will assume the 100 percent use of the index fund since that makes sense for most people. *While an 80/20 split in international bond funds is reasonable, it is probably more realistic to put 100 percent in the index fund only because international bonds do not represent a high proportion of anyone's portfolio.*

Canadian Equities (70 percent indexed)

The TSE 300 is a little odd. It has a heavy weighting in both resource stocks and financial stocks. Financial companies make up almost 25 percent of the TSE 300, and resource stocks, including oil, gas, gold, forestry, and minerals, make up another 23 percent. While financial companies have accounted for between 15 and 25 percent of the TSE 300 over the last 15 years, resource stocks have been as high as 37 percent. This is a heavy weighting compared to the S&P 500, which has only 16 percent in financials and 7 percent in resource stocks. Whereas the TSE 300 has only about a 14 percent weighting in technology stocks, the US market has almost double that — around 26 percent. The last thing I'll say about our index is that it is heavily weighted by a small number of stocks. Whereas 10 stocks make up about 20 percent of the S&P 500 index, only five stocks make up about 25 percent of the TSE 300, and two of those companies are related — BCE and Nortel Networks. Finally, international money managers tend to invest in Canadian stocks only when they want to increase their exposure to the resource sector. So the TSE 300 can be subject to price swings that result from changing demand by international investors for our gold and forestry companies.

Additionally, the stocks of the Canadian market aren't nearly as closely tracked by as many people as are American stocks, because there are fewer people in the world that are interested in owning Canadian stocks. For these two reasons — the odd nature of our index and the fact that fewer investors are assessing our stocks every day — a good active manager has a reasonable shot at beating the TSE 300. The performance numbers bear this out, as we've seen.

Having said all this, I still want to insulate the Canadian stock portion of my portfolio from underperformance. There have been more years when the index beat the majority of active managers than years when the majority beat the index. And as we saw, the managers that did beat the index didn't beat it by much. So it only makes sense that the core holding of my Canadian equities should be indexed. If I could find an active manager that I was *certain* would consistently beat the index, then I'd allocate all of my Canadian equities to her. But I do not have the confidence that I could find such a manager. So I split the Canadian stock portion 70/30, so that 70 percent is indexed. There is no impressive mathematical formula or computer program that told me it should be 70/30, instead of any other split. It is not unreasonable to put 50 percent in an active fund and index only 50 percent. But the odds are not symmetrical because it does not make sense to put 100 percent in active, whereas it is perfectly sensible to put 100 percent in the index. Given the performance record of active managers and the challenge of picking the ones that will consistently outperform, a higher allocation in indexing can be justified, right up to 100 percent. But unless by some mysterious power you are able to pick out an active manager that you know will do better than the index, I would limit the active part of your Canadian stock portfolio to a maximum of 50 percent. The extra 2 percent return from a good active manager adds up, but a manager who subtracts 2 percent from your returns will detract from your portfolio just as fast.

The percent that you allocate to active management should be geared toward an active manager whose style is very different from the index. Otherwise you might as well just index completely. That means that the 30 or so percent in an active fund should be in a small-companies fund or a fund with a very specific style. Small companies are less followed than the big companies, so the odds of a manager adding value are greater in this sector. We'll talk more about styles and picking managers shortly. One note of caution: If you do invest in an actively managed small-companies fund, make sure that it definitely holds small companies. Some small-cap funds cheat by investing a significant portion in larger-company stocks, and then you end up getting closer to the index, which defeats the purpose of going active. *Index anywhere between 50 and 100 percent of your Canadian equities.*

US Equities (85 percent indexed)

This is easy — the numbers speak for themselves. If you want the odds to work in your favour, this is not a difficult decision — most of a portfolio's US stock exposure should be indexed. If the earlier charts didn't convince you that indexing makes sense in the US, then . . .

Brenda: Believe me, I'm convinced.

Ted: Don't get me wrong. I'm not saying that the US index will always beat most managers over every time period. Don't come looking for my head if a bunch of active funds beat the index next year or the year after. I'm not saying that you are *guaranteed* to have a top-performing fund by investing in an index fund —

Bob: We know, we know. You're saying that the probability is higher that we can outperform by investing in the index —

Brenda: Over the long term. Not necessarily in any given year, although it's likely that in most years the index will beat most active managers.

Ted: I couldn't have put it better myself.

Bob: So why put anything in an actively managed US equity fund? Why do you allocate 15 percent to active management?

Ted: Same as Canada. There is the opportunity for some managers to pick smaller companies in certain sectors that have a good chance of beating the index. I'm not going to put too much of my US exposure at risk, but I want to at least have the benefit of some active management.

Brenda: But if the odds are so overwhelmingly in favour of indexing, why not just stick with it?

Ted: There would be nothing wrong with putting 100 percent in an index fund in the US, or Canada for that matter. But there's an element of regret that I'm trying to avoid, as I mentioned earlier when we were talking about the use of active management in a portfolio. Some academics actually define risk as the likelihood that an investor will regret his decision. You'd certainly regret investing everything in technology stocks if they went down by 25 percent and never recovered, right? Well, I'd also regret putting absolutely everything in an index fund just to see the index underperform many managers in any given year.

This is commonly referred to as "regret aversion," a term used by behavioural economists to describe the natural psychological impulse to avoid regret. Studies in the field of psychology and behavioural economics indicate that most people hate bad things more than they like good things. In other words, it is typical human behaviour to put more emphasis on avoiding the feeling of regret from a decision, than on pursuing the feeling of satisfaction from a decision. This is why many people chase after the "hot" funds — because they are determined not to regret missing out. On the flip side, this same impulse encourages many to invest too conservatively — because they are avoiding the regret of losing money, even if it means giving up higher returns. The benefit of investing some of your portfolio in actively managed funds is that you can appease that part of you that doesn't want to regret the decision to not invest in some of the good active funds. But you're not caving in to that impulse too impetuously, since the base of your investments is still indexed.

Brenda: And that compromise makes sense, even if over the long term the index beats all the active managers?

Ted: If I were *guaranteed* to beat all active managers by investing in an index fund, it would be purely irrational to invest in an active fund. But remember that there are no guarantees. Just reasonable projections of the future based on probabilities. It is probable that the index will outperform the majority of active US equity managers over the long term. But I want to hedge my bets just a little, so I don't lose out on a possible 2 percent and have to live with the regret of missing out. And I'm willing to take the risk that I'll underperform with that allocation in active management.

If I had no confidence that I could pick a good active US manager, I'd put it all in the index. But I don't want to regret missing the returns of a manager that I think can outperform. So I put just a little into an active US fund. *Keep the active part of your US equities limited to no more than 20 percent of your US investments, and the best bet for this part is in the stocks of smaller companies that are marginally less efficiently traded and priced.*

European Equities (100 percent indexed)

It's hard to make a case for putting a lot into actively managed European equities when you look at the track record of the index. There are some good reasons to think an active manager can beat the index, though. The equity markets of Continental Europe are not as developed as those of North America or Britain. Continental Europeans have traditionally been investors in bonds. This stems from the ownership structure of many large European companies, which are owned and often controlled by large banks. However, since the implementation of the Economic Monetary Union, the European market has been undergoing some restructuring. The result is that the stock markets will become much broader and more companies will be issuing public shares. The stock market in the UK is a different story. It is very developed and very efficient.

An allocation of 20 percent in actively managed European equities is not reckless but the same argument made for international bonds holds for European equities: because they constitute at most just over 10 percent of your portfolio, you might as well index the whole allocation. If you're a millionaire, then it makes sense to have 20 percent of your total European holdings in active funds; otherwise it's not worth splitting off. Again, it's the smaller companies that make the most sense when allocating a portion to an actively managed European fund, because they are less closely followed and therefore provide the active manager with a better chance of beating the index.

It used to be the case that a manager could add value by altering the country weights of an actively managed European fund. This would entail putting more investment into the countries that the manager anticipated were going to do better. If Britain appeared to have a stronger economy than France, the manager could try to beat the index by investing more of the fund in the UK and less in France. This strategy still makes sense but not indefinitely. As the economies of European countries become more closely integrated with the introduction of the Euro common currency, they will tend to perform more as a unit. Ultimately, when the UK joins the European Union, as most people believe it will, the ability of an active manager to add value by selectively under- and over-weighting countries will diminish. There are probably about two more years of opportunity in country selection, before an active manager will have to rely more on stock or economic sector selection. *If you find an active manager you like, I wouldn't recommend more than 20 percent in her fund.*

Asian Equities (zero percent indexed)

The Asian indexes are easier to beat. Not *easy*, just *easier*. Besides, there aren't many Asian index funds. I favour a good actively managed Asian fund where a skilled manager can weight each country differently, depending on her view of their respective economies. Unlike Continental Europe, the economies of Japan, Hong Kong, China, Singapore, South Korea, the Philippines, Thailand, Malaysia, and Indonesia tend to have their own political and economic characteristics. The problem is that some of the best Asian funds exclude Japan from their mandates. But you definitely don't want to have zero exposure to one of the largest economies in the world. All Asian economies are largely dependent upon Japan for their economic success because of the enormous amount of trade that occurs between Japan and the other Asian countries. Japan represents about 10 percent of the total world stock market. It is the largest single-country market after the US, although from time to time it switches with England, which also represents around 10 percent. Japan is far too large and important for investors to leave out of their portfolios.

When it comes to country exposure, there are therefore two basic strategies to choose from: Go with a great Asian fund that excludes Japan, and then add a Japanese fund to your mix. Or go with a good Asian fund that includes Japan as a core holding. I prefer to choose a good Asian fund that holds few or no Japanese stocks, to which I can add a good Japanese fund. That way I don't have to worry about my exposure to Japan being reduced or eliminated if a particular Asian-fund manager isn't optimistic about the Japanese stock market at a given moment in time.

Unlike the rest of Asia, where active managers have a good shot at beating the index, and indexing is difficult to implement anyway, Japanese equities *can* be passively managed, so you can't go very wrong with an index fund. Many Japanese active funds, however, have done very well, at least over the short history available to assess them. The Japanese index — the Nikkei 225 — is not necessarily reflective of the true value of Japanese companies, since in that economy there is so much cross-ownership between different but related companies. A better index for a Japanese fund is the MSCI Japanese index. But there are some good Japanese fund managers out there, so use an active fund if you have confidence in one. Some actively managed Japanese funds hedge the yen exposure when they think that the yen will decline. I get nervous about managers who attempt this, since they can often wipe out any equity gains with a bad currency call. An active Japanese fund that does not take large bets on currency can be as good a choice — even better — than an index fund.

A winning formula for covering off the whole region is to combine a good actively managed Asian fund that does not invest in Japan with a good actively managed Japanese fund that does not make substantial currency bets on the yen. The amount of Japanese stock you hold should not deviate too significantly from its natural weight in the Asian market — currently around 70 percent — so the final result of your Asian stock holdings is *70 percent in a Japanese fund and 30 percent in an Asian fund that excludes Japan*. If you choose to index the Japanese portion, you will end up with a maximum of 70 percent of your total Asian equities in index funds.

Emerging Markets (zero percent indexed)

The least efficient of all the markets. Nonetheless, as we've seen, active managers have only been able to beat the index about half the time. Emerging markets index funds are hard to come by, for two main reasons: some stocks in the emerging markets index are very illiquid; and the restrictive trading regulations of some countries make the funds difficult to manage. Emerging markets should represent a small portion of anyone's total investments, as we'll see when we construct the portfolios. The MSCI index that tracks emerging economies is weighted about 44 percent in Latin America, 40 percent in Asia, and 16 percent in Eastern Europe, South Africa, and the Middle East. A good active manager will therefore have to have a demonstrated talent in picking Latin American companies and an excellent sense of global economic trends and how they affect the developing countries, most of which are extremely dependent upon exporting their resources and goods to developed countries.

Specialty Sectors (zero percent indexed)

There is no need to hold specialty funds in a portfolio. These are funds with very narrow mandates such as precious metals, technology, oil and gas, or health care. I call these "fun funds." You can invest in them for fun. Your Canadian equity index fund already gives you plenty of exposure to resource and gold stocks. Your US equity index fund contains a reasonable helping of technology stocks. You will not miss out on any short-term sectors that are hot if you are properly diversified. The problem with sector and specialty funds is that by investing in them, you are overweighting them in your portfolio, and putting yourself at risk of generating poor performance over time. We all know that today's hot funds are tomorrow's losers.

If you have extra money you want to have fun with, and you think you know something about the technology or gold sector that the market as a whole doesn't, or you have faith in an adviser whom you believe has special knowledge, then play with some of these funds. And there's no point in indexing these sectors if you are playing. A good active manager who has developed a deep understanding of a particular sector is in the best position to choose stocks within that sector. Just make sure you don't seriously overweight certain sectors because this contravenes the laws of prudent diversification. And don't load up on a bunch of sector funds, each of which only represents a small portion of your total investment, but which collectively account for a large portion of your portfolio. Ten percent is the maximum that most investors should contemplate for the *total* allocation in active specialty funds, with no more than 5 percent in any one of the sectors. And if you do use sector funds, don't use them to time the market. If even the best active managers have difficulty timing the market, it's not very likely that you or I are going to have better luck. "Luck" being the operative word. *But I still favour zero percent in specialty or sector funds, especially if your objective is to maximize your long-term returns.* You can find fun in a variety of other ways — some of which are definitely more exciting, and not as dangerous.

So that's how I justify the split between active and passive for each asset class. There's no mathematical equation or computer model that gives the one and only answer. Common sense, based on everything we've talked about so far, dictates the splits I've shown.

Brenda: So what does your actual portfolio look like, then? After you've split up the index part from the active part.

Ted: We'll get to the actual portfolios themselves later.

Bob: Later? Are you planning to sleep over?

Ted: For now I wanted to show you what kind of a mix of indexing and active management makes sense for your portfolio. You can see that the mix depends on which market we're addressing. It can range as high as 100 percent indexing for international bonds or as low as zero percent indexing for emerging markets. There is nothing wrong, however, in indexing the entire portion of bond, Canadian, US, and European equities. In fact, you will do a lot better indexing all of these markets than you would be if you were gambling on an active manager that you aren't sure has a good shot at outperforming the index in each category.

Brenda: But if there aren't any Asian or emerging markets index funds in Canada, you wouldn't be able to index your whole portfolio, even if you wanted to.

Ted: Not true. You'd have to sacrifice some exposure to the emerging markets, and Latin America in particular. But there are some good international index funds available in Canada that track the MSCI EAFE index, which covers Europe, Australia, and the Far East regions. So, you can stick to indexing exclusively if you aren't confident that you or your adviser can choose active funds that are highly likely to generate superior returns in the future.

Bob: Okay. I've been holding off up until now. But you made a rather dramatic point of demonstrating earlier that it is impossible to choose a "winning" manager. Are you contradicting yourself or am I missing something? Even if some indexes are easier to beat, how are we supposed to be able to pick a good manager who is going to beat the index, when you've insisted that it's impossible to choose a winner?

Ted: Well, you'll remember that I made a point of saying that it's *very* *difficult* to predict a winner and perhaps impossible to pick a long-term winner *if* you're relying on past performance exclusively.

Bob: Sounds vaguely familiar.

Ted: We're not guaranteed to pick a manager that *will* generate 2 percent extra for us — the trick is to choose a manager that is *likely* to be able to add 2 percent above the index. And it's an important decision because a poor manager can subtract from your portfolio just as quickly as he can add.

Bob: So why not avoid the risk of underperforming the index by investing in index funds only? Why even bother suggesting that a portion here and a portion there could be actively managed?

Ted: There's nothing crazy about not taking the risk. Some people do prefer to put all of their money into the index. There are a few reasons why I don't. First, I am confident that I can pick a manager who is likely to beat the index and add 2 percent per year to my portfolio on average. Second, I want to avoid the regret I would have if I didn't act on my confidence in choosing good active managers. For me, because I have some knowledge and a system for choosing managers that is fairly rigorous, I'd rather add some active management to my portfolio than forego the opportunity to generate an extra 2 percent. I don't want to lose the opportunity to add to my portfolio talented active managers that will *probably* beat the index by a small amount over time.

Brenda: But that's risky as well because the active managers you choose may not beat the index, in which case you'll lose out.

Ted: I'm prepared to take that risk because I believe I can minimize it with my approach to choosing active funds. If I had no confidence in my ability to pick a good manager who is likely to outperform the index by 2 percent, then I would index my whole portfolio, instead of most of it.

Brenda: Well, I'm dying to hear what your secret formula is for choosing a winning manager, after you spent so much time telling us it can't be done.

Ted: It's not that it *can't* be done —

Brenda: I know, I know. Slip of the tongue. I meant to say, "After telling us how hard it is to pick winning funds."

Ted: When you're talking probabilities, there's a big difference between "can't" and "hard to do." An important distinction we can't gloss over.

Brenda: Point taken. So what's the secret to choosing an active manager?

Bob: Wait a minute. I don't even understand how we're supposed to index. Why are we worrying about how to pick an active manager for the smallest part of our portfolio when I don't have a clue how to do the bigger part, which is indexing?

Ted: Let's take one at a time. Since we're talking about active management, I'll explain how to choose a good manager. Then I'll cover off the indexing part. And, as promised, since you've been such patient listeners, I'll even cover off the process of building a whole portfolio that matches your individual goals and risk tolerances.

Brenda: Let's get on with it then.

The Bottom Line

There's a place for active management in everyone's portfolio. The most relevant role for active management is in those markets that are less efficient and therefore offer the greatest opportunity for the active manager to add value beyond the index. The more efficient the market, the harder it is for the active manager to "know something" that the majority of investors do not, and therefore the harder it is for the manager to add incremental value.

The percent allocation to active management depends on the probability that the manager will add value above the index returns. It is very unlikely that a manager can add much more than 2 percent each year over a long period of time. So the objective of adding active management to a portfolio whose core is indexed is to increase the likelihood of marginally higher returns. There is nothing wrong with indexing the entire portfolio. But if you do, you lose the opportunity to add 2 percent, which is only relevant if you have a high level of confidence in the active managers you choose. *The degree to which you use active management depends on the upper limit that I have recommended for each asset category, and the confidence you have in your ability, or your adviser's, to choose a skilled active manager.* It is far better to go all index, than to invest part of your portfolio with an active manager that you are not sure has a high probability of outperforming over the long term.

6

How to Distinguish the Talented from the Lucky

Considering how little agreement there is on which mutual funds are "winners," the popularity of books that purport to rate the top performers is startling. Most of these books rely exclusively on analyzing past performance. But this method is fatally flawed, as we know from the coin-tossing competition we examined in Chapter 4.

You simply can't distinguish talent from luck by looking exclusively at past performance. The math tells us that with a big enough sample size, there will always be some managers lucky enough to flip 10 tails in a row, or beat the index 10 years in a row. Just as you can't predict who will flip the 10 tails, you can't use only performance to predict who will beat the index over the next 10 years. Do not buy a book or believe an adviser who focuses on past performance exclusively in choosing a winning fund.

Risk is a critical measure, as we've seen, that must be considered in choosing a potential winner. But that's not as easy as it sounds. How do you define, never mind evaluate, risk? There is little consensus in the academic community on the best method of measuring risk. In fact, "risk" can be defined differently depending on the investment objective. An investor who is contemplating putting money into a mutual fund in order to retire comfortably probably has a different feeling about risk than one who is saving for a sports car. And both of these investors would have different attitudes toward risk than would a pension manager who is investing the money of a large pension plan, to fund the retirement of many employees over successive years.

Most of the mutual fund books employ reasonably good methods of assessing risk, and the more measures an author uses to assess risk, the more legitimate is the analysis. For example, an assessment that combines volatility, number and degree of past negative returns, and number of years in which the fund underperformed T-bills or GICs is sufficiently well-rounded to give readers a sense of the manager's investment style.

Performance, risk, and the level of fees charged by the fund are the three essential *quantitative* criteria for assessing it. But other equally important *qualitative* elements must be examined to find a truly skilled manager. *The **quantitative** analysis helps you focus on **possible** winners by eliminating the losers. The **qualitative** analysis helps you focus on **probable** winners by separating the lucky from the skilled managers.* I'll show Bob and Brenda how to use both types of analyses to find a good active manager, one who is likely to outperform the index.

Ted: The first step in assessing a manager is the easiest: Was the performance of her fund good?

Performance assessment

Ted: Were the fund's returns better than the index and its peers over a variety of periods? A good manager should have above-average performance in each year since the fund was started, and cumulatively over one, three, five, and 10 years. Above average, in this case, means above the average active manager in the particular category, as well as above the index.

Bob: Does a manager have to have superior performance in all of those time periods?

Ted: No. But most time periods must be above average. It is crucial to assess the individual calendar years because some managers may have one or two incredible years that pull up their 10-year returns artificially. Also, I tend to disqualify managers who do not yet have three-year track records on their funds since there is just not enough history in one or two years to even hope to separate luck from skill.

Bob: So if a manager underperforms, they should be rejected.

Ted: If a manager has had year after year of performance that is below the index, the only forgivable reason might be that she is purposefully taking less risk in the fund: her aim might be to limit the fund's volatility, rather than beat the index. There is nothing wrong with that. However, it's generally more effective for an investor to manage risk in the entire portfolio, rather than with a particular fund. Portfolio risk is managed with asset allocation — the mix of cash, bonds, and stocks — and this is a more direct and effective method of managing risk than using a conservative fund manager. Often the conservative fund manager is simply holding more cash than usual to reduce risk, but still charges a fee that applies to an all-equity fund; in my view, this is not value for money, especially since we've seen that most managers can't time the market. It is debatable whether or not conservatively managed funds can really safeguard the investor in the long term. Some of the biggest companies that everyone assumed were safe ended up facing some trouble: Royal Trust, Dome Petroleum, Olympia and York all come to mind. The so-called "safe" funds are not necessarily safe, and if they are, it's often because they're holding more cash — but then they are not good complements to a core holding of indexed product. *The best way to achieve safety is by combining cash with an index fund — not by paying over 2 percent in fees for a manager to hold a lot of cash in his fund.*

Brenda: So what else do you look at after a fund has passed the performance test?

Risk assessment

Ted: Here's an important question to ask if a manager has had spectacular returns: How much risk did he take to get those returns? The problem with some funds, as I showed you earlier, is that they take on unusual risk to generate unusual performance.

Bob: What's wrong with a little extra risk if you can generate better returns?

Ted: Nothing, as long as you're prepared for that risk. But extra risk doesn't always mean better performance; it can often lead to severe underperformance. The factors that increase risk and generate higher performance are the same factors that can cause a fund to do poorly. For example, a fund manager could make big bets on just a few companies, put a lot of money in one or two sectors of the economy instead of diversifying it among different sectors, or pick stocks of companies that have very little earnings but potentially explosive future growth. As long as you know the possible outcomes of your investment, there is nothing inherently wrong with a riskier fund. But you should limit how much you invest in riskier funds since their great performance can easily turn into dramatic underperformance.

Bob: So how do you know if a fund is risky?

Ted: Risk is a hard concept to define. Some people like to measure risk as the degree to which a fund goes up and down. This is referred to as its volatility, and it is measured by standard deviation, which is simply the degree to which returns deviate from their average. Others like to define risk as the likelihood that a fund will underperform a safe investment like a GIC or T-bill. Still others prefer to define it as the number of times a fund has generated a negative return or the extent to which a fund's return deviates from the market index.

All of these methods are appropriate and *the best assessment of risk is a combination of many different measures.* There are lots of mutual fund books on the market that give a risk rating to funds and even the major newspapers that track fund performance once a month include a measure of risk that is usually related to volatility. So it's wise to look at what the books and newspapers have to say, but don't forget to look at the actual holdings of the fund, since volatility doesn't tell the whole story. What percentage of the fund is invested in the top 10 stocks? A fund that puts a lot of its investments in just a few holdings is less diversified and potentially riskier. What kind of companies does the fund hold? A fund that holds a lot of very small companies that you have never heard of and can't get much information on is probably a lot riskier than a fund that holds BCE and big bank stocks. If you can't determine a fund's risk on your own, you can get help from an adviser. Don't accept advice from someone who can't tell you about the risk of the fund they are selling you.

Brenda: Okay. I get it. Performance is only relevant in the context of how much risk the manager took to get it.

Ted: Very well put. Good past performance — a record of beating the index over most years — is a necessary but not sufficient criterion for a good active manager. The second quantitative test is whether or not the manager achieved his track record without taking excessive risk. But here's an important point: The risk that a fund took on to achieve its return is often incidental to the objective of the manager. In other words, the risk of a fund may be *coincidental* and not *purposeful*. The manager may have made stock-picking decisions without much regard for the overall risk of his fund. When analysts assess a fund's risk characteristics, they may be making certain unwarranted conclusions about the manager's style or risk objectives. The only way around this is to use a qualitative assessment to determine whether the risk of the fund was the result of the manager's deliberate intent, or merely an after-effect of his stock choices. You'll hear me say over and over again that looking at the numbers alone is not sufficient to assess a manager's skill. *You have to dig beneath the numbers to determine whether the numbers truly reflect intentional decisions. Often the numbers that demonstrate both performance and risk are merely incidental.*

You'd be surprised to know how many newspaper articles give fund managers a lot of credit when they deserve very little, or blame a manager unfairly when underperformance may be very short-term. I've read articles that heaped glowing praise on a manager when in fact the manager's responsibility in the fund was to pick stocks while other people made the country allocation decisions. The example I'm thinking of is a European equity fund. In reality, the stock-picking decisions detracted from the performance of the fund, while the choices of which European countries to invest in added all the value — and even made up for the bad stock picks. Only half of the equation was working and it wasn't the half that the celebrated manager was responsible for!

Bob: What if a manager has performed poorly for so long he has nowhere to go but up?

Ted: A manager who doesn't have skill can only get lucky; he can't get skilled all of a sudden. A fund with substandard performance or risk characteristics is not a good investment.

Fees

Ted: There's one final quantitative measure to consider besides performance history and risk: a fund's fees. As we saw when we were discussing indexing, fees can eat up a huge part of our returns. This holds true for actively managed funds as well. Fees should not be much higher than the average fees for all funds in the category; preferably, they should be lower than the average. The odds of an active manager outperforming the index and adding the 2 percent we're looking for are greatly increased if the fees on her fund are below average.

To summarize then, the *quantitative* tests that an active manager must pass are three-fold:

1. Above average performance and above index performance over each year since the fund's inception and cumulatively over one, three, five, and 10 years. Funds with less than three-year track records are too young to assess.
2. Risk that is not excessive. It should be at most only marginally higher than the risk of the index itself, if not lower.
3. Fees that are, at most, only marginally above average in the fund category, if not lower.

Brenda: Well, I don't have to look at much more than performance to pick out an investment genius like Warren Buffett. Obviously there are real live gurus who have shown that they have skill because they have generated superior returns for very long periods of time.

Ted: But what's a sufficiently long period of time?

Brenda: I would say that if a manager can pick stocks that outperform the index for 10 years or more, she has clearly demonstrated skill.

Ted: Many academics would disagree with you. The general assumption these days is that it could take a track record of at least 25 years to be able to properly distinguish skill in a manager. Some feel that even 25 years isn't long enough. One study suggests that 70 years are required to really be confident of calling a manager skilled, and that only about 4 percent of all active managers are really capable of beating the market over the long term.

Brenda: That's ridiculous.

Ted: It's not so ridiculous when you consider the coin-tossing competition. How many tosses does it take before you eliminate the effect of statistical probabilities? We already saw that with enough tossers, someone can toss 10 tails in a row. In fact, we can predict that someone will toss 20 tails. We don't know who it will be in advance. But we know it's likely that someone will. And when the contest is over, maybe that person's name is Warren Buffett. I believe Warren Buffett is a skilled stock picker. Most research suggests that in order for a manager to be called skilled, with a high degree of confidence, she has to generate 5 percent over the index over 10 years, or 3 percent over the index over 20 years. But your ability to determine, with confidence, that a manager is skilled, is greatly enhanced by looking beyond just the numbers themselves, especially if you don't want to wait for 20 years before you hand over your money.

Once the quantitative tests are passed, the real work begins. Unfortunately, most investors and many "experts" stop at this point. But we've seen that if they do, their ability to distinguish luck from talent is reduced.

Bob: I'd call number crunching real work. Can't imagine it getting tougher.

Qualitative tests

Ted: The numbers are just the start. If you like a manager's track record, you still have to look at qualitative factors to assess whether or not he is skilled or just lucky. While the numbers may tell you that you have a *potential* winner, only the qualitative factors can tell you why, and give you a sense of whether good performance is likely to persist. This is especially true when a manager's track record is shorter than 10 years.

Bob: So what are these qualitative factors?

Ted: They all focus on the decision-making process of the manager and the probability of his process being successful in the future. Let me list them:

1. The degree to which the manager's strategy can be clearly articulated.
2. The extent to which the manager adheres to a strategy.
3. The extent to which the strategy is complementary to indexing.
4. The length of time that the manager has been employing the strategy.
5. The manager's relationship to the investment firm he or she works for.
6. The organization of the firm.

The most important step, and often the most instantly revealing, in your qualitative research is to get the manager to explain her strategy. You would be amazed what many managers say, when asked to describe their process for choosing stocks. Many simply mumble and say things like, "It depends on the market conditions" or "It's a variety of factors, and the importance of each element can't be quantified" or "We look at this, we look at that, we do the hokey-pokey and we turn ourselves about . . ."

Bob: Come on.

Ted: Well, maybe that's a little extreme. But it's simply amazing how many managers can't articulate their process. In order to be assured that underlying the numbers is something more substantial than the "hokey-pokey," you need to know what the strategy is. How do they arrive at a decision to buy or sell? In fact, one of the best ways to assess a manager's strategy is to ask him to describe his most recent buy, sell, and hold decision. I can't tell you the number of blank looks I've seen in response to this question. You know there's something missing when a manager cannot explain the rationale behind her decisions, especially if she's been given prior notice of the questions you want answered!

There are all kinds of stock-picking strategies. The three most popular strategies are (1) to buy stocks when they are perceived to be undervalued; (2) to buy stocks of companies that are expected to grow rapidly; and (3) to buy stocks in industry sectors that are expected to benefit from different economic cycles. I won't go into detail on all the different approaches, because *what's important is that the active manager* ***has*** *a strategy* of some sort. There is little academic agreement on which strategies generate superior performance over the long run. But if a manager is relying on his intuition or indefinable hunches and gut feelings, he is more than likely playing a coin-tossing game — with your money! If he can't explain his strategy, you won't be able to see how the fund is any different from the index that it's trying to beat. There's no point in paying a fee that is at least twice as large as that of an index fund if you are going to be buying a broadly diversified equity fund with heavy weightings in large companies and industry weightings that do not deviate much from the index. You want to own something that is complementary to, and therefore different from, the index.

Mind you, some managers are just not good communicators. They may have perfectly legitimate and rigorous ways of picking stocks, but they can't describe their methods very convincingly. I wouldn't take a chance on these types, no matter how wonderful their track records are, because I have difficulty distinguishing them from the lucky coin tossers. So play it safe, and stick to the ones who have a strategy, and can describe it clearly and convincingly.

Brenda: And that's it?

Ted: Not quite. You see, having a strategy is one thing; applying it consistently over time is another. Discipline is a rare quality in most managers because they are human beings. We've already talked about how our emotions affect our decision-making. Remember, *one of the principal reasons why active managers have trouble beating the index is that they do not apply their strategies in a strictly rational and disciplined way*. They get nervous about falling prices even if they know that the fundamentals of the stock are still good. Or they hold on to a stock with a rising price even though their system indicates that the stock has become overvalued. They let emotions interfere with the systems that they have designed to buy and sell. That's when things fall apart for many managers.

The opposite approach can be a problem as well — there are managers who stubbornly cling to their systems when their strategies no longer work. They refuse to acknowledge that what worked for them for years is no longer effective. Perhaps their system only worked when markets were going up, and they discover that the approach is not useful in a down market, but they are not willing to change fast enough. Or maybe they focused all their attention on resource stocks, which were really hot for a number of years, and now have no expertise in banks or other stocks, which may be the current winners. Their pride and stubbornness may not let them see that they need to adapt their approach to different markets.

Consistent investment success requires extremely rigorous discipline: the discipline to stick to a strategy even when a manager's emotions are pulling him away from it; the discipline to acknowledge that the strategy is no longer applicable if market conditions or circumstances change; the discipline to recognize the difference between the need to stay the course, and the need to adapt to changing markets. Sometimes, despite the best application of discipline, a manager can neither stay the course, nor adapt to changing markets. This occurs when the manager is struck with what I call the "success syndrome" of investment management. For example, perhaps a manager has generated stellar returns by finding undervalued small-company stocks. All of a sudden his success attracts a lot of new money and he can no longer invest in smaller companies because there isn't enough outstanding stock in particular companies to take meaningful positions in with the larger pool of money.

Bob: Whoa. You lost me there.

Ted: I'm glad you stopped me, because this is actually a common problem, especially with small-stock funds. A manager might amass a great track record by investing in small companies. Her great returns will attract a lot of attention and many investors will pour money into her fund. But with a larger fund, she can't invest in the same small companies that she used to build her reputation. In the early years, when the fund had maybe only $50 million in assets, she could take 5 percent of the fund and invest the $2.5 million in the stock of a small company. But as her fund gets bigger and reaches $500 million in assets, the same 5 percent position would require a $25 million investment. The problem is that the same small company and many like it might not have enough publicly traded stock to allow the manager to buy $25 million worth easily.

Bob: So why doesn't she just leave the investment at $2.5 million?

Ted: Because then it represents only half of a percent of the whole fund. So even if the stock does extraordinarily well and triples, it won't have much impact on the total returns. In fact it will only add one percent to the whole portfolio, which isn't even enough to cover the extra trading costs and management fees of the active fund. The great little companies that the manager invested in when she started the fund are no longer realistic investments because her fund is too big to take meaningful positions in very small companies.

Bob: I get it.

Ted: The important point is that a manager must have a system, and then he can neither deviate from it too impetuously, nor stubbornly cling to it if it is no longer working. The system has to be as applicable in the future as it was in the past, and if the market dynamics change, the manager must be prepared to adjust his strategy in order to continue a winning streak. When strategies change, for whatever reason, you can almost be assured that fund performance will suffer. I have never met an investment manager who could change his strategy and continue to generate extraordinary returns. How many times would you expect anyone to invent or implement a series of distinct winning formulae? Do you think that Laurence Olivier used a different preparation technique for each part he played? Do you think that Pavarotti approaches his arias with a different singing technique each time?

Bob: I'll bet there is a nice sports analogy in there somewhere that you could have used instead.

Brenda: The whole thing sounds like a coin toss to me. System or no system.

Ted: I'll be honest. It is as much of an art as a science. And probably more of an art. If there were people who could make the markets scientific by analyzing them and coming up with reliable ways of predicting price movements, they would be rich beyond their wildest dreams.

Brenda: Like Warren Buffett.

Ted: He is a great example of someone who is religious about keeping to his strategy. One of the key reasons for his success is that he has been so disciplined in his approach to picking stocks, which is based on long-term investments in companies at prices that he determines are not excessive. He can articulate his strategy clearly and the strategy has not gone out of style and probably never will.

But where many managers get caught is in the short term, because it's then that the market is not sufficiently scientific to be predictable.

Brenda: What do you mean by that?

Ted: It's what we talked about earlier — how the market is based on rational drivers in the long run, but can be affected by short-run, irrational drivers that exaggerate its movements.

Most active managers believe that there is an opportunity to trade when the market is "acting irrationally." The question is, how does a manager determine exactly what these opportunities are and when they will occur? A talented manager must be able to articulate her strategy for taking advantage of these opportunities. She must explain how she does her research and explain how she decides to buy a stock and sell another. What drove her thinking? How did she arrive at a price that she thought was the right one at which to buy or sell? She must demonstrate discipline around her strategy. What kinds of processes does she have in place to ensure that she sells at prices she thinks are overvalued? How exactly does she determine if a stock is overvalued? Does she consider the risk of her overall fund and how does she manage this risk? Why does she think her strategy will continue to work in the future? If her method seems haphazard and more intuitive than logical, then I want no part of it. It may work for her, but it's probably because she's been lucky. *Performance generated from luck doesn't have as good a chance of persisting as does performance based on a disciplined strategy.* The essential question, therefore, focuses on how a manager executes her strategy in the short term. Does she ignore the short term because her strategy, like Buffett's, is based on long-term thinking? Or does she provide superior long-term gains by exploiting short-term opportunities? If the latter, how does she identify these opportunities and what exactly is her strategy for exploiting them?

Brenda: So as long as she can articulate her strategy and demonstrate that she adheres to it, you hand over your money. Providing of course that she has a good track record, realized with reasonable risks, and the fees on her fund are not much higher than average.

Ted: Not quite. But almost. I want to know that she's been practising her strategy for some time and has confidence in it. I also want some reassurance that she is going to be around for awhile. Does she have an ownership position in the investment firm she's in? Does she have some of her own savings in the fund she's managing?

I also want to be assured that she is not distracted by other things. As we've seen, some of the best managers find themselves attracting a lot of investors' money, to the point where they spend more time administrating their money management business than they do picking stocks. Some managers claim to operate independently but when you go to watch them at their place of business, you discover that they are actually splitting their time among a few funds while junior analysts make most of the trading decisions.

Do you see how important it is to go behind the numbers?

Bob: Yeah, but how can we ask all those questions when I don't even have the time to interview these people? In fact, I don't even know who they are. Would they even agree to see me in the first place?

Ted: Unfortunately, you'd need a lot of money to have firsthand access to the managers. But that's not a problem because most financial advisers do have enough money, when you add up all their accounts, so the mutual fund companies will often bring the fund managers to meet the financial advisers. In many brokerage firms or larger planning organizations, the fund managers will meet with some people from the head office of the brokerage company. The head office people — usually a mutual fund research group — or the financial advisers themselves will ask these questions on your behalf so they can properly advise you on what funds to invest in.

Bob: What if we want to go it alone? Without an adviser?

Ted: Then be sure you get the information you need. You can call the mutual fund company and ask them for their materials. And you can use those books that recommend funds on the basis of quantitative *and* qualitative judgements. Because most active funds are not sold directly to the public, if you want to go it alone, you'll need to use a discount brokerage account. Most of the discount brokers have special mutual fund help desks that should be able to provide you with some information, but you'll have to rely more on the mutual fund recommendation books if you're doing your own research.

The Bottom Line

There is a place for active management in a portfolio. While I wouldn't fault anyone for using indexed products for their entire portfolio, I personally like to have some of my money working toward the extra 2 percent that a good active manager is capable of generating. The trick is to choose a good active manager. Looking at past performance alone will not adequately protect you from naively choosing a lucky coin tosser. The past performance numbers can help eliminate the losers, especially when the risk that was taken to achieve the results is considered. *But by themselves, past performance numbers don't eliminate the lucky winners from the talented winners.* The quantitative factors to consider, in addition to past performance, are risk and the fund's fees, which should not be much higher than the average fees in the industry.

A thorough investigation of the qualitative factors is necessary to increase the probability of choosing a talented winner. While there are no guarantees that analyzing both the qualitative and quantitative factors will turn up talented winners, the odds are more in your favour if you consider both. Make sure that whatever source you use to pick active managers — the advice of your financial adviser, a book, or a newsletter — incorporates consideration of both the numbers (i.e., performance, risk, and fees) and the rationale that helps to explain the numbers. You have to be satisfied that the good performance numbers are not random; otherwise, you're better off staying in indexed products, where you know exactly what you're getting and you're likely to get above-average long-term returns.

7

How to Index Your Portfolio

Now the easy part: how to index the part of your portfolio that you want managed passively. It's easy because the choices are more limited (thankfully) than they are in active management, where there are more than 2,000 funds to choose from.

There are three basic ways to index: index mutual funds, unit investment trusts, and index-linked GICs. There are also index-linked structured notes, but these products are a very specialized form of indexing that would require you to seek advice from a knowledgeable broker. Most of the discussion in this book is centered on index funds because they are the most common and convenient way to index. But unit trusts have unique benefits that you may want to take advantage of, depending on the size of your portfolio and how you invest your money.

If you do a lot of your own investing, you can structure a portfolio of index funds through some of the major banks. Or you can buy either the funds or the unit trusts through a discount brokerage operation. If you manage your investments with some assistance (usually the best way for most people), you can work with a financial adviser to index. Your adviser may use funds or unit trusts. We will explore the advantages and disadvantages of the unit trusts and compare them with index funds. But the best way to invest in markets outside of

North America is by using index funds. Altamira, a direct mutual fund company that sells its funds to the public over the phone or at its branches, offers some index funds, and is also an alternative.

There are also index-linked GICs at most of the major banks. If you have a short-term time horizon, or longer time horizon but can't get comfortable with short-term market volatility, the GICs are an option. But you must be prepared to give up some of the upside potential of your investment in order to enjoy the safety of an indexed GIC.

Brenda: You've already got us paralyzed over the decision of picking an active manager. I'm not sure we can cope with deciding how to index the bigger part of our portfolio.

Ted: Fortunately, the bigger part is the easier part. Once you decide on an allocation for each asset class . . .

Bob: Whoa. What?

Ted: First you have to determine how much you want to put in bonds, Canadian stocks, US stocks, and other asset classes. Then you have to decide how much you want to index in each of these categories. Then you have to decide how you want to index. And finally you have to pick an active manager for parts of your portfolio if you don't want to index your whole portfolio.

Bob: How am I supposed to do the asset allocation thing, and the index thing, when I barely understand what you're talking about?

Ted: I promise I will take you step by step through the whole process. It's actually very simple. A qualified adviser — a broker, planner, or accredited bank employee — can help you with the first steps. But I promise I won't finish our discussion without giving you some help on the "asset allocation thing" if you want to take a crack at it on your own. Let's focus on how to index. Then we'll back up and look at the whole investing process before concluding.

Bob: Sounds reasonable.

Ted: There are essentially three basic methods of indexing: index funds, unit investment trusts, and index-linked GICs. There are also index asset allocation services that will rebalance a portfolio of index mutual funds for you. Because these services are based on index mutual funds,

I'll consider them along with the funds themselves. So let's start with the funds.

The first way to index: index funds

Ted: As we know, an index fund is nothing more than a mutual fund that tracks a particular index. For every index, there could be, in theory, a fund that tracks it. The number and types of index funds are quickly expanding in the US and slowly but surely in the Canadian market as well. The most common index funds track a bond index, Canadian stock index, US stock index, or international stock index.

The market leader in the US, an organization called Vanguard, offers over 25 index funds. Vanguard has very low fees and what many people don't know is that Vanguard is sort of like a non-profit organization. Their philosophy is to operate solely for the benefit of their investors, so that all the money they make is put back into reducing the fees of their funds. The organization is actually owned by the fund holders, much like a mutual insurance company.

While there aren't as many choices in Canada, the no-load mutual fund companies are starting to bring out more index funds in an effort to compete for leadership in the category.

Index funds operate in the exact same way as other mutual funds, except that they track a particular index, rather than attempting to do better (and risk doing worse!). They are entirely liquid, meaning that you can redeem your investment any business day and get your money back within three days and often sooner. You get a statement — usually every three months — that shows you how your investment is doing. Most of the major banks offer index funds so you can purchase them the same way you would buy any of the banks' funds — at their branches or over the phone, if they offer telephone purchasing.

Brenda: I've heard that bank no-load mutual funds are not as good as other mutual funds. I guess that was referring to their actively managed funds.

Ted: First of all, that is patently false. Just open up your newspaper and check out the monthly mutual fund returns and you can see for yourself that many of the banks have wonderful funds. The actively managed funds at banks are subject to the same assessment criteria that we spoke of earlier: many of the bank funds have fantastic performance records, but you have to dig deeper than just the numbers to separate the talented managers from the lucky ones.

More importantly, you're right in that we're not talking about the actively managed funds, where there can be big discrepancies between the "winners" and "losers." When we're talking about index funds, there is less variance among funds.

Bob: So if one index fund is like another, does it matter where we buy index funds?

Ted: Good question . . . and the answer is that it *does* matter.

Bob: How do you distinguish one index fund from another? If you're looking for a Canadian index fund, they must all be the same since they all track the index.

Check what the index fund tracks

Ted: There are three essential things to look for. **First**, you want to *determine which index it is that the manager is tracking*. In Canada, for instance, an equity manager could track any number of indexes. There is the large-company index, the S&P/TSE 60. There is the broader TSE 300. And there are smaller stock indexes as well.

Bob: Brother. I knew this would be more complicated than you said! How many indexes are there in the States?

Ted: In the US there are, as you might imagine, many more indexes. The most popular for indexing is the S&P 500. When it was started, the 500 stocks in it covered 90 percent of the total value of the American stock market. Now it covers about 75 percent. But there is also the Dow Jones Industrial Average, the Wilshire 5000, the Russell 2000, the NASDAQ 100 . . .

Bob: Okay, you've convinced me. I'll never be able to pick the right index fund.

Ted: It's actually not as intimidating as it sounds. It pretty much comes down to what the index holds. Your choices are quite limited at the moment, but as indexing continues to increase in popularity, the choices will expand. Choosing the right index depends on your portfolio. For instance, if you hold only one Canadian index fund, then you probably want the TSE 300 since it's the broadest-based index in Canada. The TSE 300 covers about 85 percent of the entire Canadian stock market. In the US, the most popular index, used by most funds, is the S&P 500. In fact, Standard and Poor's, which is the company that developed and maintains the index, partnered with the Toronto Stock Exchange in late 1998 to develop the S&P/TSE 60, Canada's newest index. The S&P/TSE 60 tracks the stocks of the 60 largest and most heavily traded companies in Canada. This index may eventually eclipse the TSE 300 as the most popular index in Canada.

Bob: So the best index funds are indexed on the S&P/TSE 60 in Canada and on the S&P 500 in the States.

Ted: Not necessarily. The problem, with both of these indexes, if you remember, is that they have a "large-cap" bias, which means that they consist of the stocks of large companies. They don't include stocks of smaller companies. For instance, while the S&P 500 represents about 75 percent of the entire US stock market, it excludes the other 25 percent, which are stocks of smaller companies.

Bob: So what?

Ted: The point of indexing is to generate the returns of the market. So the question becomes, what is "the market"? The market is more than just the stocks of big companies. Once you exclude certain stocks, like smaller-company stocks, you are starting to make bets on which stocks will do better in the long run. But we've already seen that trying to pick the outperforming stocks is a challenge that only a very few active managers can master. So if you invest only in the 60 largest stocks in Canada and the 500 largest in the US, you're essentially making a bet against the smaller companies.

I recommend funds that track the TSE 300 and the Wilshire 5000 because they represent a larger percentage of the stock markets of each country. The Wilshire 5000 actually covers about 99 percent of the entire US stock market.

Bob: It has 5,000 stocks in it? How can a manager buy 5,000 stocks?

Ted: It actually has over 7,000 stocks in it. It started at 5,000 in 1974 but has been expanded as more companies have issued stock. But the index fund manager doesn't hold all the stocks, just about 2,000 or so.

By picking the right 2,000 stocks, the manager can track the index very closely, since those stocks are the main drivers of the Wilshire's returns. The process of buying some but not all of the stocks in an index is called "optimization," since the manager is *optimizing* the returns of the fund as it relates to the index. It is sometimes called "sampling" as well since it relies on *samples* — some but not all of the stocks or bonds from the index.

Bob: I remember you told us that earlier.

Ted: The only reason not to hold a fund that tracks the broader indexes is if you are already investing a large portion of your portfolio in small-cap stocks. If you don't want to overweight your portfolio in small companies, you might want to just track the larger companies with your index funds.

Bob: Can't you buy funds that track the indexes of smaller companies?

Ted: Yes. But they are hard to find right now in Canada. They are popular in the US and they will probably become available in Canada eventually. The Russell 2000 is the most common small-stock index in the US. There isn't a widely accepted index for small stocks in Canada. The TSE 200 separates the 200 smaller stocks from the TSE 300 but there aren't any funds currently that track it. There is also the Nesbitt Burns Small Cap index, which we used when we were looking at index returns. It contains very small companies, many of which would be hard for a manager to purchase. That's why I generally recommend sticking with funds that track the TSE 300 and the Wilshire 5000. Both indexes are market-capitalization weighted — meaning that greater weight is given to stocks that are higher-priced and more highly traded because there are more issued.

Bob: What about the rest of the world, besides Canada and the States?

Ted: That's reasonably straightforward. Remember Morgan Stanley Capital International? MSCI is US-based, but it's developed a number of indexes that are used for most international index funds.

Brenda: I've heard about Morgan Stanley, but I don't understand why everyone uses the indexes they developed for other countries. Don't England and Germany have their own indexes? Why don't managers just use the indexes of each country separately when they manage their index funds?

Ted: It's easier for managers to gather all the data they need from one source like Morgan Stanley than to have to rely on stock exchanges all over the world to provide data. If index managers had funds based on the British FTSE 100 and the German DAX, they would have to get all the prices and stock information from each different exchange. The Morgan Stanley indexes are so popular because Morgan does all the work of gathering data and providing it to managers. The other big advantage is that Morgan is very selective about choosing the stocks they put in their indexes. Some of the stocks in the local index are not traded that much, so they are difficult for an index manager to buy and sell. Morgan makes sure that all of the stocks in their indexes are traded actively.

The most popular MSCI index is the EAFE index, which tracks stocks in Europe, Australia, and the Far East. You can also buy funds that track separate countries or regions, like the MSCI Europe Index. Morgan Stanley also has an Emerging Markets index, which tracks stocks in Africa, Latin America, and other developing countries.

Bob: And they are all "market-ization-something" weighted?

Ted: Yes, they are market-capitalization weighted. Morgan Stanley's methodology is to ensure that 60 percent of the market capitalization of each country is captured in their index. In addition, 60 percent of the capitalization of each industry group must be reflected within the index. In its regional indexes, such as the MSCI EAFE, each country is weighted according to its overall market capitalization, compared with that of other countries.

Brenda: So why does Morgan Stanley only pick 60 percent as the number for both total market capitalization and industry capitalization?

Ted: Because they have so many indexes to track from different markets all over the world. They wanted their indexes to be easily replicated by managers, which is hard if they had used all the stocks in each country since, as I mentioned, many of the stocks in the local indexes are small and don't trade as much. So they build their indexes by starting with the largest stocks and working their way down. When they reach 60 percent, they stop adding any more stocks to the index. Morgan also wanted to make sure that each country index was constructed in the same way; otherwise the indexes would not fairly and consistently represent the market activity in each country. Morgan's system actually works very well and is a fair representation of each market. If they didn't have a standardized approach, they might run into trouble in dealing with indexes such as the Dow Jones Industrial Average in the US.

Bob: But that's the one that is always quoted for the US market! What's the problem with it?

Ted: Unfortunately, it is the one that is often quoted. The problem with the "Dow," as it's often referred to, is that it is price-weighted. That means that the stocks with the highest prices have the most influence on the index.

Bob: That sounds fair.

Ted: Actually, it's not. Why should a stock that is trading at $75 have more weight or influence than a stock that trades at $25? If the $75 stock goes down by 2 percent and the $25 stock goes up by 3 percent, the index will go down, even if far more $25 stocks are publicly available. The investment community does not take the Dow that seriously, except that it is generally quoted in the mass media. Market-capitalization weighted indexes are best because they reflect not just the price of the stock, but how many shares are publicly available.

Bob: Why is the Dow quoted so often if it's not reflective of the market activity?

Ted: Because it's been in existence the longest. It was started in 1896, whereas the S&P 500 wasn't created until 1957. The 30 stocks that make up the Dow are chosen by Dow Jones & Co., the company that also publishes *The Wall Street Journal*. But I wouldn't advise investing in an index fund that tracks the Dow because it doesn't track the market in a meaningful way. Investment managers never compare themselves to the Dow, only to the other indexes like the S&P, Wilshire, or Russell indexes.

That brings out another very important point. Watch out for funds that use "index" in their names but are not pure index funds in the traditional sense. They are funds that use an index as a base from which the manager uses active management techniques to attempt to add value to the index.

Bob: Sounds interesting.

Ted: We know how few managers are able to add value to the index. It is only those rare ones that have the skill to do it over the long term and believe me, they aren't the ones managing index funds. I much prefer to use a good active manager on the allocation I put into active funds and leave my index funds to be run as index funds. Also, some of these quasi-index funds use their own manufactured indexes, which are not publicly quoted. I recommend keeping a clean distinction between indexing and active management. That way you can invest in the best of either, since they require unique skill sets. It doesn't make sense to mix them up. *Stick with good index funds that track the publicly recognized indexes of specific markets.* That's the only way to get the benefits of indexing working for you.

Finally, when choosing an international index to track, you have to consider how the manager treats currencies. Like actively managed international equity funds, index funds that invest in the stocks of an international index are almost always fully exposed to foreign currencies. This means that a US equity index fund will do even better when the Canadian dollar drops since it purchases US stocks in US dollars. Similarly, a European equity index fund will do even better when the Canadian dollar drops against the euro. Of course, these funds do less well when the Canadian dollar rises. The complication arises for index funds that use derivatives to get exposure to foreign markets in order to be 100 percent RRSP eligible. These derivatives-based RRSP index funds can be invested in Canadian or foreign currencies, depending on how the fund is run. The manager may invest in Canadian-dollar T-bills, or he may prefer US-dollar T-bills issued by Canadian governments. I favour index funds that are based on the local currency of the stocks that are bought — for example, a US RRSP index fund that is based on the US dollar, or a European RRSP index fund that is based on the euro. Although they will underperform when the Canadian dollar rises, they generate returns in the same way as most foreign equity mutual funds — in foreign currencies. And you get the benefit of both foreign stock and currency diversification.

Bob: I think I've learned as much as I want to about the indexes themselves. What about the other things to look for in an index fund?

Check what the index fund charges

Ted: The **second** thing to look for in an index fund, after determining which index is being tracked, is fees. We've seen that *fees have a huge impact on long-term returns* and this is one of the primary reasons why index funds outperform active funds in the first place. You want to make sure that you are not paying excessive fees for your index fund. There can be a large discrepancy in fees between funds:

Canadian Equity Index Funds		
Highest Fee	**Lowest Fee**	**Average Fee**
1.25%	0.25%	0.85%

The larger the fee, the more the fund will underperform the index that it is tracking, and the less you'll get in returns.

Bob: So lowest fee wins, obviously.

Ted: Not necessarily. *I wouldn't pay more than one percent in total MER fees for an index fund.* But there are other factors to consider besides fees.

Check the tracking error

There is a **third** consideration to make in choosing an index fund: as always, *check the track record of the index fund manager.* Who is managing the fund and how long have they been managing index funds? What is the organization's performance record?

Bob: But index funds just track an index, so what performance is there to look at? I guess you mean we should look at the index to see how it's done?

Ted: No, I don't mean looking at the index. What I mean is that not all index managers are created equally, believe it or not. Managing an index is not a job devoid of skill. The challenge in managing an index fund is not, as it is for active funds, to outperform everyone else over time. The challenge is to match the index as closely as possible.

Brenda: Why wouldn't an index fund match the index, if that's what the manager's objective is?

Ted: Because it's not as easy as it sounds. For instance, say a Canadian index fund brings in $100,000 of new money on a given day. That's not enough for the manager to invest in all 300 stocks of the TSE 300 index. So the manager has to decide which stocks to buy with the cash. The next day there might be $200,000 in cash so the same decision has to be made. The next day there might be a withdrawal of $50,000 so the manager has to decide which stocks to sell, since he can't reasonably sell just a few shares of each of the 300 companies represented in the TSE 300 index.

Brenda: Why can't he just buy or sell a few shares of each stock in the TSE 300?

Ted: Because it's hard to buy just a few shares — who would want to sell just three shares of BCE?

Brenda: There's a price at which anyone would sell anything. I'm sure of that.

Ted: You're right. But that's exactly the point. The manager can't afford to pay *any* price for the shares since then he will be deviating from the common market price of the index. Most of the buying and selling of stocks, or bonds for a bond index fund, occurs near the market close at end of day or first thing in the morning the following day, when the market opens. By buying and selling near the market close, the manager increases her ability to track the index closely by trading at the prices that are at or near the closing index prices for the day.

Brenda: So you're saying an index manager has to have as much skill as an active manager?

Ted: It's a different skill. Managing an index fund does require a special skill. The manager needs to know how to get as close as possible to the index. The further he is from the index, the greater is the tracking error that he accumulates. And one big mistake cannot be undone easily. If he buys at prices that are way off from the closing market prices, he will underperform the index. Or if he's using optimization techniques, but he doesn't pick the right stocks to optimize the returns and get them as close as possible to the index, he can generate a large tracking error. It's very difficult to make up for a big mistake since he is always trying to get as close to the index as possible and he can't overcompensate for prior mistakes without risking that he will increase the tracking error even more.

Brenda: Sounds like a pretty stressful job.

Ted: It's not as "passive" as many people might assume. *Tracking error — the extent to which the fund deviates from the index over time — is what you must consider when you assess an index fund manager's record.* Part of the tracking error is obviously due to the fees, since unlike an index fund, the index itself doesn't have any MER fees deducted from it. But the other part of the tracking error reflects the manager's skill in tracking the index.

A good index manager should generate returns that are within 0.5 percent of the index over one year or longer. For international index funds, one percent error is reasonable. Both of these benchmarks exclude MER fees, so total deviation from the index should not exceed fees plus 0.5 percent — or fees plus one percent for international funds.

Bob: So what do I do once I've picked out some good index funds?

Ted: You can work with your adviser to construct a portfolio that suits you. Or you could go into one of the index rebalancing programs we discussed earlier. These programs allow you to invest in a portfolio that is made up exclusively of index funds covering the global market. CIBC was the first to introduce these types of programs, and they now offer two services that are versatile enough to suit any type of investor. For both services there are seven portfolios to choose from, each with a different asset allocation, and therefore a different level of risk. TD brought out a similar program, also with a number of portfolios to choose from, based on the Green Line index funds.

One of the CIBC programs rebalances the chosen portfolio back to its original asset allocation every six months. So if the portfolio starts you off with 25 percent in Canadian equities by investing in the Canadian index fund, then you will be rebalanced twice a year to ensure that you always come back to 25 percent. The other program makes small changes in asset mixes based on the investment managers' view of the markets.

Bob: Here's a better idea. I save some fees and invest the money myself. I could buy all the stocks in the TSE 300 — that's not such a big deal. I could buy a bunch of bonds, some US stocks . . .

Ted: Before you get too far down the road on that idea, let me tell you why that is not as easy as it sounds. First of all, the cost to you of buying all the stocks in the TSE could be quite high since you will pay higher brokerage commissions than a manager who is buying on a much bigger scale. It takes about $5 million to start up an index fund properly and avoid the risk of significant tracking error. And that's just one fund. If you've got $50 million to invest, you might have a shot at designing your own portfolio. And that assumes you know what proportions of stocks to buy. Imagine all the paperwork involved in tracking your portfolio of hundreds of stocks and bonds. What if you need some cash? Can you imagine the ordeal and expense of selling part of the portfolio off while still maintaining the right proportions? Don't forget about all the tax reporting you have to do on your own as well . . .

Bob: Okay, okay. Not such a great idea. Just asking. What about those GICs I've heard about that are called "index-linked GICs"? What have they got to do with an index? Are they a good investment?

A second way to index: index-linked GICs

Ted: They're good investments, but only for the right type of person. They combine the safety of a GIC with the upside potential of the stock markets because their returns are linked to a particular index.

Bob: Sounds like a dream come true to me!

Ted: For some people they are a dream. But there's no free lunch, as we all know. The cost or tradeoff of the safety feature is that some of the upside is sacrificed. And because Revenue Canada taxes the gains on an index-linked GIC as income, you don't get the capital gains tax benefit, where only 75 percent of a gain is taxed. Of course, in an RRSP, the tax issue is irrelevant since no gains are taxed in a registered account.

For someone who is just not comfortable with the ups and downs of the market, no matter how well they understand that in the long run the market is not that risky, index-linked GICs can make sense.

Bob: How much upside is traded off?

Ted: It depends on the particular GIC. Some have a cap on them so that if the market goes up by 40 percent over a three-year period, the

GIC might only return a maximum of 30 percent to the investor. Others don't cap the upside, but they don't allow for full participation in the upside either. These GICs usually allow the investor to enjoy 60 to 80 percent of the upside of the market. This condition is called the participation factor. The lower it is, the less upside you'll enjoy if the market rises. And even then, the market returns are calculated by averaging out the month-end prices for the last year of the GIC, so if the market goes up in only the last month of a three-year term, the return isn't very impressive. The averaging part of the calculation can be useful for three-year indexed GICs since the market is more volatile in the short term; the averaging protects the investor from getting nothing if the market drops in the last month of the term. But the five-year indexed GICs are better suited to as little averaging as possible. When you inquire about the GICs, make sure you ask whether they cap the maximum you can earn, no matter how high the market goes, or limit the extent to which you get to participate in the upside, by only giving you a percentage of the market gain. The GICs are always structured one way or the other. The best have low or no caps and high participation factors.

On the flip side, the GICs do offer some reasonable growth potential. There are TSE-linked GICs as well as GICs that are linked to international stock markets. One of their unique benefits is that they come in short terms — most of them are three- or five-year terms. So they are good for investors who have short time horizons and can't afford to lose money, but also want some exposure to the stock markets.

Bob: So do you recommend them?

Ted: I only recommend them for very particular circumstances. Because they limit your upside and because you lose the capital gains tax benefit outside of an RRSP, they are generally suitable for investors who simply can't stomach the short-term volatility of the market but still want to have some stock exposure. Or for investors who want to have market exposure but have very short time horizons such as three years, where the market could go down. Don't forget, they are like GICs in that your money is locked in for the term of the GIC. You cannot get your money back any day you want, the way you can with a mutual fund.

If you are considering them, be sure to ask three things: What index do they track? Is there a cap or maximum that you can earn over the period? If not, what is the participation factor? Finally, how are the returns calculated — by averaging the last 12 months or by simply taking the price of the index at the end of the term?

If your time horizon is five years or longer, and you aren't going to lose too much sleep as the markets gyrate from day to day, you're better off in mutual funds because you get full upside potential and the capital gains tax benefit.

All of the major banks offer indexed GICs. The best offers come from TD, Bank of Montreal, and CIBC. TD and BMO offer Canadian-, US-, and world market–linked GICs. CIBC has a Canadian-linked GIC and a number of portfolios that represent the entire spectrum of world markets. The GICs of all three institutions come in three- and five-year terms, and use participation rates. Only BMO has a cap in addition to a participation rate, but it's 60 percent per year, so it's not very limiting. National Bank is the only bank to offer a two-year index-linked GIC — it's based on the Toronto 35 index and has a cap of around 20 percent.

Brenda: So the two choices for indexing are index mutual funds and index-linked GICs. Sounds like the funds are the better choice for most investors.

Ted: There is a third way to index. It is effective for investors who do a lot of their own trading. You need a brokerage account to index this way, which means you have to either work with a broker, or trade on your own through a discount brokerage account.

A third way to index: unit investment trusts

Ted: These index products are called unit investment trusts and they trade on the stock exchanges in the same way that a stock does. As with stocks, you pay a commission to buy and sell them. They are called "trusts" because the investor is buying units of a trust that holds all the stocks in the index. So owning the trust units is basically the same as owning all the stocks in an index. The trust units never stray far from the actual price of the index stocks for one simple reason: large investors are allowed to trade their units in for the actual stocks at any time. TIPS, or Toronto Index Participation Units, are a good example of a unit investment trust. TIPS 35 include the 35 largest stocks in the TSE 300. In fact, the Toronto Stock Exchange can take credit for launching the first exchange-traded index trusts in the world.

Brenda: Are there others?

Ted: There are SPDRs, which track the S&P 500, DIAMONDS, which track the Dow Jones Industrial Average, and NASDAQ 100 shares, which track the most liquid stocks on the NASDAQ index. All of these are traded on the American Stock Exchange. There are nine Select Sector SPDR Funds which track subsets of S&P 500 stocks that belong to specific industry sectors such as energy. There are also WEBS, or World Equity Benchmark Shares, which also trade on the American Stock Exchange. There are 17 different WEBS trust units that track indexes that are based on 17 country indexes developed by Morgan Stanley Capital International.

Bob: So why would you use any of these trust units when you can just buy a fund and pay no brokerage commission?

Ted: Two reasons — the trust units have lower ongoing management fees in some cases, and you can track single countries with WEBS if you want, whereas most international index funds track larger regions. Here is a chart that outlines the advantages and disadvantages of the unit trusts, in comparison with index funds:

Index Funds	TIPS, SPDRs, WEBS
✗ Management fees are higher on Cdn. and US index funds (0.5–1%).	✓ Low management fees on TIPS (0.05%) and SPDRs (0.18%). This is the biggest advantage of all.
✗ Fund units can only be bought or sold at closing day prices.	✓ Continuous pricing on stock exchanges allows investor to buy or sell at current prices throughout the day.
✗ Capital gains tax can be marginally higher if manager sells stock to fund investor redemptions, thereby generating a capital gains distribution on which tax must be paid.	✓ Capital gains distributions on TIPS and SPDRs are potentially lower than on index funds since stocks do not have to be sold to fund investor redemptions. Some capital gains tax is usually owed by investors when the trust sells stocks to meet the demand of large investors who redeem their units for the actual stocks.

Index Funds	TIPS, SPDRs, WEBS
✗ Very few single foreign country index funds exist.	✓ Investors can separate out each foreign market (e.g., using France WEBS, Italy WEBS).
✗ There is a small risk of tracking error since fund manager must be skilled in investing cashflows in and out of fund.	✓ There is no risk of tracking error since investment is in a trust that holds the identical stocks in the index.
✓ Management expense ratios for international index funds average around 0.9%.	✗ Management fees for WEBs are high, averaging around 1.5%.
✓ Usually no commissions are charged for buying or selling fund units.	✗ Brokerage commissions must be paid to buy and sell trust units.
✓ Can be purchased through most bank branches or through a broker or discount broker.	✗ Must be purchased through a broker or discount brokerage operation.
✓ Involves automatic dividend reinvestment so benefit of compounding returns is maximized.	✗ Dividends must be reinvested manually and applicable commissions paid for the purchases.
✓ Easy to set up a regular investment plan at most banks, allowing money to be automatically transferred from bank account to fund each month. Systematic withdrawal plans are also easy to set up. Some banks (CIBC, TD) have automatic rebalancing programs for index funds.	✗ No eligibility for regular investment plans, systematic withdrawal plans, or automatic rebalancing programs.
✓ Derivatives-based index funds use futures so you can exceed the 20% foreign content limit in registered accounts.	✗ WEBS do not allow an investor to exceed 20% foreign content limit in RRSPs and RRIFs.
✓ Dividends accrue immediately when paid out by each stock.	✗ Dividends are withheld and paid out at certain points so compounding on reinvestment is reduced (TIPS and SPDRs pay out quarterly, WEBS pay out semi-annually).

So the bottom line on unit investment trusts is that they can be good for some investors. If you are working with a broker or have a discount brokerage account, you can invest in them, but you must be prepared to reinvest the income that is paid out, since the dividends do not reinvest automatically. And you must keep them long enough to mitigate the brokerage commissions you'll have to pay when you buy and sell them.

For individuals with high investment balances, the index funds make more sense. Royal Bank charges 0.3 percent for minimum investments of $250,000 for its "Premium" funds. CIBC, through a fee rebate, charges only 0.3 percent for investments in its index funds for accounts of $150,000 or more and only 0.25 percent for accounts of $500,000 or more. These fees are only marginally higher than TIPS and SPDRs, and much lower than WEBS, and there are no commissions to buy and sell the funds as there are for the unit trusts. With the funds, you get automatic dividend-reinvestment, as well as other services, such as rebalancing, if you want them. Also, I prefer the Wilshire 5000 as the US index to track but no investment trusts exist for this index; you'll have to go with index funds if you want the Wilshire.

For investors with more modest portfolios, the funds are easier to buy because they have low minimums. The minimum investment at Canada Trust and CIBC is $500, or lower if you set up an investment plan to automatically move money out of your account and into an index fund on a regular basis. TD's minimum for RRSP accounts is only $100.

For investors who want the flexibility to buy into and sell out of the stock market — even though we all know you can't win in the long term by trying to time the market — the funds are better because they charge no purchase or selling commissions. If you want to exit and then re-enter the market, you can sell and buy the index funds at no cost. But beware that most fund companies limit buying and selling of their funds to a few times a year at most. Anyway, buy-and-hold is the only effective way to invest.

For investors with long time horizons, who don't mind reinvesting the dividends on their own, and who do not meet the high balance requirements for the lower fees of some funds, TIPS and SPDRs make a lot of sense. WEBS are too expensive and I don't recommend them unless an investor is looking to get exposure to just one single country. International index mutual funds are almost always a better choice because their fees are generally lower and you don't have to pay commissions to buy and sell them.

Bob: I think the funds make sense for us. Although I do have to say that I like the idea of the guarantee on the index-linked GICs.

Ted: There's nothing stopping you from combining the indexed GICs and the funds. But if your time horizon is five years or longer, the funds make more sense, since you're not likely to lose money over that time period. It's not impossible to lose money, though, so it ultimately depends on your risk tolerance. If it would really make the difference between sleeping at night or not, the indexed GICs are a good option — perhaps for part of your portfolio.

Some segregated mutual funds, offered by insurance-licensed representatives, are based on indexes. They have 10-year guarantees. But I have to say that the value of a 10-year guarantee is questionable. The odds of the TSE and S&P generating a loss over 10 years is extremely low. The segregated index funds are only useful, in my mind, for the other benefits that derive from their being an insurance contract. They offer creditor proofing and a death benefit, so if you have a small company and you want to protect your investments against bankruptcy, then it might be worth talking to a broker or insurance-licensed adviser about seg funds. They also have some merit for older people since after death, a beneficiary can claim the original investment without having to wait for the 10-year period to expire.

The Bottom Line

Index funds are the best method of indexing for most investors. They are easy to buy. There is no commission for purchasing or selling them. The tax consequences are straightforward and beneficial in terms of capital gains. Dividend and capital gains distributions are reinvested automatically into the fund so your money keeps working for you.

Index-linked GICs are for investors who are so uncomfortable with the ups and downs of the market that they are prepared to give up some of their return potential for the comfort of guaranteed principal. This comfort has particular benefit over a three-year period, which many index-linked GICs offer, since three years is too short a time frame for an investor to be exposed to the stock markets.

Unit investment trusts — TIPS and SPDRs in particular — are

good investments for investors with portfolios that do not meet the minimum requirements of lower-fee index funds, and who are able to trade on their own or through a broker.

When investing in an index fund, make sure you consider the index the fund is tracking. Is it a legitimate and publicly quoted index that represents the broad market? Consider the fund's fees as well as its history of tracking error, which indicates the manager's skill in matching the index.

8

The Grand Finale: The Ultimate Investor Portfolios

It's time to put it all together: to integrate indexing with the basics of investing.

The key to successful investing is nothing new. It's not mysterious and it's not complicated. *The best way to invest is in a diversified portfolio that consists of stocks, bonds, and cash securities. That is the beginning and the end of successful investing.*

There are two unanswered questions that derive from the above proposition:

1. What is the best mix of stocks, bonds, and cash?
2. Which stocks? Which bonds? What kind of cash?

The mix depends on your investment objectives and risk tolerance. If you have long-term investment goals such as saving for retirement, and you are not terrified of the stock market, then your investment in stocks should be greater than your investment in bonds, and your cash holdings should be small. If you are saving to buy a house in five years and can't afford to risk losing much of your investment, you will want a small portion in stocks, and a higher portion in bonds and cash.

The question of how to fulfill each asset allocation with certain stocks and bonds is a little less clear-cut. The purpose of this book has been to demonstrate that it makes sense to index a good portion of your investments. The degree to which you use index products to populate your portfolios is up to you.

I will walk Bob and Brenda through the process of designing an appropriate portfolio that builds on the basics of investment planning. At the same time, I will integrate the benefits of indexing and active management into their investments.

Brenda: So how do we take all this wonderful teaching and do anything useful with it?

Bob: Yeah . . . you said you'd tie it all together for us.

Ted: We're back to the starting point. We need to build you a portfolio that achieves whatever it is that you are aiming for.

Bob: Aiming to be rich, like everyone else. So what's the plan? How long before I can afford a Porsche?

Ted: Everyone has different objectives. And most people have distinct short-term and long-term objectives. Your short-term objective might be to buy a new car in a few years and your long-term objective might be to save for retirement. Or maybe your objective is to buy a home and put something aside for retirement. Or maybe you just retired and your objective is to avoid outliving the money you've got right now. You really have to determine what you want and need to achieve because this decision is what drives how you invest. The mix of stocks, bonds, and cash in your investment plan is called the asset allocation, because your money is being allocated to different asset categories.

Bob: So how would we know which assets to allocate our money to?

Ted: Every financial adviser will give you a different asset allocation recommendation . . .

Bob: Great.

Ted: It's not as problematic as it might sound because there's no right answer.

Bob: You're right. That's not problematic at all! Who needs right answers?

Ted: There really isn't one and only one best portfolio for every investor. There is a range of asset class recommendations, within which any set of recommendations makes sense.

Brenda: But portfolio recommendations usually come out of a computer model. That's what I got from my planner. So shouldn't they all be the same?

Ted: Every computer model that spits out a recommended portfolio is based on assumptions made by a human being. Computer models are only as reliable as the assumptions that go into them. That's why different planners or banks will give you a different recommendation on how much you should hold in stocks versus bonds. The models all make different assumptions about inflation, future interest rates, expected stock market returns, how an individual's investment knowledge should affect his portfolio, etc. With each different assumption comes a slight variance to the output, which is the recommended portfolio.

Bob: So why doesn't everyone just use the same assumptions?

Ted: The assumptions are unlikely to vary much, but it's true that every economist or manager will have slightly different views on the appropriate inputs. If a portfolio that is recommended to you seems odd, then a red flag should go up. For example, if you're nearing retirement and someone tells you that you should put a large amount of money in a real estate deal or small mining venture "for the tax benefits," then run the other way. But for the most part, you'll find that most financial advisers won't be too far off. Their recommended portfolios should be reasonably close to the asset mixes I'm going to show you. If they're not, ask them why. Remember, there are no right answers, but there are answers that are "more right" than others. Many planners will recommend a higher percentage in Canadian equities than I will. I would urge you to challenge them on why Canada, which makes up 2 percent of world stock markets, should have a heavier weighting than US stocks, which make up 50 percent of world stock markets.

Some believe investment knowledge should play a very small role in an investor's asset allocation. If you have a long time horizon and need to build a retirement nest egg that will let you live comfortably at a certain level of income, it is not particularly relevant how scary you find the stock market. Either you maximize your long-term returns or you don't. This position is a little extreme but there is considerable merit in it. Why should your portfolio returns be undermined by your lack of understanding of the markets and the nature of short-term volatility? Do you want to retire comfortably or not?

Others believe that your personal knowledge of the markets and your comfort with market volatility should play an integral role in the development of your portfolio. If your portfolio is not personalized so that it takes into account your distinct preferences and attitudes, what good is it?

Brenda: So what do you believe?

Ted: I lean toward the school of thought that investor sophistication should play a minor role in the design of a portfolio, and your objectives should play the major role. Exercise is good for you but it's not that much fun. Same with eating broccoli. Similarly, investing in stocks is good for you, even if it can be a little disconcerting in the short term. The point is that if you want to generate sufficient returns on your investment, you need to be invested in stocks, no matter what your level of personal investment knowledge.

As we discussed earlier, many people mistakenly believe that risk is best measured by the degree to which the market goes up and down, commonly known as "volatility." But volatility is a short-term phenomenon. Over a 10-year period, the return from stocks is much more predictable than over a one-year period. The real risk in investing is not having enough money to do what you want or need to do. For most people, that means not having enough capital at retirement to generate sufficient income for a comfortable lifestyle. So I tend to put a lot of weight on an investor's time horizon and ultimate objectives. Those factors are crucial since they help determine an appropriate mix of stocks, bonds, and cash.

There's no perfect asset mix decision. It's just that some mixes are better than others.

Bob: Okay. So what's a better mix for my Porsche?

Ted: The mixes are relatively straightforward. I will give you some general recommendations, recognizing that every book, broker, bank, or planner will give you variations on a theme. I've classified asset allocations for five different types of investors. I will walk you through the different categories and help you decide where you belong. Then I will help you construct a portfolio that integrates the best of indexing with the best of active management.

Bob: Can't we just skip to the part where you tell us which funds to buy?

Brenda: Just ignore him. It's getting late.

Ted: Before getting into the exact recommendations, let me define the five portfolios. It's important to spend a bit of time determining the best asset mix for you. Most investors can fit into one of the five portfolios depending on two factors: their objectives and time horizon.

I like to describe objectives as a tradeoff between *avoiding loss*, which is typically referred to as risk tolerance, and *growing your money*. Unfortunately, you simply can't have a low risk tolerance and, at the same time, an ambition to grow your money as much as possible. The two are incompatible since you have to take a certain amount of risk in order to meet a high-growth objective. *What is most important are your objectives and how you make your tradeoff between growth and safety.* If you are not focused on growing your money as much as possible, but need regular income, as you might after retiring, then the tradeoff favours avoiding loss. If you are saving for retirement 10 to 30 years from now, you will probably favour growth and not be too concerned about the risk of loss.

Brenda: Why wouldn't you be worried about losing your money? Everyone worries about that.

Bob: Why wouldn't you want to grow your money as much as possible? Everyone wants to be rich.

Ted: Everyone wants to grow their money *and* avoid loss. But you have to take risk to grow your money. That's the natural law of investing. If you think about it, no one would be willing to sell you a stock at a reasonable price if there wasn't some risk associated with owning it. Likewise, no one would be willing to offer you a GIC that was safe *and* gave you the possibility of earning 15 percent. If everyone had identical tradeoff preferences, the market couldn't function, since there would be no reason for people to trade. The investment process only works because some people are willing to trade off growth for safety, while others are willing to trade off safety for growth. That's the beauty of the capitalist economic system.

Bob: Amen. What about time horizon?

Ted: Time horizon poses somewhat of a constraint on your objectives, because no matter how growth-oriented you are, you can't expect to grow your money aggressively over a short time period. Just as you need to accept some risk in order to maximize growth, you also need a longer time horizon. You'd have to have an extremely high risk tolerance and no interest in preserving your money if you wanted to maximize growth over a period of less than five years. So I've added time horizon as a secondary factor to consider when you determine which portfolio suits you.

Here's the breakdown of the five investor types, according to objectives and time horizon. The sizes of the "loss" and "growth" boxes indicate their relative importance as part of the investment objectives. I've attached a numeric value to each objective just to illustrate their importance, relative to each other. The numbers themselves don't mean anything. You can see that you have to end up with a score of 100, but how you get there depends on how you trade off the risk of loss against the objective of growing your investment. You have to pick between an 80/20 split and a 20/80 split, and three options in between. The time horizons I've listed under each investor profile are the minimum number of years you need in order to achieve the objectives.

	Safe	Conservative	Balanced	Aggressive	Very Aggressive
Objective (avoid loss vs. achieve growth)	Loss (80)	Loss(60)	Loss (50)	Loss (40)	Loss (20)
	Growth (20)	Growth (40)	Growth (50)	Growth (60)	Growth (80)
Min. Time Horizon	**3 yrs**	**5 yrs**	**5 yrs**	**7 yrs**	**7 yrs**

Each investor can fit into one of the five categories depending on their objectives, which are defined by the tradeoff decision they have to make, and by respecting the corresponding time horizon constraints.

Bob: What if someone has a three-year time horizon to buy a Porsche but doesn't want to risk losing his money?

Ted: Easy answer: Can't be done. That, my friend, is the tyranny of tradeoffs. You have to pick because you can't have it all.

Brenda: So in designing portfolios, you don't consider an investor's knowledge of the markets or comfort with market volatility?

Ted: What I've shown are generic categories only. If you are working with a financial adviser you trust, he or she can take you into the finer details of your personality and situation. But for the ease of demonstration, I am just going to focus on the one tradeoff that matters the most in designing a portfolio: the avoidance of loss versus the achievement of growth of your investment.

Bob: So we're obviously in the "very aggressive" category since we have around 20 years before we retire and we want growth at any cost.

Brenda: Not so fast Mr. Race Car Driver. I don't think we want growth "at any cost." I'm not prepared to take any risk at all on our retirement savings.

Bob: But no risk means a safe or conservative portfolio and I'll never get a Porsche with that kind of attitude.

Ted: Actually, the risk of losing money over 20 years is very slim. Definitely less than one percent. So you can still save for a Porsche, but it will take you longer than three years.

Brenda: I think we're only disagreeing on whether we're "aggressive" or "very aggressive."

Ted: That's right. That's where a financial adviser can help you sort out some of the nuances of your objectives. Making tradeoffs isn't easy — in any aspect of life. Neither category would be wrong. In fact "very aggressive" is probably right for Bob and "aggressive" is right for you, Brenda. Although I'd be inclined to advise you toward the "very aggressive" portfolio since you have such a long time horizon.

Bob: I like this man.

Brenda: Well, how would we really know which category we fit into?

Ted: *First*, consider your time horizon — how long you plan to invest the money. Use the minimum time periods that I've listed as an indicator of which category suits you best. *Second*, consider whether you need income to live off in the short to medium term, or whether you are trying to grow your capital for use in the longer term. The generation of income is suited to the safe, conservative, and balanced portfolios. Growth is geared toward the aggressive and very aggressive ones. When you are thinking about your objectives, keep in mind your financial situation. If you might lose your job and you don't have a lot of savings, then short- to medium-term income will be important, even if you have a long time horizon. *Third*, you have to decide how much risk you can tolerate, since the very aggressive portfolios will be more volatile than the other ones. The ups and downs of a very aggressive portfolio don't matter in the short term, as long as you don't need the money for seven years or longer. But you have to know yourself well enough to know that you won't panic when things get bumpy. Can you be disciplined enough to forget about your investments until your annual financial check-up comes due? If not, drop down to an aggressive or balanced portfolio, if that allows you to get through the times when the markets aren't going in the right direction. But remember, if you drop down a portfolio, you are trading off long-term performance for short-term peace of mind. You will likely have less money seven years later and beyond, so you have to consider how much lower volatility is worth to you.

Let's look at sample portfolios for each category, then get into the good stuff.

Portfolio:	Safe	Conservative	Balanced	Aggressive	Very Aggressive
Cash	20%	5%	5%		
Canadian Bonds	70%	50%	40%	25%	15%
Intl. Bonds	10%	10%	10%	10%	10%
Canadian Stocks		10%	15%	15%	15%
US Stocks		15%	20%	30%	35%
Intl. Stocks		10%	10%	20%	25%

Bob: So, seeing as we're "very aggressive," we should hold nothing in cash, 25 percent in bonds, 15 percent in Canadian stocks, 35 percent in US stocks, and 25 percent in international stocks.

Ted: You got it.

Bob: Tell me again why there is more in US stocks than in Canadian.

Ted: The American market is much larger than ours. As much as I love this dear country of ours, the US market has generated superior returns for many years. It has a much more diversified economy. Canadian stocks represent only 2 percent of the world's total stock market. That's not to say that the TSE 300 won't beat the US market every once in a while, and maybe even a couple of years in a row when resource stocks are really hot. But in the long run, I prefer a heavier weighting in the broader economic engine south of us.

Brenda: Why didn't you split the Canadian and US stocks into "large-cap" and "small-cap" categories?

Ted: That's a finer detail that I could have included, but I wanted to keep it simple. I generally recommend separate consideration of small-caps for aggressive and very aggressive investors only. These investors can put around 20 to 30 percent of the Canadian stock allocation and 20 to 30 percent of the US stock allocation into small-caps. So that ends up being about 5 percent Canadian small-caps and 10 percent US small-caps when you look at the whole "very aggressive" portfolio. But you don't have to worry about this because both the index funds and the active funds that I'm going to recommend hold some small-caps.

Bob: What's "cap" again?

Ted: Sorry. "Cap" stands for capitalization and refers to the size of the company's outstanding stock issue. "Large-cap" and "small-cap" are shorthand for large-company stock and small-company stock. Since the stock of smaller companies is riskier, it makes sense for the aggressive investor to hold more of it than the less aggressive investor would.

Bob: Why hold international bonds?

Ted: Currency and issuer diversification. In some years, the bonds of other countries do much better than our own. This is especially true when our beloved Canadian dollar falls in value or the interest rates of other countries fall more than ours do. This was the case in 1998 when returns of international bonds were 9 percent higher than Canadian bonds.

The key to diversification is to get the right balance between all the different asset categories. In theory, you could break down the asset categories even further.

Bob: Some other time, perhaps.

Brenda: So now that we have our recommended asset classes, how do we integrate the whole indexing strategy into these portfolios?

Ted: We can now integrate our five portfolios with the market splits we looked at earlier. Remember, the recommended allocation in active funds is only to go for the extra 2 percent. There's nothing wrong with indexing all of the bonds as well as North American and European equities.

Here is a reminder of how we approached each market:

Market	Passive Target Allocation	Active Target Allocation
Canadian Bonds	80%	20%
International Bonds	100%	0%
Canadian Equities	70%	30%
US Equities	85%	15%
European Equities	100%	0%
Asian Equities	0%	100%
Emerging Markets Equities	0%	100%
Specialty Sectors	0%	100%

If we integrate these splits between passive and active into our five portfolios and divide international stocks into 55 percent Europe, 30 percent Asia, and 15 percent emerging markets, we get this:

Portfolio:	Safe	Conservative	Balanced	Aggressive	Very Aggressive
Cash	**20%**	**5%**	**5%**		
Canadian Bonds	**70%**	**50%**	**40%**	**25%**	**15%**
Index	*55%*	*40%*	*32%*	*20%*	*12%*
Active	*15%*	*10%*	*8%*	*5%*	*3%*
International Bonds	**10%**	**10%**	**10%**	**10%**	**10%**
Canadian Stocks		**10%**	**15%**	**15%**	**15%**
Index		*10%*	*10%*	*10%*	*10%*
Active			*5%*	*5%*	*5%*
US Stocks		**15%**	**20%**	**30%**	**35%**
Index		*15%*	*17%*	*25%*	*30%*
Active			*3%*	*5%*	*5%*
International Stocks		**10%**	**10%**	**20%**	**25%**
Intl. Index		*10%*	*10%*		
Europe Index				*11%*	*14%*
Japan Active				*3%*	*4%*
Asia Active				*3%*	*3%*
Emerg. Mkt. Active				*3%*	*4%*

There you have it. The final portfolio recommendations that integrate both active and index funds.

Bob: Why didn't you just show us the chart at the very beginning? Then I wouldn't have missed the game on TV.

Ted: I was hoping to educate you a little on why the chart is the way it is. I doubt you would have just accepted it without understanding why indexing is such a dominant part of the portfolios.

Brenda: Don't tell me you're going to leave us without making specific recommendations on which funds to hold?

Ted: I really just wanted you to understand the basics of indexing and how to use it in your portfolios.

Brenda: But we'd be left hanging now if you didn't finish up by telling us which funds to buy. Surely you don't want us relying on the books that you already demonstrated are not reliable.

Ted: It's not that the books are unreliable. It's just that when it comes to active funds, it's very difficult to predict who the talented managers really are and which active funds will outperform over the long run. Most of the books don't recommend many index funds since the experts pride themselves on choosing funds that they expect will beat the market. I think that most of the books that recommend the best funds are actually very useful tools for assessing active funds.

Bob: So which books do you recommend and which should we avoid?

Ted: Listen, I may write a book some day myself, so I'm not going to attack any one person's methodology for choosing funds. It's worth looking at two or more of the books to help you get a feel for a particular active fund. But I will say this: no matter whether you rely on a financial adviser or a book to pick your active funds, make sure they consider *qualitative* as well as quantitative factors before making their recommendations.

Anyone that relies exclusively on past performance numbers and past risk assessments has only done half the job as far as I'm concerned. To predict *future* returns, you must consider the qualitative factors.

Brenda: So you're not going to tell us which index funds are best and which actively managed funds you recommend? Why are you so reluctant to give us your "picks"?

Ted: Because my purpose wasn't to give you yet another set of "expert picks." First and foremost I want to be sure you are equipped to construct a portfolio that has *probabilities working in your favour.* Whether you do that in conjunction with a financial adviser or on your own, make sure you have the odds working for you, not against you.

But I don't want to leave you hanging, so I will give you the funds that I think make up solid portfolios. One final point before I do. The beauty of index funds is that you can pretty much forget about them once you've invested in them. Just check once a year to see how the tracking error is against the index that the fund is following. And make sure that the fund company hasn't increased the management expense ratio.

With the active funds, you have to keep on top of them, or rely on an adviser who will. The qualitative factors that lead you to invest in the active funds, including the ones I'm going to recommend, can change quickly. For example, the manager could leave, or the company could become too big to maintain its original investment strategy. So someone has to monitor the active funds. Also, you should review your portfolio once a year to rebalance it back to the right asset allocations. At that time you can also make any adjustments that might be necessary if your personal circumstances have changed. If your investment objectives or time frame change for any reason, you should consider one of the other portfolios — either a more conservative or a more aggressive one.

Brenda: Maybe we could be so forward as to suggest that you come back to tell us if we should make changes next year.

Ted: I'd be happy to. My "picks" for active funds were chosen because they have a good shot at beating the index and they are complementary to a core holding in index funds, meaning that their managers have styles that are different from the index itself. Here they are:

	Index	Active
Cash		Any money market fund
Canadian Bond	CIBC Canadian Bond Index Canada Trust Canadian Bond Index	Altamira Income Altamira Bond Trimark Advantage Bond C.I. Canadian Bond
International Bonds	CIBC Global Bond Index	Guardian International Income
Canadian Equity	CIBC Canadian Index Green Line Canadian Index Canada Trust Canadian Equity Index Royal Canadian Index Altamira Precision Canadian Index	Talvest/Hyperion Small Cap Cdn. Equity Atlas Canadian Large Cap Growth Fidelity Canadian Growth CIBC Canadian Imperial Equity
US Equity	CIBC US Equity Index CIBC US Index RRSP Green Line US Index Canada Trust US Equity Index Royal US Index Royal US RSP Index	Ethical North American Equity AGF American Growth Class
Europe Equity	CIBC European Index Green Line European Index	Universal European Opportunities Fidelity European Growth
Asia Equity		Fidelity Far East
Japanese Equity	Green Line Japanese Index	AGF Japan Class
Emerging Markets Equity		Spectrum United Emerging Markets
International: *Europe, Japan, Asia, and Australia combined*	CIBC International Index CIBC International RRSP Index Canada Trust International Index Green Line International RRSP Index Royal International RRSP Index	AGF International Stock Class Templeton International Stock

You'll note that you can choose to either separate the regions of Europe, Asia, and emerging markets or combine them into one international fund. I generally favour separating them so you can manage how much you put into each region; otherwise you are captive to the weights of the MSCI EAFE index. The EAFE index is about 20 percent invested in Japan, 10 percent invested in the rest of Asia, including Australia, and 70 percent invested in Europe. These weights can change quite a bit as one of the regions outperforms the others.

However, for the conservative and balanced portfolios, the international weighting is small enough — at 10 percent — that it makes sense to use the EAFE index funds. For a registered account — either an RRSP or a RRIF — you need to make use of the EAFE RSP index funds since that's the only way you can meet the asset allocations that I have specified, which exceed 20 percent foreign content.

Bob: So can you show us what our actual portfolio would look like?

Ted: Yes. Here is the breakdown for each of the five investor profiles. I'll separate the registered portfolios from the non-registered ones, since they have to be structured a little differently on account of the 20 percent foreign constraint. We'll have to forego some active management in the registered portfolios because of this constraint, even though we will make use of derivatives-based RSP index funds. Since many of the index funds are sufficiently similar to be interchangeable, I've listed them all together, separated by a backslash.

	Safe	Cons. Non-Reg.	Cons. Reg.	Balanced Non-Reg.	Balanced Reg.	Aggr. Non-Reg.	Aggr. Reg.	Very Aggr. Non-Reg.	Very Aggr. Reg.
Any Money Market Fund	20%	5%	5%	5%	5%				
CT/CIBC Cdn. Bond Index	55%	40%	40%	32%	32%	20%	20%	12%	12%
Altamira Income	15%	10%	10%	8%	8%				
Trimark Advantage						5%	5%	3%	3%
CIBC Global Bond Index	10%	10%	10%	10%	10%	10%	10%	10%	10%
RB/TD/CT/CIBC Cdn. Index		10%	10%	10%	10%	10%	10%	10%	10%
Talvest/Hyp Small Cap Cdn.				5%	5%	5%	5%	5%	5%
CIBC US Equity Index		15%	15%	17%	15%	25%	15%	30%	15%
RB/TD/CIBC US RSP Index					5%		15%		20%
Ethical North Amer. Equity				3%		5%		5%	
RB/TD/CIBC Intl. RSP Index			10%		10%		17%		22%
CIBC/CT Intl. Index		10%		10%					
CIBC/TD European Index						11%		14%	
AGF Japan Class						3%		4%	
Fidelity Far East						3%		3%	
Spectrum United Emerg. Mkt.						3%	3%	4%	3%

Brenda: Why did you use CIBC, TD, Canada Trust, and Royal index funds, but not all of them in all cases?

Ted: I chose the best index funds in each category, except where there was little difference, in which case I chose the cheapest few available. Some of the banks don't offer certain index funds. I could have also included the Altamira Precision index funds, but there are only three of them, and they have high minimums of $5,000. But the most convenient way to put together a portfolio of index funds is using the funds of one supplier. This is especially the case if you are dealing with one of the banks, or one of their discount brokerage arms. If you are working with an independent adviser, you can mix and match to your heart's content. You'll note that in this case I split the US portion between the CIBC US Equity Index fund and the RRSP version offered by CIBC, Royal Bank, and TD. This is because the first one tracks the Wilshire 5000 while the US RRSP index funds track the S&P 500. I like using both since the first one gives you exposure to some smaller-company stocks, but it's not a derivatives-based fund so it is considered foreign content and uses up part of the 20 percent limit. If you limit yourself to the TD or Royal index fund families, you would just put the entire US stock portion into their US RRSP index funds since they don't offer index funds that track the broader Wilshire 5000.

Brenda: How do we buy the index funds and the active funds that go with them?

Ted: Some of the banks, notably TD and CIBC, are starting to offer active funds other than their own. But the best way is to work with a broker or planner who can put the portfolios together for you.

The alternative is to stick to the index funds only and then you don't have to worry about how to buy a Fidelity or AGF fund; just buy the index funds at your bank.

You can use my outline of different portfolios, or for a more personalized portfolio, you should speak to a financial adviser with reputable credentials at a bank, brokerage firm, financial planning organization, or to someone else that you trust.

Bob: But if I want to do it on my own, where do I go?

Ted: If you are confident that you can proceed on your own without any more guidance than I've given you tonight, and you want to mix index with active funds, you can put a portfolio together by purchasing the funds through a discount brokerage account. The index funds from the banks are no-load, which means there is no commission to purchase them; however, most banks impose a $40 redemption charge on no-load funds that are not from their own bank. So to sell a CIBC index fund through TD Waterhouse discount brokerage or to sell a Green Line index fund through CIBC Investor's Edge discount brokerage will cost you $40.

There *is* a charge for purchasing the actively managed funds, since the ones that I have recommended are "load" funds. You can choose between paying an up-front "load" commission, or a "rear" load where you pay only if you sell your funds before a certain number of years have transpired. The number of years depends on each fund company, but usually you have to hold for about seven years before there is no redemption charge.

Brenda: What about the bonuses that some discount brokerage companies are paying to customers who buy rear-load funds? They sound like a pretty good deal.

Ted: I would not make a decision based on those bonus inducements. The problem with rear-load funds is that they sometimes have a higher ongoing fee, or management expense ratio. More importantly, you might have good reason to sell your fund before the commission schedule runs out after about seven years. We discussed all of the qualitative factors that go into choosing an active fund. But any of those factors could change. If the manager of a fund leaves and you want to sell and invest in another fund, the rear-load funds limit your flexibility, since there is a penalty for selling early. That's why I prefer the front-load option — because the ongoing fund fees are often lower and you can sell anytime without penalty.

Bob: So which discount brokerage firm should we deal with?

Ted: The discount brokerage firms are all pretty similar when it comes to buying and selling mutual funds. Your best bet is to choose one that provides some mutual fund research. The best discounters for price and mutual fund assistance are TD Waterhouse, Royal Bank Action Direct, CT Market Partner, and CIBC Investor's Edge. They are currently the only discounters to offer comprehensive over-the-phone assistance in choosing mutual funds, although Schwab Canada offers guidance to its clients as well.

Brenda: I think we're better off using a financial adviser to help us. I don't want to get into trouble just as we're starting. How do we find a good adviser?

Ted: That is the question I'm most often asked. It's wonderful if you have the time and interest to do your own research. But most people don't. So how do you find good help? Just before I leave, I'll address this last question.

The Bottom Line

Every investor is unique because he has a distinct investment profile defined by his objectives, risk tolerance, and time horizon; however, most investors can fit into broad categories, of which I've defined five. Each category is distinguished by the tradeoff between two conflicting objectives: the desire to grow the investment and the desire to avoid losing money. The objectives are constrained by a second factor, the investor's time horizon, because each reward-risk tradeoff decision requires a minimum amount of time to work. For instance, if an investor weighs growth and loss avoidance equally, she would be suited to a balanced portfolio of stocks and bonds. But if her time horizon was only three years, at the end of which she needed the money, her allocation to stocks should be zero. Stock investments require five years or more in order to reduce their risk to a reasonable level. In this example, although the investor's objectives favour a 50/50 split between stocks and bonds, her time horizon forces her into a more conservative portfolio that only holds bonds and some cash.

Once the tradeoff decision is made in the form of an investment objective, and the minimum time horizon test is passed, an appropriate asset mix of cash, bonds, and stocks can be determined. This asset mix must then be fulfilled with either indexed products exclusively, or a mix of index and actively managed products.

Actively managed mutual funds should only be used to complement a core holding of index funds in most asset classes. And active funds should only be added if the investor is confident in her or her adviser's ability to choose a fund that is likely to outperform the index.

Do-it-yourself investors can put together a portfolio at one of the banks that offer a good selection of index funds. Alternatively, they can construct a portfolio of index funds by using the services of a discount brokerage operation.

Investors who prefer more advice and assistance in the investment process, as many do, can find a financial adviser that they trust to help them design a largely indexed portfolio that suits their needs.

9

Getting Good Help

The hardest part of the investment planning process is finding an adviser with experience, the right credentials, and a demonstrable track record. Even these three criteria are not enough. You have to find someone you can trust and relate to.

The search is not dissimilar to finding a good doctor, dentist, lawyer, accountant, real estate agent, repair person, or house painter. How does anyone find a professional that they are comfortable with and who does good work?

I'm going to go out on a limb and say that any adviser who refuses to sell you an indexed product is someone you probably don't want to do a lot of business with. After all, I wrote this book to convince you that indexing should be a significant part of your portfolio. This book also covers related topics, such as how to pick a good active manager and how to pick a financial adviser, so that you know how to use indexed products effectively. If all I did was to make a compelling intellectual argument for indexing, you wouldn't necessarily know what next steps to take.

But if you are not convinced by the arguments in favour of indexing, then there's no point in taking my recommendation on how to choose a financial adviser, since you will have already rejected my portfolio recommendations. If you buy into the power of indexing, then it would be illogical to take the advice of someone who did not believe in indexing. Remember that advisers do not usually make as much money selling index products as they do by selling stocks and active funds that charge commissions. They may have many reasons for telling you why indexing is not a good idea — probably more objections than I could even dream of, despite my best effort to tackle the more common ones.

A good investment adviser will understand, or at least be prepared to learn, that indexing should be the base of everyone's portfolio. The role of the adviser is critical to your investment success because the adviser will help you put together a portfolio that mixes the right asset classes together for your particular situation. Her advice will be more personalized than the five investor profiles I outlined in the previous chapter. She will take into consideration your income and tax situation and your cash needs, and she can assess your tolerance for risk much more rigorously and comprehensively than this or any book can. Finally, a good adviser can help you integrate active management into a portfolio of core index holdings by recommending good active funds, much as I've done.

In addition to advising you on indexed products, the adviser must have some methodology for choosing the active funds that are likely to outperform. After assuring yourself that you are not going to be waging World War III in order to get the larger part of your portfolio indexed, ask the prospective adviser how he chooses active funds. Does he pick the funds himself and, if so, on what basis? Does his company have a recommended list of active funds? Most brokerage firms, financial planning organizations, and even some banks have head-office recommendations on active funds from which the adviser can choose. But beware. Many of the funds on the recommended lists carry high commissions and adviser fees (called trailers), so be cautious about why a fund is being recommended to you.

It will be hard to ascertain exactly how the active funds are chosen. Just because a broker or planner doesn't know exactly how decisions are made by head office doesn't mean they aren't based on a good methodology that blends quantitative and qualitative factors. If you do not get a satisfactory answer to your questions about how the funds are chosen, be persistent and don't be shy. *This is your money*. You would never buy a car or house without probing for answers on critical issues such as the horsepower and warranty of the car, or the age and recent repairs of the house. If the car salesperson mumbled cryptically about the warranty, would you buy the car? Your finances are more important than a car purchase. Your money deserves a lot of attention. And you deserve answers on how it will be managed, before you hand it over.

There's no fool-proof way to find a good financial adviser, but I'll do my best to give Bob and Brenda some ideas.

Bob: My buddy has a broker but I've heard him complain about how much money he pays in commissions and how he never really understands what he owns. I tried to get some help from the branch where we do our banking, but I could tell that the teller was way out of her league.

Brenda: And we've read about those financial planning firms where everyone seems to get in trouble with the law. It's no wonder we aren't properly diversified in our investments. There's no one out there to help us that is qualified, knowledgeable, and trustworthy.

Ted: I'm glad to say that there are in fact many people who meet those criteria. But I'm sympathetic to how hard it can be to find them.

Bob: So how do we do it?

Ted: The first and most obvious answer is to find them the same way you find a good painter, plumber, insurance agent, or car mechanic — word of mouth. You'd be surprised how many friends, colleagues at work, neighbours, or family members do have an adviser that they are comfortable with. Don't be shy about asking. The best painters are always the ones that someone recommends to you. The best movers I ever hired didn't come from the Yellow Pages; they came through a referral. Ask your doctor, ask your accountant, ask your gardener. You'd be surprised how many good leads you'll uncover if you ask around.

Here's another tip. Don't underestimate your bank.

Bob: Give me a break.

Ted: No. I'm serious. The Canadian banks have earned a lot of money over the years from baby boomers borrowing money to buy homes, cars, university educations for their kids. But the boomers aren't borrowing anymore. They're investing. And the banks woke up to this fact about five years ago and decided that they were not going to lose their business just because their customers' needs were changing. They have invested very heavily in hiring and training staff to become legitimate financial planners. Some employ specialized people who are trained financial planners. The old notion that "bank tellers can't give advice" is an outdated criticism.

I'm not saying that every bank is overflowing with highly qualified and reliable advisers in each branch. I'm saying that, for example, of the 5,000 or so people who are registered to sell mutual funds at a typical Canadian bank, there are many who are eminently qualified to help you with all of your investment planning needs, and many that you will feel very comfortable with.

As the banks continue to spend money on hiring and training staff, they will increasingly be a realistic alternative in your search for an adviser.

Brenda: How will we know if they are qualified?

Ted: As with any professional, ask them what credentials they have. The bare minimum requirement is the completion of the Canadian Securities Course. Many professionals in the banks are enrolled or have completed the courses to become bona fide financial advisers. Once you start talking to them, you'll be able to determine quite quickly whether you think they can help you. Ask them some basic questions to gauge their response. Whatever you do, don't rely on a title. You won't find "Teller" on anyone's business card these days. An impressive title such as "Investment Specialist" can mean something completely different from one bank to another. For instance, an "Investment Specialist" at one bank is a highly trained and accredited financial-planning sales professional, but at another bank, the same title applies to anyone who sells mutual funds. So ask potential advisers about their experience and credentials, and make sure you assess their knowledge on topics such as indexing and asset allocation.

Brenda: The problem with the banks is that as soon as you find someone good, they move to another branch and you have to start all over again.

Ted: That is a potential problem, but it is becoming less severe. As more bank personnel are hired and trained to be investment professionals, there is less staff turnover or transfers. Both the staff and the bank executives recognize that the continuity of relationships is key to retaining their clients. In the old days, a banker's career path was clear: from a teller position, he would learn about the lending side of the business and gradually make his way up the branch ladder to become a branch manager and then a regional or district manager. In order to make his way up, he had to move around a lot to different branches to get the experience and promotions that were required. A "banker" was essentially a lender of money.

Today, bank employees are less focused on lending; in fact, many are entirely devoted to the "wealth management" business, which keeps them focused on investing. And they do not necessarily aspire to be branch managers. Many bank branches don't even have branch managers in the traditional sense.

The new "banker" is more often than not someone who specializes in financial planning, only a part of which is lending. The new "banker" is compensated differently as a result. She is likely to have a base salary that is complemented with some sort of a commission based on increasing the client assets she manages. She is less concerned about promotion and more focused on helping people invest properly so that she can retain her client base and earn her commission.

Bob: Sounds kind of sleazy.

Ted: Not at all. An increasing part of a bank adviser's compensation is commission or bonus. But the bonus or commission depends on his ability to attract new clients to the bank and keep the existing ones. He can only do that by offering good and trustworthy advice. The leading banks actually penalize him by reducing his bonus if he loses clients, so he has a huge incentive to keep his customers satisfied.

Brenda: How hard is it to find a good investment planner at a bank?

Ted: It depends on which bank, and the personnel at your particular branch. You just have to shop around a little, and don't feel bound to one bank or branch just because it's where you have your chequing account. It's a lot easier to transfer a chequing account to another bank than it is to find a financial planner that's right for you. Besides, there's nothing wrong with having your chequing account and a mortgage at one bank, and your investments at another.

Brenda: Anything else?

Ted: Assess what investment tools the adviser has at her disposal. Does she use sophisticated software to build a portfolio, or scribble notes on the back of a lunch bag? If the adviser isn't interested in talking to you about index funds, or if she doesn't have many index funds to offer you, I'd keep looking. Finally, the best bank advisers are able to offer you more mutual funds than just their own.

Bob: Why would they ever do that?

Ted: As I said earlier, the banks are becoming very aggressive in their quest to dominate the wealth management business in Canada the way they dominate the mortgage and lending business. They are shrewd enough to know that in order to keep their clients' business, they cannot just push their proprietary product. As you construct a portfolio based on a core holding of index funds, you need to be able to add only the active funds that are likely to outperform. Those active funds may or may not be the bank's own funds. If you don't have the option to use other funds, your returns may be severely limited. There's no point in holding an active fund unless you have good reason to believe that it will outperform the index over time.

Brenda: So if the bank doesn't offer other companies' mutual funds, we shouldn't deal with them?

Ted: I wouldn't go that far. It depends on the quality of their actively managed funds. Interestingly, the two banks that have been the most aggressive in offering other companies' funds are the same two banks that are the leaders in indexing: CIBC and TD. They are the two strongest players in terms of offering a good mix of index, active, and other companies' funds. So one of those banks would be my first choice.

Brenda: What if we find a planner or broker that we like, who seems very qualified and knowledgeable, but strongly discourages us from indexing?

Ted: Bottom line: It just ain't going to work.

If you believe in indexing, then you have to find someone who shares your conviction, which may be difficult, given that there is less financial incentive for planners to do so. However, a good adviser will realize that by doing the best thing for you, he will benefit in the long run by keeping you as a client, and getting some referrals from you.

I'll add one qualifier. Many good advisers are simply not that educated about index funds. So don't discount a good one who needs to be persuaded to make indexing the core holding of your portfolio. Maybe you can educate your adviser!

Brenda: So other than by referrals or checking out a few banks, are there any other ways to find a good adviser?

Ted: You can call the Canadian Association of Financial Planners at 1-800-346-2237, or 416-593-6592, or visit their web site at *www.cafp.org* for a referral to a financial planner in your city. All of the big banks have subsidiaries that operate full-service brokerage services. The investment advisers that work at these subsidiaries are eminently qualified to help you put together a portfolio. Some are focused on picking stocks for their clients, and while I'm skeptical that many have the ability to pick a group of stocks that will beat the index over time, some are able to. Plus they can tailor their stock recommendations to your particular needs, as long as they are willing to start with a base of indexed product. You can get a referral from your local bank branch for an investment adviser near you. Just be sure to be assertive and thorough when you interview anyone who wants to manage your money, no matter how fancy their office is or how expensive their watch appears to be.

One last thing: You are paying for advice so you need to know if you're getting value. Meet with your adviser annually and be sure he shows you how your portfolio did in comparison with the market indexes. If your investments underperformed a simple balanced fund, be sure you are satisfied with an explanation as to why. If you have any trouble getting your portfolio returns, or getting reasonable answers about why you underperformed, it's time to find another adviser.

The Bottom Line

Choosing an adviser can be a time-consuming process. But it is no less important than finding a doctor that you trust and like. In some ways it's harder to find a good adviser, because there is a much broader range of skills and abilities in the investment planning profession than there are in the medical profession.

Ask around to see if any of your contacts — friends, family, colleagues, your doctor — have an adviser that they think is good. Don't underestimate some of the talent that resides in the banks. The banks employ an expanding group of professionals that are in most cases highly trained and very knowledgeable. The banks take the wealth management business very seriously. And the risk is low that a bank will sell you something inappropriate, since the banks take great precautions to avoid risking their strong reputations. The greater risk at a bank is that you will end up in underperforming active funds. So test the receptivity of your bank adviser to indexing. And ask a lot of questions before committing to a bank's active funds, although some of the bank funds are great. The best combination of investment products is offered at banks where index funds can be combined with active funds managed by either the bank or by another company.

A broker or planner will likely charge you a commission on the funds you buy; alternatively, she may charge you an ongoing fee of one percent or less. One, but not both, of these fees is legitimate since it's hard to earn a living by selling index funds. Good advice is worth paying for. And to be sure that you *are* getting good advice, have your adviser review and compare your returns annually.

When you are assessing an adviser, ask about their qualifications and experience. Test them on their investment knowledge. And of course, determine whether or not they are champions of indexing. If they're not, ask them why. Judge their response for yourself.

10

My Work Here Is Done

Bob: Okay. My head is full. I think that's all I can take.

Ted: I think you've got enough to get started. In fact, I hope you feel you've got enough to take you on a long but steady journey toward financial security.

Bob: Can you guarantee us that we'll be rich by indexing?

Ted: I can't give you a guarantee because it depends a lot on you. It depends on how much you save, how long you've been saving, how committed you are to taking a long-term view of your investments and not reacting to market ups and downs . . .

Brenda: Say we did all those things. Then we'd be assured of financial security, right?

Bob: He already said we would.

Ted: Not quite. I can't give you a guarantee. No one can. You have to remember that investing is all about probabilities — successful investment strategies are based on putting the odds in your favour. Because active managers are human and fallible, and because markets are efficient to varying degrees, indexing provides the "safest" bet for a long-term investor. A buy-and-hold strategy has proven to be very successful, both as a historical fact, and because it actually reduces taxes and trading costs.

Brenda: And you're sure that indexing is not just a fad?

Ted: The logic that underpins it is very sound. That's not to say that there won't be years in which a majority of active managers beat the TSE 300, Wilshire 5000, or S&P 500. A majority may beat the index for a few years running. But the fact is that over a longer period of time, the index will *likely* be in the top half of all mutual funds, and probably in the top 25 percent. Why would you not want to have the odds in your favour?

There's no law of nature that allows me to say that indexing will always beat active management. It's not necessarily true by definition or scientific formula. Nor is it mathematically undeniable that stocks will outperform GICs, for that matter.

However, you're not guaranteed to live happily ever after when you get married, and you can't be assured that you won't get hit by a bus on the way to work in the morning. But you still fall in love and get engaged, and you still get out of bed to earn a living each day. You take calculated risks every day of your life. Investing is no different. As we've seen, investing is about tradeoffs just like every other decision you ever make. Your best interest is served by trading off the stable returns of a GIC in favour of investing in a diversified portfolio that includes bonds and stocks. Equally important is the decision to trade off the potentially super-high returns of some active managers, for the more probable better-than-average returns of the index.

Bob: Thanks. I'll call you in a few years when I finally buy my Porsche.

Brenda: Yes. I'll call you then as well. We might need a lesson in life insurance at that point.

Ted: Night.

The Bottom Line of the Bottom Line

1. We've seen that very few managers are able to consistently outperform the index over time, even after deducting fees from the index to simulate a typical index fund.
2. We've seen that the very few managers that do outperform don't beat the index by much.

3. We've seen that many of the managers that underperform the index lose by a large margin.
4. We've seen that it is very difficult to pick out, in advance, those managers that are able to outperform. The so-called experts don't even agree on which funds are winners, and past winners often become losers.
5. We've seen that the index is consistently one of the top long-term performers in the mutual fund industry. The most consistent and predictable winning funds are index funds.

If you accept these premises, you are bound to this conclusion:

> *Indexing is an investment strategy that is strongly favoured by probabilities — more so than any other investment strategy.*

Don't let anyone tell you that indexing doesn't make sense by arguing that there are lots of great managers who have consistently outperformed the market. No one can dispute that. But that's not the point. The point is that you can't predict with great confidence who the *future* outperformers are going to be. For markets such as Canadian stocks, and to a greater extent Asian and emerging market stocks, you can make a reasonable judgement of who is likely to outperform based on their past performance *and* other qualitative factors. But that doesn't negate the power of indexing. It only suggests that you can benefit from a selective use of active management, added to a core holding of indexed product. I ask you: No matter what your net worth, or how sophisticated your investment knowledge, why wouldn't you want to have investment probabilities working for you, instead of against you?

APPENDIX

1

The Best Index Products

Index Fund Families

The banks dominate the index category, simply because they dominate the no-load category of mutual funds, of which index funds are a part. That is not to say you can't buy index funds from a broker or planner. If you go the route of working with an independent adviser — either a planner or broker — you can request any of the bank funds from them since most can sell them. If they want to charge you a purchase commission on the index funds, make sure it is 2 percent or less. It is perfectly legitimate for them to charge a commission, even though you wouldn't have to pay one by investing at the bank directly. They have to earn a living and be compensated for the advice they are giving you. Index funds, as we know, are among the least lucrative products for independent advisers to sell.

Here is a rundown of the index fund families in Canada:

1. **CIBC**: The largest offering of index funds in Canada as well as the most comprehensive index rebalancing services. CIBC has the only US index fund in Canada that tracks the Wilshire 5000, which is the broadest and best index to track for US stocks since it is less dominated by large companies than the S&P 500. CIBC is also the

only bank to offer an international bond index fund. Significant fee discounts are available for investors with over $150,000 to invest; fees on smaller investments are competitive, but not as low as either Royal Bank or Altamira. The CIBC family of index funds was designed to address any investor's basic index requirements. Minimum investment is only $500, and $25 per month for an investment plan that automatically debits a client's account and invests the money in any of the CIBC funds. 1-800-465-3863

2. **TD**: Runner up with a solid index offer. Minimum investment is $100 for an RRSP. Unfortunately, outside an RRSP, the minimum investment is higher, at $2,000. The monthly minimum for a regular investment plan is $25. TD is the only supplier of index portfolios other than CIBC. TD's fees are quite competitive, and in some cases lower than CIBC's. 1-800-268-8166

3. **Canada Trust**: Good selection of index funds, including Canada's only balanced index fund, which is comparable to, but less effective than, the rebalancing index portfolios offered by TD and CIBC. Low minimums at $500. 1-800-386-3757

4. **Royal Bank**: Got into the game long after CIBC and TD with a smaller index offer but very competitive fees. They have two "Premium" index funds with lower fees for minimum investments of $250,000. While their offer is limited, they are likely to expand it over time. Their fees are very competitive, ranging from 0.3 to 0.5 percent. 1-800-769-2563

5. **Altamira**: Got into the game late and their offer is very small but likely to expand. Their fees are very competitive, but minimums are very high at $5,000, although only $50 per month for a regular investment plan. 1-800-263-7396

6. **Bank of Montreal, Scotiabank, and National Bank**: None is championing the index story. All have Canadian and US stock index funds, but their fees are high. Will be interesting to see if they follow the other banks in getting more aggressive with their index offers.

Unit Investment Trusts

If you choose to go the unit trust route, you have to have a brokerage account, since they are all traded on stock exchanges. You can buy TIPS, SPDRs, and WEBS through a broker and some planners. If you prefer to do your own investing, any discount broker in Canada will allow you to buy and sell them for a commission. Note that unit trusts are also known as index participation units.

Index-Linked GICs

Finally, if you opt for index-linked GICs, because you want to index some of your portfolio but also want the safety of a GIC, all of the major banks have solid products. Most offer a TSE-linked GIC as well as a GIC that is linked to international markets. Investors can pick a portfolio that matches their particular investment objectives. Bank of Montreal and TD are the only banks to offer a GIC whose returns are indexed to the S&P 500 — a nice product given how robust the US markets have been. National Bank is the only one to offer an index-linked GIC with a two-year term. The other banks offer three- and five-year terms.

I'm hard pressed to pick one bank over another when it comes to index-linked GICs. Each offers a slight variation and none is a clear leader in this area. Some set maximum returns, or "caps," on the investments; those that do not have participation factors that mean investors don't get the full upside of the markets. TD stands out as having the most options because it offers GICs linked to the TSE 100, S&P 500, and a global markets index, as well as to three of its own active mutual funds, which is quite innovative. CIBC also stands out because they offer portfolios of index-linked GICs that offer you diversification in all major asset classes and world markets, and also guarantee you a small return even if the markets go down.

The best products have the two- and three-year terms, since the five-year terms are long enough that an investor is better off by investing directly in an index fund and getting the full upside potential of the markets. The only problem with the two- and three-year GICs is that you can't enjoy as much upside because either the maximum return caps are lower, or the rate at which you can participate in rising markets is lower. Don't forget that index-linked GICs are designed for very conservative investors or investors with very short time horizons. In order to get the benefit of safety, you have to trade off the upside potential that you would enjoy by investing in a fund.

APPENDIX

The Best Active Funds

Here's a bit of background on the active funds I've chosen as potential complements to the index funds that make up the core investments in the recommended portfolios. Since the allocation to any one active fund is quite low, an investor could combine two in each category, but the most sensible approach is to pick just one. I've listed them in order of my preference.

Canadian Bond: Altamira Income

Although the long-time manager of this fund, Will Sutherland, left Altamira in 1998, his replacement, Robert Marcus, has been managing the alternative Altamira Bond Fund for nearly as long. The Altamira Income Fund is managed more conservatively than Altamira Bond. When I met with Robert, it was readily apparent that he has a clear vision and strategy for running bond funds. While his predecessor was a very active trader, Robert generally takes a longer-term view of his investment decisions. This fund is an excellent, but more conservative, complement to a bond index fund. Robert will shorten or lengthen the average term of the fund, depending on his view of interest rates, so that it can benefit from rate changes more than the bond index can. In the current interest rate environment, rates have a greater probability of rising than of falling, so I prefer the more conservative Altamira Income Fund. If economic dynamics change such that interest rates are more likely to fall, the Altamira Bond Fund is a better choice, especially for more aggressive investors.

Canadian Bond: Altamira Bond

Robert Marcus has managed this fund for almost nine years and it is easily one of the best bond funds available in Canada. Robert is a long-term bull, meaning that he generally sees long-term interest rates declining, which benefits bonds with longer maturities. Compared with his more conservative Altamira Income Fund, which is an equally good complement to an index fund, the Bond Fund is better suited to the aggressive and very aggressive portfolios that I outlined, because they have longer time horizons and can withstand some of the short-term volatility that this fund will suffer from if interest rates increase.

Canadian Bond: Trimark Advantage

This fund is an even more aggressive complement to the bond index because it has a much higher holding of corporate bonds than the Altamira funds. Patrick Farmer has been managing this fund for five years and his strategy is to hold some government bonds, to which he adds a large allocation of corporate bonds, including some high-yield bonds. Patrick is more focused on the spread between the government and corporate bond yields than is Robert Marcus, whose attention is geared toward the average term of the portfolio. Whereas Patrick holds between 40 and 70 percent in corporate bonds, Robert sticks, for the most part, to government bonds. Patrick is another manager who can clearly articulate his strategy; his fund is well suited to the aggressive and very aggressive portfolios.

Canadian Bond: C.I. Canadian Bond

John Zechner manages this bond fund, as well as other equity funds at C.I. I like this fund because John's style is not reflective of the index.

He is not afraid to take bets on the direction of interest rates, and this makes the fund a good addition to a core index fund. He beat the index in three of the last five years, but his underperforming years were only about half of one percent less than the index. In addition to making interest rate bets, he is very aggressive in his holdings of corporate bonds. The extra element — he will often hold double the index weight in high-grade corporate bonds — differentiates this fund from the index, and from the Altamira funds. My only concern is John's ability to continue to generate good results on this bond fund while also managing other funds for C.I.

International Bond: Guardian International Income

If your portfolio is sufficiently large to justify splitting the international bond part of your investments between active and index funds, this fund is a good choice. It is fully RRSP eligible, which means that it does not use up any of that precious 20 percent foreign content that you're allowed in an RRSP or RRIF. There is no point in wasting that 20 percent on an international bond fund when there are good international bond funds that are 100 percent RRSP eligible. Laurence Linklater of Dresdner RCM Global Investors manages this fund and he is quite adept at using active currency management to change the exposure of the fund to different currencies. I would consider this fund as a small component — 25 percent — of the international bond part of your portfolio. Because international bonds should only make up 10 percent of the whole portfolio, indexing the entire portion is suitable for most investors. But if you are lucky enough to have investable assets that exceed $1 million, you might want to add this fund to the international bond index fund. I would use this fund only as a complement to an index fund, since the international bond index, as we've seen, is a tough competitor.

Canadian Equity: Talvest/Hyperion Small Cap Canadian Equity

I have met Sebastian Van Berkom a number of times and he is a very compelling and engaging manager with a clear philosophy and extremely disciplined strategy. There are very few pure small-stock managers in Canada, since most hold some medium- and larger-cap stocks in their portfolios, and most don't have long track records. Sebastian has been managing this fund since its launch in 1993 and has generated very impressive results. He has also overcome some stumbles, which are inevitable in the small-cap sector. As long as the fund doesn't get too large for him to keep to his strategy of looking for high-growth companies that are fairly valued, this fund will continue to be a great complement to an index fund, because it is very different in its structure and return characteristics. It's probably 12 to 24 months away from getting to the point of being too big to continue to do well, at which time Sebastian is likely to close the fund to new investors. This fund beat the index in every year of its existence, except 1998. This fund is especially well suited to the aggressive and very aggressive portfolios.

Canadian Equity: Atlas Canadian Large Cap Growth

Fred Pynn of Bissett & Associates is the manager of this fund and his style is to focus on medium to large growth-oriented companies. This fund has a great track record and a proven strategy behind it. It is not higher on my list because I'm concerned that Fred and Bissett in general have received so much positive publicity in the last couple of years that the increasing amount of money flowing into their Canadian equity funds may cause them to change their strategies. Since there is a limited number of medium-sized companies to invest in, as the fund gets bigger Fred might have to increasingly rely on buying large-company stocks in order to invest all the investors' cash contributions. This change might jeopardize the strategy that has made the fund successful in the past. If you meet the $10,000 minimum investment, you're better off to invest in the Bissett Canadian Equity Fund, which Fred co-manages with Michael Quinn. The Bissett fund has a much lower MER fee. Both funds have been able to consistently beat the TSE 300 in most years.

Canadian Equity: Fidelity Canadian Growth

Alan Radlo manages this fund at Fidelity and has been very successful in taking on the index. His mandate is primarily focused on small caps, but he mixes in larger companies so the fund is not as pure as the Talvest/Hyperion alternative. He is very adept at investing in high-growth but lesser-known companies and so this fund is a nice complement to a Canadian index fund.

Canadian Equity: CIBC Canadian Imperial Equity

Réal Trépanier was hired by TAL Global Asset Management to take over the CIBC Core Canadian Equity Fund a couple of years ago; since then he has turned that fund, formerly a chronic bottom-half performer, into a consistent top-half performer. CIBC started up the new Canadian Imperial Equity Fund to let him really show his stuff. This fund has a "best of" strategy, in which Réal uses stringent value criteria to choose his favourite growth stocks in the Canadian market. He keeps the number of stocks in this fund limited so that it doesn't become over-diversified and "index-like" in its behaviour. Although this fund does not have the three-year track record that I normally require before making it one of my picks, I have spent a fair amount of time with him assessing his strategy and style, and have confirmed to my satisfaction that the stellar two-year performance on this fund is not just coincidental. In 1998, Réal blew away the index by over 10 percent, and unlike most of his competitors, he didn't hold one US stock to do it.

US Equity: Ethical North American Equity

I don't believe in ethical funds. First, the criteria of what constitutes "ethical" are never agreed upon by everyone. Second, the idea of limiting the universe of possible investments is simply anathema to the objective of maximizing returns. I'm also very skeptical about any manager's ability to consistently outperform the US index. But when I met Cynthia Frick of Alliance Capital Management, I was almost converted. This is a woman whose intelligence and clarity of thinking are exactly what you look for in an investment manager who has a shot at beating the index. And the fact that she has done it within the confines of an "ethical" mandate is even more impressive. This fund invests exclusively in US equities, despite its name. It is an ideal complement to the Wilshire 5000 for all portfolios. Cynthia may not continue to outperform the index, but if anyone has a chance, her discipline and that of Alliance Capital make the fund a strong contender. She beat the index in three of the past six years, and tied it once.

US Equity: AGF American Growth Class

It's tough to beat the index in the US market. Stephen Rogers has been able to do it in three of the last six years that he's been managing this fund. This fund is more conservatively run than many active funds because it focuses on large companies, which has helped its performance because large caps drove the market over the past few years. Stephen's approach is a consistent and straightforward search for high-growth companies that are well capitalized and established in their markets. This fund is a good complement to the index in the balanced portfolio.

European Equity: Universal European Opportunities

Stephen Peak of Henderson International, based in London, has managed to beat the MSCI Europe index in two of the four years that this fund has been running. While there are other European funds with longer track records, none has been able to beat the index more than 50 percent of the time. In fact, the closest runner up to this fund only beat the index in two of the past six years. I think the Universal fund is the best complement to a European index fund because it uses a distinct strategy of investing in small companies of larger countries, as well as investing some of its assets in emerging Eastern European countries. Although I don't like that Stephen Peak holds a small percentage in US stocks, almost all European managers "cheat" a bit in this way, so I am still confident in recommending this for the aggressive portfolios it was designed for.

European Equity: Fidelity European Growth

Beating the MSCI Europe index isn't any easier for an active manager than beating the Wilshire 5000 or S&P 500. Sally Walden and Thierry Serero of Fidelity, based in London, only beat the MSCI Europe index in two of the past six years. That doesn't sound impressive, but compared with almost all other European managers, it's quite an accomplishment for these growth-oriented managers.

Asian Equity: Fidelity Far East

It's difficult to compare Asian funds because their mandates can vary quite widely. One fund may exclude Japan entirely, while another may have over 50 percent of the fund invested in Japan. Still another may hold 40 percent in cash. The best Asian funds do not hold excessive cash because that represents a market timing decision that is too easy to get wrong. Fidelity has one of the best Asian funds available. K.C. Lee has been managing the fund since its inception in 1991. He has a disciplined approach of buying and holding large Asian companies that have solid long-term prospects. His approach is quite conservative in that he does not look for small, unknown Asian companies. His aim is to take advantage of the growth in particular Asian countries by investing in established larger companies. My only discomfort with this fund is that its mandate excludes Japan. But that's an easy fix — we simply add a good index or active Japanese fund to the portfolio.

Japanese Equity: AGF Japan Class

The manager of this fund, Sumio Sakamoto from Nomura Investment Management, takes a reasonably conservative approach to managing this fund. He focuses on large Japanese companies that are household names in Japan and around the world. Sumio does make currency bets, but he is usually modest in the extent to which he hedges the yen exposure, which is preferable since you don't want to give up solid stock returns because of a bad currency call.

Emerging Markets Equity: Spectrum United Emerging Markets

I never fail to learn something from time spent with Ewen Cameron-Watt of Mercury Asset Management in London, England. He and his team scour the emerging markets to come up with the best stocks they can find. Each person on the team specializes in a different part of the world and they layer on macro-economic forecasts to determine which parts of the emerging markets are likely to outperform over the next 12 months. His knowledge and the resources he taps are as impressive as the rigour with which he applies his strategies to pick stocks. There are some emerging markets funds that have posted marginally better returns. But this is only because they raised cash to avoid some of the downdraft that all emerging markets suffered in the last two years. I don't have faith in a manager's ability to correctly identify the market tops and bottoms, so I prefer a manager who *invests* my small allocation to emerging markets, which is exactly what Ewen does.

International Equity: AGF International Stock Class

This fund is managed out of San Diego by Charles Brandes and his partner Jeff Busby. Both are disciples of the legendary Benjamin Graham, who originated the value approach to investing. While this international stock fund is only two years old, Brandes and Busby have managed the AGF International Value Fund over five years, and they have proved to be consistent and disciplined in their stock-picking strategies. I prefer the International Stock Fund to the International Value Fund because it excludes US equities, making it better suited to a portfolio that already has a US allocation.

International Equity: Templeton International Stock

This fund took a real hit in 1998, mostly because of a heavy weighting in Asia. But even good funds stumble and the Templeton strategy that has worked for years has not changed. Templeton invests in undervalued stocks no matter which countries they trade in, so the country allocations are purely incidental. Don Reed oversees this fund, but the stocks he invests in are chosen from the famous list of approved equities picked by Templeton analysts from all over the world. Analysts at Templeton typically specialize in both industry sectors and global regions. Because it excludes North America, this fund provides a clean approach to international investing, without skewing the country allocations in a portfolio.

APPENDIX

3

Reviewing the Mutual Fund Rating Books

No single mutual fund rating book does the entire job. Some are stronger on the quantitative side, while others are stronger at evaluating qualitative factors. Here I've briefly evaluated the most popular Canadian rating books, outlining their strengths and weaknesses. Although I am rating the books on their methodologies for picking active funds, I am also keenly interested in their views on index funds. Indexing is not a glamorous thing to recommend. And it takes some courage to recommend index funds, since they reduce the need for recommendations on active funds, the raison d'être of the fund rating books.

Smart Funds

Jonathan Chevreau, whom you'll know if you are a regular reader of the *National Post*, is a columnist and general public commentator on the fund industry. He teamed up with Stephen Kangas and Susan Heinrich in the most recent edition of this book, published by Key Porter. *Smart Funds* assesses not just individual funds — of which 100 are recommended — but also the major fund families and how they rank against each other. The funds of 50 fund companies are rated as either "smart," "noteworthy," or "available." Strengths and weaknesses of each fund family are listed, and while this is useful, most investors do not limit themselves to just one fund family. A strong element of the book is the research that goes into each assessment of "smart" and "noteworthy" funds — my only concern is the rigour with which they are chosen. While I wouldn't dispute any of the choices, there are some good funds that are rated as only "available." The best part of the book remains the assessment of the top 100 funds. The analysis is a strong combination of all elements including risk, returns, and manager style — all very adeptly captured on one page. Among the most interesting aspects of the book are the manager interviews featured at the beginning; and because each new edition contains new interviews, back copies are worth holding on to. The authors deserve enormous credit for including a couple of index funds in their list of "smart" funds.

Gordon Pape's Buyer's Guide to Mutual Funds

Gordon Pape is the originator of Canadian mutual fund ratings. His book, published by Prentice Hall, provides the most comprehensive coverage because it has detailed commentary on over 900 funds. The greatest strength of Pape's approach is his qualitative assessment of absolutely crucial information that some of the other books omit. If a new manager has taken over the fund, it will be recorded in the book, and Pape will adjust his rating accordingly. Because the future performance of a fund is only as promising as the manager's skill, it is surprising that few other authors track this information consistently. On the weaker side, Pape's ratings are often influenced by his expectations of how certain markets will do in the coming year. For instance, Asian and emerging market funds were rated quite low in his 1999 edition because of the turmoil those markets have suffered. I believe that a fund should be compared with its peers, not with other funds in different asset classes — asset allocations should remain reasonably static, given how difficult it is to predict which markets will outperform in a given year. Quantitative assessments are not as explicit as in the other books (no fancy charts or graphs) but Pape does consider these assessments in his evaluation. He merely chooses to fill his pages with the qualitative factors, having used the numbers to screen his selections. Pape is not a big fan of index funds and so index funds do not rate highly in his book, which is a disappointment.

The Year 2000 edition of Pape's book will incorporate the work of Eric Kirzner and Richard Croft (see *FundLine Adviser*, below); it will be interesting to see how these mutual fund gurus combine their talents to deliver superior recommendations that combine Pape's qualitative strengths with the quantitative approach of the other two.

The Best of the Best

Wilfred Vos is the analyst who invented the "all time periods" methodology of evaluating fund performance. This is a breakthrough approach to assessing returns because it doesn't just look at discrete years, or periods, but combines them to more accurately assess a fund's performance. He has co-authored this Prentice Hall book with Bruce McDougall. The basis of each fund assessment is Wilfred's quantitative methodology, which he applies rigorously to generate a recommended list of 50 funds. The second half of the book looks at the performance and details of each stock in the Toronto 35, but the more interesting and useful part is the mutual fund section. No one can fault Wilfred's mathematical approach to assessing risk and returns. It is comprehensive and detailed. Each recommended fund is awarded a rating based on how the fund does against similar funds (e.g., Canadian small-cap equity funds), and how it does against all mutual funds in its asset category (e.g., Canadian equity funds). These comparisons are made on the basis of risk, return, and the balance between the two. Wilfred's approach is clearly head and shoulders above other quantitative approaches, and this is probably one of the reasons why Gordon Pape acknowledges and uses some of Wilfred's analysis in his own *Buyer's Guide*. One weakness of the book is how light it is on the qualitative factors, such as manager turnover. It surprises me that no index funds managed to pass the severe tests that are applied to other funds — none is recommended.

Duff Young's Fund Monitor

Duff runs a portfolio analysis company and is a commentator for the *Globe and Mail*. His bi-weekly columns are always fresh and insightful. While some of his past picks wouldn't win any awards, his Prentice Hall book is very easy to read and his quantitative assessments of risk, MER fees, and performance consistency are very useful. His treatment of risk assessment is comprehensive; it includes multiple methods, and grades how each fund does in a bull and bear market. If you like charts and colours, his book is full of them. Of particular note are his consistency charts, which show the quartile ranking of each fund over each calendar year. He has a short list of 66 recommended funds followed by a quantitative assessment of many Canadian funds at the back of the book. These brief summaries at the back are useful, but give too much weight to his quantitative assessment and don't sufficiently assess information such as manager or style changes and how they may affect a fund's performance. Duff does not include index funds in his 66 recommended funds, but at least he gives them good ratings in his overview at the back.

FundLine Adviser

Richard Croft, an investment guru known for his skills in options trading, and Eric Kirzner, a finance professor at the University of Toronto, teamed up with a unique approach to evaluating funds. They provide details on their 97 "best bet" funds and include statistics on hundreds of other funds at the back of the book, which is published by HarperCollins. Their unique approach is extremely useful because instead of considering a particular fund in isolation, it shows how the fund can be used in a portfolio. Their system is founded on the principle that different styles should be combined in order to construct good portfolios. This is a methodology that is consistent with the best thinking in investment theory. I only wonder why no one ever did it before! Croft and Kirzner's style assessments allow investors to generate portfolio returns that are not the random outcome of many funds, but the expected results of a carefully chosen *combination* of funds. Additionally, the two authors are determined to convey the actual skill of a manager. To this end they developed a "Manager Value Added" score, which rates a fund manager's ability to outperform an appropriate risk-adjusted benchmark. Where the book is weak is in its lack of qualitative assessments. A change of managers, for example, would not be registered in their rating system. Much of the first part of the book is a worthwhile read on the basics of investment theory and how to put a portfolio together. Unfortunately, only one index fund gets into their "best bets" list.

Although there will not be a Year 2000 version of this book, the good news is that Croft and Kirzner are teaming up with Gordon Pape on his mutual fund guide to make it even more comprehensive than it already is.

The Money Coach's Guide to Top Funds

Riley Moynes has been producing this book for a few years now, most recently with Michael Nairne. Previously his co-author was Duff Young, so it's no surprise that this book, published by Addison Wesley Longman, is strikingly similar in layout and methodology to Duff Young's *Fund Monitor*. The Moynes and Nairne book includes 100 recommended funds and then some quick facts, at the back of the book, on hundreds of other funds. The statistical pages at the back of the book are useful, but they're missing the key qualitative comments that Duff includes in his book. Moynes and Nairne have added a useful feature: for each recommended fund, they list a complementary fund and a similar fund. This helps investors put funds together without duplicating investment styles. Their "complementary" recommendations are sometimes confusing though, since European funds are listed as complementary to US funds; and they don't do a good job of *explaining* the important concept of complementary funds. There is only one index fund in their recommended list, and it is included grudgingly. However, there is another index fund listed in the exclusive "up and comers" category.

Chand's World of Mutual Funds

Ranga Chand definitely focuses on the quantitative side of assessing mutual funds, often at the expense of qualitative factors. Of 1,500 funds examined, 237 pass his tests, which are based on performance and risk assessments. Because his method of screening is purely quantitative, index funds do manage to get onto a few of his lists. While his analysis is easy to follow and consistently applied, it is not as rigorous as Wilfred Vos's. Ranga writes a small amount about each fund, but this is insufficient qualitative analysis to be able to predict that the past performance of a fund is likely to continue. Ranga's book, published by Stoddart, is an excellent screening device since the thoroughness of his quantitative assessment provides a solid point from which further analysis can be done, or comparisons made with other authors' recommendations. Ranga is also not shy about listing the underachieving funds. While he may be overly reliant on quantitative assessments, his mathematical approach does not lend itself to the human interference that might selectively exclude winners such as index funds: guess what — index funds are more represented in this book than in any other!

APPENDIX

Recommended Reading on Indexing

Books

A Random Walk Down Wall Street, by Burton G. Malkiel
(New York: W.W. Norton & Company, 1973)
A controversial look at the predictability of stock prices and whether it is possible to outperform the market, given the randomness of stock price movements.

Bogle on Mutual Funds: New Perspectives for the Intelligent Investor, by John C. Bogle
(New York: Dell Publishing, 1994)
The original guru of indexing explores mutual fund investing and why indexing is such a powerful investment strategy.

Common Sense on Mutual Funds: New Imperatives for the Intelligent Investor, by John C. Bogle
(New York: John Wiley & Sons, 1999)
A follow-up to the original book that continues the exploration of mutual fund investing and includes some personal insights on leadership and the Vanguard philosophy.

Investment Policy: How to Win the Loser's Game, by Charles D. Ellis
(Homewood, Illinois: Business One Irwin, 1985)
Easy read with powerful insights on how investing is a loser's game; the thesis is that because investors as an entire group are "the market," they can't beat it.

Stocks for the Long Run (second edition), by Jeremy J. Siegel
(New York: McGraw-Hill, 1998)
Excellent overview of investing from many angles. Full of statistics and interesting facts.

Web Sites

www.indexfundsonline.com
An independent American site that explores many aspects of index investing. A great source of information and education.

www.fundlibrary.com
Independent Canadian fund site with information on particular funds, repeats of investment shows, and lots to explore.

www.globefund.com
Globe and Mail fund site with lots of information that makes it easy to compare the returns of different funds.

www.vanguard.com
Site of the largest index fund company in the world, complete with many articles on indexing, as well as education on mutual funds in general.

www.msci.com
Overview of the Morgan Stanley Capital International indexes and how they are calculated.

www.efficientfrontier.com
Personal site built by a doctor in the US who has downloaded research and information about investing, much of which relates to indexing.

Subject Index

Page numbers for charts are indicated in boldface.

About the Author

Ted Cadsby is a senior executive of the CIBC group of companies, where his responsibilities include overseeing the CIBC mutual fund family. He is much sought after by the media for his commentary on the topic of index investing, and is a regular speaker at industry conferences. Cadsby was awarded the Medal in Philosophy at Queen's University, obtained his MBA at the University of Western Ontario, and has also earned the Chartered Financial Analyst designation. He is actively involved in the community through work at the Investment Funds Institute of Canada and volunteer work with the Canadian Blood Services organization.